A Love of the Land

A Love of the Land

By Darrell Sifford

With photographs
by David Cupp

Farm Journal, Inc.
Philadelphia, Pennsylvania

Picture Credits:
All photographs are by David Cupp except the
following: Michael P. Durning, page 18; Jim
Schroeder, page 183, and B. E. Fichte, page 250.

Book Design: Michael P. Durning

Library of Congress Cataloging in Publication Data
Sifford, Darrell, 1931-
A love of the land.
1. Farm life—United States. 2. Rural families—United States. I. Title.
S521.5.A2S58   973'.09734   80-18379
ISBN 0-89795-010-0

First Edition

*To Marilyn, who sent me on my way
and welcomed me when I returned.*

Acknowledgments

No one person could have completed this book without the cooperation, help and kindness of many others. I want to thank *Farm Journal's* Sharon Nelton, who conceived the idea for this book, who helped me keep the goals in focus and whose rare kind of professionalism enabled her to be my friend while she was my editor.

I also want to thank the many others from *Farm Journal*, especially Dick Braun, whose help was given generously.

And last, but certainly not least, I want to thank those who welcomed me to their homes, farms and ranches, answered my many questions and treated me not as a writer but as part of the family. Their patience is a testimonial to their humanity.

Contents

Introduction

At 8:30 on a July morning I put on a wool-and-polyester-blend gray suit, seized my briefcase and rode an elevator 400 feet down to ground level. Then I walked four-fifths of a mile along Philadelphia's Broad Street to the *Philadelphia Inquirer*, where I am a columnist.

At that same hour, almost halfway across the country, Glen Harder moved briskly into his barn to check the feeding of 13,000 deep-breasted turkeys that soon would be shipped from his farm in southwest Minnesota to a slaughterhouse in Iowa.

In Cedarburg, Wisconsin, twenty miles north of Milwaukee, Henry Retzlaff and his father had finished milking their twenty-seven cows and were cleaning out the barn, anticipating a breakfast of scrambled eggs and sausage, before the son would drive a tractor into the fields and the father would tend the family produce stand near the highway.

In Alice, Texas, fifty miles west of Corpus Christi, Jack Dunn frowned at the brilliant sunrise and wondered when, oh when, would rain come to soak his range and transform brown into green and give his cattle something more to eat.

In Lodi, California, Jerry Fry already was up, sipping coffee from a brown mug and waiting for dawn to bring enough light to allow him to get into his vineyards. Larry Sanders, a cotton farmer, was in his pickup truck, driving toward Monette, Arkansas, for a load of liquid fertilizer. Glenn Matsuura, a Japanese-American Buddhist who is a potato farmer in Blackfoot, Idaho, was on his way to a cup of coffee at the Riverside Inn, next to the Snake River, before heading into the fields.

At that time I knew none of these people. But in the weeks that followed I would come to know all of them—and their families. They would invite me into their homes and they would share their hopes and fears, their victories and defeats, their joys and sadnesses. They were among a dozen families that I visited during a summer in which I traveled more than 23,000 miles, from coast to coast and almost from Mexico to Canada, as I sought to find out what it is like to live in rural America, to farm, to pray for rain when the skies are cloudless, to bring up children geographically far removed from the classic problems that we tend to associate with big cities.

I was surprised when *Farm Journal* asked if I would discuss the possibility of writing such a book. After all, I'd never lived on a farm and I'd never spent much time in the country. To the contrary, I had lived mostly in cities—near St. Louis, in Louisville, in Charlotte and now in Philadelphia. I'm reasonably citified and I like it that way. My wife and I live on the thirty-seventh floor of a downtown condominium, where we seem closer to the jumbo jets than to the spindly trees that are planted in squares cut from the sidewalks below.

If you live in a city or town, you may wonder why this book matters. If you live on a farm, you may wonder why I, an outsider to farming, was asked to write it. Because, *Farm Journal* editors said, they wanted a city person to go out and examine rural America and try to deal with the conceptions and misconceptions that so many of us urban Americans have—that farmers are rich; that mechanization has eliminated hard work; that farmers are uneducated; that government doles keep them in business; that it is the good life free of stress and anxiety; that farm children are marvelously advantaged; that farm children are culturally deprived.

Perhaps someone like myself, as filled with misconceptions about farming and farm families as most Americans, could take a fresh look at rural life and come closer to the truth about people who till the soil.

Could we make it work? Could we find the right people to visit? Would they be open with me? Would it be possible to write a book that, on the one hand, would tell urban Americans how it is on the farm and, on the other hand, give rural Americans a chance to meet and find out about each other?

Our discussions continued, on and off, for a year and a half. Finally, we agreed, it was time for us to stop refining ideas and for me to go to work. That's when I packed my bags on what seemed like every Monday morning and headed for the airport and another flight, another layover in Chicago, another rental car and another drive along gleaming superhighways and dusty back roads.

This book, *A Love of the Land*, is the result of those trips. It has been a learning experience for me and a learning experience, perhaps, for those I visited. I learned, for example, that there exists between farmers and their land a bond of love that transcends discouragement, discontent and even total disaster. I learned that a farmer's commitment to the land can be as sacred as commitment to the family.

What about those I visited? What did they learn from me? My guess is that the awe that obviously was present in me at times reinforced something they knew but perhaps tended to take for granted—that rural America is vibrant, diversified, beautiful and busy. I think they also learned that some of us from the city know even less than they thought about what goes on in the country. With a frankness I can understand, one farmer told me: "I believe you're about as green as anybody I've met."

In my exploration I met some wonderful people and made what I hope will be some lasting friendships. I hope that what I have written in this book will leave those of us in the city and those of us in the country with the feeling that we're a little closer than we thought and that all of us would be friends if we had the good fortune of crossing paths.

Darrell Sifford
February, 1980

A Love of the Land

1 ✺ Hard work and tender moments

In the middle of a North Carolina summer the heat can seem almost suffocating—even at ten o'clock in the evening.

That's how it is on this June evening, as the thermometer out by the well shows eighty-four degrees, as the greenish-blue Japanese beetles buzz inside the glass jars hanging from gate posts, apple trees and clotheslines—jars that have been baited and turned into death traps for the beetles that by day munch the tobacco leaves that are Osborne Oakley's livelihood.

Tomorrow Oakley will empty the traps, spilling clusters of beetles on the ground, some still crawling and fluttering. He will pour kerosene on the clusters, set them afire and then bait the traps again—a ritual he repeats every day until cold weather comes and does the killing for him.

This summer is not going to be good for him and other tobacco farmers, he says. There has not been a soaking rain for six weeks. The two ponds from which he irrigates part of his twenty acres of tobacco are in danger of running dry from the heavy pumping. The pastureland on which his twelve cows graze is turning brown—and the weather forecast from a Raleigh radio station offers no relief: "Clear skies and continued hot tomorrow and Saturday. Afternoon highs in the middle to upper 90s."

Osborne ("Big Oz") Oakley, a North Carolina tobacco grower . . . and proud of it.

Oakley sighs, leans back in his aluminum-frame rocking chair and looks at the stars. "You know, tobacco doesn't have to have the most water in the world to make a good crop—if you get it at the right time. The perfect rainfall would be about an inch every seven days—from planting through the growing season. Since I've been farming, I've never seen a perfect season. Some are close to perfect and some are terrible. But never a perfect one."

Osborne Oakley is my father-in-law, and my wife, Marilyn, and I come to his tobacco farm every summer, a week's respite not from the heat but from the noise, the litter, the haste and the pushing and shoving of the big city. Even when it's a long, hot summer—as this one promises to be—the Oakley farm, where Marilyn grew up, still is one of my favorite places on earth.

Why? It's the incredible quiet of it all, a place where we can regenerate, think about who we are, where we've been and where we're going. Almost every day, usually late in the afternoon, Marilyn and I walk down the hill behind the house of white aluminum siding to the larger of the two ponds, the one that's spring-fed, and we sit on a waist-high flat rock, listen to the frogs and tell each other that this is how life was meant to be lived.

Even in the midst of drought it's the kind of place I want to come home to. Marilyn's parents, Osborne and Remell, make it that way, and they have from the very beginning. I was separated but not yet divorced when Marilyn and I told them how we felt about each other, that we planned eventually to marry, that I was leaving my job as executive editor of the *Charlotte News* to become a columnist for the *Philadelphia Inquirer* and that Marilyn eventually would be leaving her job in Charlotte, too, and moving to Philadelphia.

The "divorced-man" syndrome had bothered me because I didn't know how her parents would feel about that. I also am seventeen years older than Marilyn—and I didn't know how they'd feel about that either. My apprehension about that had been fueled by a question one of Marilyn's brothers had asked her after I first met him: "Hey, how old is that guy anyway?"

We had sat that afternoon in the den and told Osborne and Remell what we planned to do. There was a silence. I excused myself and walked to the flat rock by the pond—I wanted the three of them to be able to talk by themselves. Twenty minutes later I saw Marilyn and her father walking down the hill toward me, their arms linked together. Osborne first shook my hand.

Then he hugged me. Then he said, "We're proud to have you as part of the family. We know Marilyn will be happy with you."

Together we walked back to the house and there was Remell, who told me, "I sure hope you like cherry cobbler, because that's what I'm baking." Do I like cherry cobbler? Does a bear have hair? She knew it was my favorite and it was her way of welcoming me to the family.

Oz Oakley has been farming this family-owned land since he bought out his eleven brothers and sisters in 1948. From the tobacco he grows, he has paid for 13½ years of college education for five of his seven children—although he never went beyond high school himself. The 100-acre farm is just outside Roxboro, twenty miles south of the Virginia border, a sleepy town of 7,000 where the low cost of living seems to be equaled by the low income of the people who live there. It's a $3-an-hour town, basically, Oz tells me, a town in which you could live like a king if you made $6 an hour. But few people make that much. Oz's seventh child, Mark, twenty-three, who lives in a separate house on the farm, works in the tobacco fields with Oz and they share expenses and income, which don't balance in some years.

What happens then? Well, first you've got to understand how tobacco farmers, many of them at least, operate. Early in the year they borrow enough money from the bank to tide them over until late summer or fall, when their tobacco is sold and when their income for the year is realized. Then they repay the loan and use whatever is left to live on for the rest of the year, when they go back to the bank and borrow again.

Some years, Oz tells me, "you don't make enough to pay back the money to the bank. Maybe you don't even make enough to pay the interest. So you go to the bank and tell them: 'It's not as good as I'd hoped.' If you've been straight with them in the past, if your payment record is good, if your reputation is good, they'll usually refinance you. That's the hope you live with."

Oz is a big man—almost six feet, three inches and 230 pounds—and in the face he looks a lot like Enos "Country" Slaughter, the legendary baseball hero who lives on a tobacco farm five miles away. They're the same age—sixty-two—and they were boyhood friends. They went to school together and played baseball with and against each other before Slaughter, as a teen-ager, signed a contract with the St. Louis Cardinals. When I was growing up in

Missouri, Slaughter was my hero. I painted his uniform number—9—on all my sweatshirts and I even tried to bat left-handed.

Would Oz introduce me to Slaughter? Yes, he would do that. If Slaughter's not off hunting, fishing or playing in a golf tournament, he undoubtedly will talk with me. Oz seems amused that this is so important to me and puzzled by the awe I obviously convey in talking about Slaughter.

The introduction will have to wait, however. Tonight we sit out under the stars, and then we go to bed early to get ready for tomorrow. That's a big day, the time when Marilyn and I work on the farm—not because I want to work while I'm on vacation but because I do want to get the feel of what it's like to pull the tobacco plants from their beds and feed them into the mechanical planter. I want some personal sense of how it is out there in the fields. But before bedtime I remind Oz of something he told me earlier—that it takes enormous hope to survive as a farmer.

He's always had hope, Oz says. "You accept a bad year and hope that next year will be better. God gives us that hope. I don't know anyplace else where you could get it. If you lost hope, you'd throw up your hands and sell out. I've seen people do that—move off the farm and go into something else they think is non-risky.

"My father had that kind of hope and I've lived with it all of my life. I got my religious belief from him, too—my faith—that and what God gave to me. Faith in a higher power is what gives people like me the courage to continue. We need faith and hope because farming is a gamble—from the time you put the seed in the ground until harvest. But then life itself is a gamble, too, from the time a woman conceives. All the mother and father can do is hope and have faith that the seed will mature and the baby will appear as a perfect human. If you lose faith and hope, if you lose confidence that next year will be better, that the baby will be healthy, then you're in a bad situation—regardless of your religion or what you do for a living."

Oz says he prays when he feels like praying and "I ask for what I think I need. But that doesn't mean what I ask for will be answered. God promises to fulfill our needs—not our wants. It may not be His will to give us what we think we need. You take lack of rain—like right now. You know you're going to get rain eventually. The only question is if it comes when you think it should or when He sends it."

Still, he says, it's impossible for him not to worry when the rains don't come, when the tobacco burns in the field and the grass dries in the pasture. "I don't think I worry a lot, but I have an ulcer, and the doctor says worry is what causes ulcers."

Tomorrow evening I'm going to get a firsthand look at Osborne Oakley's religion, Primitive Baptist, because we're going to a camp meeting, with hours of preaching. I want to go because I'm working on a series of stories about fundamentalist religion. But before that, Marilyn and I are going to the tobacco fields, to sweat and get dirty and even muddy as sweat melts dirt. For a day, we're becoming tobacco farmers.

It's something I look forward to—and so does Marilyn. It surprises her, she says, her enthusiasm to do again the work that she once disliked so much that she told a sister: "I wouldn't ever marry a farmer—not if he were the last man on earth." That was when she was little, when she spent every summer in the fields, daydreaming about what life would be for her someday, envying her schoolmates who swam and had fun.

She was the fifth of the seven Oakley children and Remell gave birth to her late one afternoon after working in the tobacco fields all day and fixing dinner. Farming, then as now, was a family effort and Marilyn was in the fields by the time she was six, usually carrying gallon buckets of water from a wagon to those who were planting. One thing she remembers vividly were the calls from the field for "w-a-a-a-t e r" just about the time she got back to the wagon that carried the water tank. There was little time to goof off, even at age six.

That bothered her at the time, but, she says, it was probably the greatest discipline builder in the world. "I work long and hard now"—she's a training consultant for a big Philadelphia insurance company—"and I don't think much about it. It's a carryover from the farm. I guess it shaped my whole attitude about work and about life. I love this land. I've walked every inch of it and sometimes when I daydream, even now, I mentally go back there and walk it. It's almost like I'm there. I don't know that I could feel that way about somebody else's land. But this is *our* land. And I hope it always will be."

Would she still refuse to marry a farmer? "Not if you were a farmer, silly." Could any husband ask for a better answer than that?

Well, here it is, morning, and I *am* a farmer—sort of, anyway.

Tobacco, it seems to me, is a crazy crop to grow because you don't just drop the seeds in the ground, fertilize, spray and irrigate. You have to do a lot more than that and there's a limit to how much anybody can mechanize a tobacco farm. Some of the work just has to be done by hand. And that's what we're going to do now.

Today we're going to replant an acre and a half of tobacco that didn't make it the first time around. We go down to the plant beds—about 1,000 yards from the house—to remove the baby plants from the beds, which contain 1,000 square feet of fertilized, sandy soil. Back in early February, Oz had scattered two ounces of tobacco seed—at about $24 an ounce—into the beds. Thousands of plants sprouted not long after that—far more than Oz customarily needs to plant twenty acres of tobacco.

It's about seven o'clock in the morning when we begin to "draw" the plants. Because many of plants already have been pulled and put into the fields, the plants that remain aren't so close together. And some of them aren't so hot-looking either—because the better ones already have been plucked. We're dealing with what's left—green, leafy stalks about six inches high. There's no sophisticated way to pluck them from the ground. That's what I call it—plucking. And Oz laughs at me and tells me again that it's "drawing, not plucking." The five of us—Oz, Remell, Mark, Marilyn and I—are there, knees bent, hunched over, plucking the plants from the sandy soil that has been softened overnight by irrigation.

I pluck plants with my right hand, transfer them to my left hand and keep plucking until my left hand can hold no more. Then I take the handful to a pile that is developing at the edge of the plant bed. Eventually Mark crates them and loads them on a wagon, which will be pulled by a tractor to the field. I watch with awe as Oz's big hands snatch the plants from the soil at what seems to me to be an uncommonly rapid pace. At least it's lots more rapid than my pace. My back is starting to hurt. I can tell that I've made a mistake in wearing tennis shorts, because I'm down on my bare knees and already they are beginning to be irritated from all my squirming around on the ground.

Oz isn't complaining. Remell isn't complaining. Neither is Marilyn nor Mark. So how can I complain? I try to work faster, but I slow down after I break off a few plants without ever getting them out of the ground. "Pull straight up," Oz tells me. "A slow, steady pull. That's what it takes."

Remell and Osborne share a moment together at day's end.

In two hours we have a dozen crates filled with plants and, after we stop to drink some tea, we're off to the field, across the road in front of the house. If I hadn't committed myself to doing this, I'd be gathering up my golf clubs now and heading for the golf course. But I can't turn back now. Remell isn't going with us. She's going to the garden beside the house to harvest some cabbages. Mark is plowing in another field. So it's just the three of us—Oz, Marilyn and myself, an unlikely threesome, I think, to turn loose together in a tobacco field.

Oz hooks the tractor to the mechanical planter, a strange-looking rig with a big wheel that revolves between the two seats on which Marilyn and I sit. As the wheel turns, Marilyn and I load it with the plants that we have put in a tray that hangs over our laps. The planter, in one revolution of the wheel, digs a hole, inserts the plant, shoots the hole full of water and covers it with soil.

I've never seen anything like this—truly a mechanical marvel. But there's no time to look at it. There's no time to look at anything except the wheel that revolves in direct ratio to how fast Oz drives the tractor. I'm having trouble keeping up. Marilyn and I load the wheel alternately and she never misses her turn. But sometimes I can't get my plant in the slot in time and, as a result, the planter leaves a watered but empty hole in the field. And that, Oz says, won't put any money in his pocket.

"Why don't you slow down the tractor?" I ask Oz. "You want to spend all day out here?" he answers. He's trying to be sober about it all, but I can tell he's breaking up underneath. In three hours we're finished and, because I dropped so much dirt from the plant roots onto my sweaty legs, I'm covered with mud. Marilyn is muddy, too, but she looks less uncomfortable than I feel. "You'll get used to it," she tells me.

What will happen to the plants we put into the ground today? Well, Oz tells me, in a month, if all goes well, the stalks will be twelve to eighteen inches high and it will be "lay-by" time. This is when more dirt is plowed up against the stalks to support them. In another month, in the first visible phase of the maturing process, the plants will begin to bloom pink blooms about an inch and a half long, open like lilies.

Oz and his hired hands—sometimes he has as many as six—will break off the blooms and "top" the plants. This keeps the blooms from sucking up moisture and taking sap from the leaves. The first harvest will come in about two weeks. In a process called

"priming," leaves are pulled off from the bottom of the stalk—
the stalk matures from the ground up. Each stalk will be primed
about every ten days, perhaps four times during the entire harvest
season, which normally ends in late September but which can run
into November. The leaves then are taken to the tobacco barns for
drying or, in a tobacco farmer's language, "curing." This is when
the leaves turn from green to golden yellow and give off the marvelous tobacco aroma that even a non-smoker like myself finds so
appealing. Curing takes four to eight days; then the tobacco is
ready for market. Oz will sell his crop in Roxboro or in South Bos-
ton, Virginia, thirty miles north, and from these sales he will earn
his year's income—enough, he hopes—to ride out the winter and
get ready for next season.

It's not likely that there will be enough this year to make it
through the winter, Oz says. It's going to be one of those years
when "living and operating expenses chew up every penny I
have."

How much does he make in "one of those years"? Grosswise, it
doesn't sound too bad—$48,000 off twenty acres. The other
eighty acres are given over to ponds, woodlands, buildings and
pasture, and the only other income the family receives comes in
those years when they sell some of the dozen or so cattle they keep.
Of the twenty acres in tobacco, only six are allotted to Oz by the
government; he is able to grow the other fourteen acres because he
leases the tobacco allotments assigned to a few other farmers in
the area. By the time he pays his lease and production costs—the
government figures production costs at $1,600 an acre—the
$48,000 has shrunk to $16,000, which he splits with his son, Mark.

"That's nothing to brag about," Oz says. "If you can't average
what the market averages or better, then it's not a good year. In a
good year I'd be 5 to 15 percent over the market average. But not
this year . . . ."

Oz borrowed $20,000 during the swirling snow of January to fi-
nance his farm operation until he sold his tobacco. "When the
bank was local, I could borrow the money just on my signature.
Now a larger bank has taken over and it calls for collateral. That
means they get a mortgage on my farm equipment and tools. They
have first claim on the land after the first mortgage holder.

"And it's tough to go to them after a bad year and say you can't
pay back the loan. Usually, they'll refinance you if your record is
good, but if you get to the point that what you owe the bank ex-

ceeds your equity, then the bank will stop the loan and sell you out—the same as with any other business.

"If you can't pay, usually you're not in it by yourself. If you're a good farmer and you still have a bad year, then other good farmers are in the same shape. But if you have a bad year when all the other good farmers are having a good year, well, you'd have a problem with the bank. That's never happened to me."

How tough is the life of the tobacco farmer?

It's tough in three ways, Oz says: Physically, because of the hard work of growing and harvesting the crop; emotionally, because of the uncertainty of what the crop will bring; financially, because of the inevitable lean years. But Oz says he wouldn't trade places with anybody he knows. "I never thought about quitting. I think this is about the most enjoyable work a man can do."

What's so enjoyable about all the uncertainties?

"I'm my own boss. I don't have to punch a clock. I can take a day off for recreation or illness and it's not held against me. When it rains, I can rest. Then when good weather comes, I can work two days in one—from sunup to sundown. There are so many young people today who want to work by the clock. And that's one reason they don't prosper. At five o'clock they want to quit. But a farmer can't work by the clock. He has to work by the weather and the season."

Oz works hard himself and he expects no less from those who work in the fields with him. "But I never ask anybody to do anything I wouldn't do myself. The Bible says God gives us different talents. If we use the talent we're capable of—the know-how to raise tobacco—if we do our part and do it adequately, then if we don't have a profitable year we still can live with the knowledge that we did the best we could."

Oz believes—without doubt, he says—the Primitive Baptist Church's doctrine of predestination: What will be will be and nothing man can do will change that which is predestined by God to happen.

When one of his sons, Wendell, was killed in a car wreck in 1959 at age seventeen, three weeks before high school graduation, Oz says both he and Remell felt it was "the will of God to take him. The Bible says He is the only one who can take and give life. A lot of people don't agree with that. But if they don't believe that, then they don't believe in an all-powerful God who rules the universe." Oz says he felt the same way when a married daughter, Dianne, died of a cerebral hemorrhage in 1969 at age twenty-two. "Nobody knows God's plan," Oz explains. "If we knew in advance what was going to happen, we might not want to live to see tomorrow. I've hit low spots. I've asked: Why did this happen to me? Why did we lose our children? Why did I lose a brother in the war when others didn't lose anybody? Why me? Why us? But there's only one answer—the belief that all things work together for good for those who love the Lord and for those who are called according to His purpose. If you believe, then you believe it was His purpose to take away the children. If I didn't believe in predestination, I couldn't have lived when Wendell was killed and Dianne died. And neither could Remell."

It's getting on toward evening now, time to go to the camp meeting and see Primitive Baptist religion, not just talk about it. This is the first day of a three-day meeting that will attract 2,000 people, most of them from an eleven-church, four-county area around Roxboro but some from as far away as northern Georgia. It's the seventy-first annual session of what is known as the Lower Country Line Primitive Baptist Association.

We drive there, dressed casually, because, we're told, that's how people dress for "the association." There are 450 seats in the eighty-by-fifty-foot building in which the preaching will take place, a building that stands in the middle of fifteen acres of church-owned property about a fifteen-minute drive from the Oakley farm.

The hinged sides of the building have been lifted to allow penetration of the scant breeze on this ninety-degree afternoon. Through the open sides I see the shelters—concrete slabs covered by tin roofs—where many of the worshipers are living for the three days. Perhaps half the seats are filled when we arrive, mostly by people with gray hair and ruddy, leather-like faces that result from toiling in the fields under the scorching sun. I see only a handful of children and most of them are playing outside.

The moderator of the meeting is Elder L.P. Martin, seventy-two, a retired door-to-door salesman, who tells me that the denomination is not growing. "We get fewer people as times goes on. This isn't a revival. We don't try to get people to join us. We believe God works in man and, when the right time comes, no power this side of hell can stop him from becoming one of God's people. We believe it's all in the hands of God." That's why the church not only doesn't seek out new members but also holds no Christian education classes for young people. ("To try to teach children about this is useless," Elder Martin explains. "It only can come from God. The love of God puts it into their hearts—not man's teaching.") Nor does the church pay preachers a salary. ("If God calls you to preach, He supplies your every need.") Nor does it require that preachers be formally educated. ("The power of God enables us to preach. Education doesn't.")

The preaching, which will run for three hours or longer, begins. The first preacher stands, sweat falling from his forehead. He's before us only by God's grace, he tells us. He describes himself as "a beggar, the lowest of the low, worst of the worst, least of the least." But he hopes for salvation—"just like you, brothers and sisters"—because he's put his trust in the Lord.

His voice trembles with emotion: "Man will fail you, but God won't. God is the only one we can depend on, look to in time of trouble." Now he's almost screaming: "God can't fail or lie! He fulfills a-l-l-l-l-l promises, predestines a-l-l-l-l-l happiness!"

He drags out the L's, almost as if he's challenging his lungs to prove how much air they can expel. Then his voice fades, as if an unseen hand has turned down the volume, and he continues softly: "There are appointed dates given us to live. Age doesn't matter. When our time has come, no doctor or man can do anything to keep us from leaving this earth."

Abruptly, the boom returns to his voice: "We mayyyyyy not live to see the morning . . ." And again, he speaks quietly: "But there is no pain, no sickness, no reason we have to worry. We believe—and we are God's people."

The final words are barely audible, and some lean forward on their benches, even cup hands to ears. The preacher sits down and the singing begins: "There is a house not made with hands. . . ."

The preaching continues and each speaker's message revolves around this theme: What will happen in our lives already has been predestined by God and nothing we can do, not even our fervent prayers, can change it. So make peace, and prepare to leave this place of sorrow and go to the mansions of happiness after death.

We hear a succession of eight speakers. All of the preaching is without notes, and some of it seems disjointed, as if one sentence is completed without any knowledge of the next. Later I ask Elder Martin if there is preparation, and he says, no, there usually is none. He, himself, doesn't prepare his sermon, which, he says, comes from divine inspiration. Sometimes, if no inspiration comes, he makes a few remarks and then sits down. The result of that is a short service, unless somebody in the congregation feels inspired to preach. Often, I'm told, somebody does come forward, and the service continues.

Elder Martin says the belief in predestination comes from "everything in the Bible—from Genesis to Revelation." But the core of the belief comes from Romans 8:29: "For whom he did foreknow, he also did predestinate to be conformed to the image of his Son. . . ."

I ask him about the power of prayer—why pray at all if everything already has been worked out by God? He smiles and tells me: "Brother, that's the easiest question you could have asked me. Prayer is predestined."

We drive back to the farm, mostly in silence. Remell asks me what I thought of "the association" and I try to think of a nice way to tell her that I have some problems with predestination. But I don't say anything. One of the marks of maturity, I found out the hard way, is knowing when to keep your mouth shut.

The next day is Sunday and the Oakley family is gathering to visit from near and far: Marilyn's oldest brother, Donald, thirty-eight, who manages the production of and sells advertising for Roxboro's twice-a-week newspaper; Mark and another younger brother, David, twenty-eight, a meat market manager at a supermarket in Raleigh, an hour away; her sister, Joan, thirty-four, a schoolteacher from New Bern, North Carolina, near the coast, four hours away. They all bring their families with them, five children in all, and their dogs, five in all. At one time there are seventeen of us, plus the five dogs, in the den, all seemingly talking at once, except the dogs, all of which seem to be barking at once.

For me, an only child, it is a scene of bedlam unlike anything I expected to see in the place to which I go for peace, quiet and relaxation. I look around—and nobody else seems to be bothered. Not only are they not disturbed by the noise, they appear to be enjoying it. Later I ask Oz about that and his answer is: "The joy of having all your family with you, in your own house, is the greatest joy a man can have."

The next day Marilyn and I go shopping and I see again, firsthand, dramatic proof of how little it costs to live in Roxboro. At least it seems little to me.

We pay $4.69 for a gallon of table wine that costs $6.00 in Philadelphia, $1.88 for ground chuck that costs us $2.25. At Central Carolina Farmers, Inc., we buy two country hams at $1.75 a pound. The last ones bought in Philadelphia were almost $3.00 a pound. We ask the salesman to pick out two good hams for us, since they're wrapped in burlap bags and we can't see what they look like. By feeling the bags, he expertly makes the selections. "You can't go wrong with these," he says. "But if for any reason you're not satisfied, bring them back. Just ship them to Osborne and we'll give you new ones."

We go to an ice cream store and pay 49 cents for a double-dip cone. We're accustomed to paying $1.25. I almost pass out when I see a sign on a downtown lot that advertises parking at $5.00 a month. We pay $65.00. Even mushrooms, which probably came from Kennett Square, Pennsylvania, near Philadelphia, are a dollar a pound. If we get them at home for $1.69, we consider it a steal. Finally we have lunch at a diner and, for $2.49 each, we have barbecued pork, hush puppies, fried apples, beans and draft beer. If you even could get all that in Philadelphia, it'd be closer to $5.00 than $2.49.

We get into Oz's pickup to go back to the farm. It's a green Ford, three years old with 40,000 miles on it, and, it has a sign on the license plate holder on the front bumper that reads: "Big Oz." People honk and wave as we approach, then look bewildered when they see it's not Big Oz. We honk and wave back. Finally they recognize Marilyn. "Look, it's Osborne's daughter," they say. Almost everybody in town seems to know Oz and Remell and Marilyn, too, even though she hasn't lived there since she left for college in the late 1960s. In Roxboro the name Oakley is as common as Smith in most places. Many of the Oakleys are related. When there is a family reunion, they have to rent a hall to accommodate everybody.

To me, Oz and Remell Oakley live like king and queen—not like people who must count their money carefully and make each dollar they spend go as far as possible. Their two-story house has three bedrooms, two baths and a den with fireplace and color television set. The kitchen is as modern as ours. The food is out of this world, usually two kinds of meat at every meal, two or three homegrown vegetables, dessert. Their Sunday car is a ten-year-old Oldsmobile Oz has repainted white from its original dark green.

How do they do so well on what some might consider so little?

How did they pay for 13½ years of college for five children? How do they always seem to have enough to do just about anything they want to do?

"We only spend money on things we think are important," Remell says. "It doesn't take much to make us happy." But the irony, it seems to me, is that they do have a lot. An awful lot.

The telephone rings and it's . . . Enos Slaughter. He's returning Oz's call. Yes, any son-in-law of Osborne Oakley's is a friend of his. He'll be pleased to meet me. When? What's wrong with now? Y'all come on over.

Marilyn rides with me in Oz's truck and, in less than ten minutes, we arrive at a red brick house overlooking a valley that will soon be flooded to create a power-generating lake. The mailbox at the head of the 100-yard-long driveway is mud-spattered, and the letters on it barely are legible: E.B. Slaughter, Rt. 2, Box 179.

A golden-eyed Persian cat stands guard at the front door, then rolls over on his back and pleads to have his stomach scratched. Birds twitter from trees that line both sides of the yard and cast pencil-thin shadows from the late-afternoon sun.

It is so very peaceful—and so far removed from the noise and the glamour of the baseball parks where Slaughter played and became a national hero, where over the years hundreds of thousands of fans (including me) stood and roared, "C'm-o-n-n-n, Eno-o-o!" when he came to bat with runners on base. He'd stand at the plate, a round-waisted little man, with the bat held motionless on his left shoulder, a portrait of relaxation. Then the pitcher would throw and that bat would come alive, slashing at the ball and so many times sending it off the wall in right field, scoring all the runners and putting Slaughter at second base, where he'd dust himself off and look defiantly at the pitcher.

I think about all those times as I ring the doorbell and wait. How often, as an adult, does a person ever come face to face with his boyhood hero?

Through the partially open door I hear a woman's voice: "Come on in. We're in the kitchen." We go inside and there is Helen Slaughter, Enos's wife, and their three daughters, Gaye, twenty-one; Sharon, twenty; Rhonda, eleven. Helen Slaughter smiles and says: "He's not here yet, but he knows you're coming. I'll swear that man works all the time. He leaves here at six in the morning and sometimes I don't see him again until after dark. I

To Big Oz, legendary baseball hero Enos ''Country'' Slaughter (right) is just a boyhood friend and fellow farmer.

don't know how he does it. He never seems to get tired. When it comes to farming, he's a workaholic.''

Helen Slaughter was a TWA stewardess when she met Slaughter in the early 1950s, in the twilight of his career, which ended in 1959 when he was forty-three. "He always wanted to come back to Roxboro," she says. "This was home for him and he had this land—more than 200 acres in all—and he never considered living anyplace else."

Is he happy? She tells me to see for myself. Enos Slaughter walks into the room, freshly showered after ten hours in the tobacco fields, wearing a navy blue golf shirt, jeans, tinted eyeglasses. He is without shoes and his white feet contrast with the deep tan on his arms and face.

"Am I happy? Shoot, yes," he says, in a mellow accent that sounds as if it's a mixture of North Carolina farmer and Virginia gentleman. "I don't think about the hard work and long hours. I just go out and do it. I don't need no help. My brother, Daniel, and me do it all. I'm my own boss. I don't think I'd like working this hard if somebody made me do it. But I'm working for myself. And I can take off and go fishing or play golf when I want to. I ought to be back out in the field tomorrow but, shoot, I'm going fishing. It'll still be there Monday, now won't it?"

Slaughter plays more golf now than at any time in his life, often in fund-raising celebrity tournaments. He scores in the middle eighties, and going to the tee with Fred MacMurray, Perry Como or other show-business personalities doesn't challenge him any more than the pitchers who decades before threw him high and tight to try to silence his bat. "Shoot, I just go out and hit the ball and have a good time—like I always have. Don't nothing bother me. Never did."

He still gets dozens of letters each week from fans who want his autograph or picture, many so young they weren't yet born when he was an active player. "People remember . . . somehow. I can't go into any city in the country without being recognized. It's really amazing. I'll be walking down a street or coming out of an airport and somebody will stare at me, walk up and say: 'Hey, ain't you Country Slaughter?' And I'll say: 'I'm afraid I am.' ''

We spend an hour and a half together and Slaughter apologizes when it's time for him to leave to watch two of his daughters play in a softball game. "Any time at all when you're in these parts, come back. You're welcome here."

*Back home in Philadelphia, with William Penn behind them,
are author Darrell Sifford and his wife, Marilyn, Big Oz's
daughter.*

Tomorrow we fly back to Philadelphia. Before we leave, I want one more nose-to-nose talk with Big Oz, this time about the seeming paradox of the federal government's supporting tobacco farmers at the same time it is spending millions of dollars to encourage people to quit smoking.

I get into the subject as Big Oz and I stand near his truck, the back bumper of which holds a red sticker with white letters that proclaim: "Califano is hazardous to my health." That's a reminder of the war against cigarette smoking waged by Joseph Califano, the former U.S. Secretary of Health, Education and Welfare, a war that is widely believed to have led to his dismissal. When Califano was fired, they set off skyrockets and shot firecrackers in the tobacco country. Compared to Califano, the boogeyman is a hero. It's not that he opposed cigarette smoking, it's that he never let up in his onslaught, and tobacco farmers felt he was persecuting them.

Big Oz says he doesn't think it would matter much if the federal government did stop supporting tobacco through its guaranteed minimum prices. If that happened, farmers in tobacco states would come up with their own plan for financial support.

"We've got to have a support floor. It's the same as the base on wheat farms. When you work with the elements, when you're on a minimum production scale, if you go below the cost of production, then it won't work out. The law of supply and demand works only when farmers get above production costs. If you don't meet production costs for many years, then you go out of business. Only the ones who turn a profit year after year could stay in business, and they couldn't produce enough to satisfy the demand. Little farmers like me have got to have more than 10 percent profit to operate. Maybe big commercial farmers can operate on that, but I can't."

Oz says he doesn't worry about what he describes as the "so-called" findings by the government that cigarette smoking is hazardous to health. He says he doesn't believe the findings are accurate, and he doubts that most other people do either, since more people, based on cigarette sales, seem to be smoking now than ever before.

As for himself, Oz doesn't smoke, not for health reasons but because he doesn't enjoy smoking. "If I liked smoking as much as I like smelling tobacco, I'd smoke all the time. But I don't. It makes me cough."

I ask Oz how it feels to be in a business that yields a product the government says can contribute to cancer, heart attacks and high blood pressure. He answers with a question: "How would you feel if the government said that the newspaper business was hazardous to your health?"

Marilyn and I go back down to the pond with the flat rock one more time before Oz and Remell drive us to the airport between Raleigh and Durham. We listen to the frogs and remind ourselves that we'll be back in a year. It's so calm, so peaceful.

Then the airplane brings us back to the big city. But sometimes, on our terrace thirty-seven floors above the street, I stretch out in the canvas-back lounge chair, close my eyes and get the feeling that I'm still back beside the pond. Sometimes it seems very quiet, almost as if I can hear the frogs. At those moments the police sirens, fire engines and garbage trucks don't seem to make any noise.

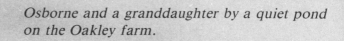

Osborne and a granddaughter by a quiet pond on the Oakley farm.

2 ⇜ The banker with a heart

In the cotton and soybean country of northeast Arkansas, wrapped around the Missouri bootheel, they tell a story about the young man who knocked on a farmer's door one evening and announced: "I'd like to be your banker."

That was unheard of in the early 1960s, a banker out in the backwoods soliciting business. The farmer was stunned. Finally he stammered: "Can you come back tomorrow?"

"What time do you get up?" the young man asked.

"A lot earlier than bankers get up," the farmer answered. Then he forgot about it and went to bed. He was jolted from sleep at 5:30 the next morning by the barking of his dogs. Groggily, he went to the window and peered into the darkness, aware that somebody was approaching the house. At last he could make out the form of a man. He continued to stare and then he ran back to the bed, shook his wife to consciousness and exclaimed: "My Gawd, it's that banker feller."

Indeed it was that banker feller, Marlin D. Jackson, who today, at forty-three, is chairman of the board and president of Security Bank of Paragould, Arkansas. But back then he was the vice-president in charge of agricultural loans for another bank, and the way he chose to drum up business was to get out and hustle, even if it meant waking up a farmer at 5:30 in the morning.

"That banker feller," Marlin D. Jackson knows what it means to be in the business of farming.

I'm in Jackson's second-floor office in Paragould, and I'm telling him that story and he's nodding, smiling and remembering.

"I told the farmer: 'Henry, I can put your whole financing into a more logical package. I can help you modernize your farm, finance your crops and equipment and take your deposits.' He was favorably impressed, not so much by what I was telling him but by my coming before daylight. Yes, I got Henry as a customer for the bank. He's a friend, and we've often talked about what happened that morning. Henry remembers it with specificity."

Jackson turns forty-five degrees in his swivel chair and repeats: " 'Specificity'—that's not a Paragould word; that's a Philadelphia word."

Marlin D. Jackson is somebody you don't forget, and one of the many things that make him appealing is that he can poke fun at himself.

I tell him that every place I go in this part of the country I find people who know him. His name must be a household word. His response, without blinking, is: "My parents were married sixty years in the spring, and the newspaper called me and asked if I'd arrange for them to be interviewed. I told the reporter that he'd have to go in by boat because the area was flooded. He didn't do that but when the water went down, he did go in by tractor. My mother couldn't figure out why he was going to such effort to interview them. I said, 'Mother, it's because you're my parents. I have some notoriety, some fame around here.' And she said, 'Fools' names and fools' faces are often seen in public places.' So there is an element of both good and bad in wide recognition."

How did Jackson, who describes himself as a "redneck country banker," become so well known? He did it the long way—from teaching vocational agriculture at Monette High School, twenty miles from Paragould, to becoming majority stockholder of a bank that makes so many farm loans that bank regulators have been known to gasp in disbelief.

At Monette he also was involved in 4-H work and "developed relationships that transcend those possible in a bank presidency." As a young banker, he tried to tear down the "artificial barriers" that separate banks from people, and he succeeded to a great extent because he was out on the farms almost daily. But he found there was a limit to how much of a good old boy he could be, a limit imposed not by him but by farmers who were more comfortable if he stayed at arm's length.

Jackson grew up in a nearby community called Dixie, so tiny that it's not listed on many maps. Dixie had a cotton gin, a pool hall and a movie theater that was open Saturday and Sunday afternoons. "They chased the pool hall out of business, and there was quite a bit of preaching about the theater being open on Sunday."

He attended Arkansas State University at Jonesboro, where he majored in agricultural economics. "But when I looked at jobs in the middle 1950s, I found a scarcity of people with any idea of hiring such an animal as an agricultural economist. So I decided to take some education courses, to qualify to teach vocational agriculture."

Along the way Jackson had a brief fling in government work, with the Veterans Administration. The only problem was that it wasn't brief enough. "When you work for the government, the object is not productivity, but to be sure you make four copies of everything you would have done if you hadn't been busy making four copies."

After four years as a teacher, Jackson was contacted by the owner of Citizens Bank of Jonesboro and asked if he wanted to become a banker.

"As ludicrous as it seems, I took a cut in pay to take the job. We never discussed salary. He asked me what I made as a teacher, and he said he'd start me at that. I quoted my teacher contract, but I forgot about the money I made with my summer jobs." The result: a 25 percent reduction, and it took Jackson four years as a banker to get his income back to where it was.

What did Jackson do as a banker? Well, in the beginning and for a while after that, Jackson wasn't sure he was a banker. The bank owner who hired him had gone on a trip to Europe, forgetting to tell the bank president that Jackson was coming on board. "I walked in on a Saturday morning and I said: 'Hi, I'm your new farm service officer. Where's my desk?' But there wasn't any desk. They weren't expecting me. As a matter of fact, the bank president wasn't pleased that I had been hired. I was not very polished. I came from the country. I was not a Jonesboro blue blood. I had no pedigree."

As farm service officer, Jackson "acted like a county agent. I took soil samples, checked for insects, helped make steers out of bull calves, doctored pinkeye, acted as midwife for the birth of calves."

Inside the bank, he was almost like a maintenance man. "I took carpets in and out, replaced light bulbs, washed windows, hauled money.''

Hauled money? "That was a very unpleasant task. I'd put eighty or ninety bags of pennies in an old truck and haul them to Memphis. It looked like I had a lot of money, but it was only $3,000. The bags weighed seventy-five pounds apiece, and I'd throw them into the truck.''

After a year Jackson decided that the bank didn't really need a farm service officer. Citizens Bank, he remembers, "was as large as all the other banks in town put together, but it was perceived as cold, indifferent, catering to the near-rich, not to farmers. We had $360,000 in farm loans. The smallest bank had more farm loans.

"So I went to the bank owner, the man who had hired me, and I told him I was quitting, that I wanted to go back to teaching. He was infuriated. He said, 'You may not resign.' And then he asked me what I wanted to do in the bank. I told him that I thought the bank should become more active in farm loans. That interested him, and he dictated a short memo. He had a way of saying a lot in a few words.''

The few words he wrote in the memo were: "Effective immediately, Marlin Jackson's job does not include maintenance, running errands or hauling pennies.''

And that was the start of Jackson's climb to something big. The bank owner asked Jackson to design a plan of action for the bank. "I wrote an elaborate memo, eight pages. He didn't like a memo longer than one page, but he read it all and accepted my recommendation that we form an agriculture committee out of bank board members with farm interests to give advice to me.''

Most of the directors hadn't been on a farm for thirty years, and they had no grasp of how things had changed. "I remember the first loan I ever presented to the bank president. He asked how many horses and mules the farmer had. None, I told him, and he turned down the loan. This was in 1960. Horses and mules were things of the past. But to this bank president they represented the highest and best collateral you could get.''

But Jackson did find four board members to serve on the agriculture committee, including one man who was a retired executive of Swift & Company, the meat-packing giant. "We convened a meeting of the agriculture committee with the board and this man got up and said, 'In fifty years this bank has been hit with only two losses from farm loans. That means we're too darned conserv-

The chairman of the board of Security Bank makes a point.

ative.' That really was a strong word for him to use—'darned.'
And then he said: 'When I was at Swift, I felt that if my salesmen
didn't incur a certain level of losses, they weren't exploiting all of
their sales opportunities. I suggest this bank now is in that same
position.' "

The directors were stunned, Jackson says, but the bank owner
liked what he heard. The bank had a mandate to serve farmers and
it adopted this motto: "Citizens Bank will meet and beat the competition with regard to agriculture."

It wasn't a very catchy motto, but it told the story. When Jackson began to beat the bushes for business—and knock on doors at
5:30 in the morning—the bank's assets were $12 million. Years
later the figure reached $150 million, but it was a long, uphill
climb.

"In Arkansas there is only one loan rate for everybody—10 percent, the legal maximum. But back then the bank had $4 million in
government bonds that were paying only 3½ percent. It was a
patriotic thing, very laudatory, to buy government bonds, but it
did zero to stimulate the local economy." It also didn't make
much money for the bank.

As Jackson was able to convince board members of the financial advantages of investing in farmers, he found fewer obstacles
in his path, fewer officers who asked about horses and mules. But
there is no question that granting farm loans can be a risky business. Jackson talks about that:

"The highest risk loan in the world is a farm production loan,
where you're lending $100,000 or more to somebody to put in his
crop. I talk about it with big-city bankers and they can't believe it.
They ask, 'You mean that you loan some farmer $100,000 on May
15 for a crop that's not even planted yet, that might not produce
anything, without knowing the price if and when the crop is delivered to the marketplace?' I say, 'Yes, that's what we do,' and then
I hear a lot of silence. City banks say they participate in all loans,
but their idea of a farm loan is when they have a warehouse [bins
full of grain] or steers in a feedlot as insulation between them and
the risk. But when it comes to production loans for rice, cotton,
soybeans, outside of Little Rock, Memphis, St. Louis and Dallas,
banks don't know what you're talking about."

By 1969 Jackson had become executive vice-president of Citizens Bank, still employed by the bank owner who had hired him

out of Monette High School. "He never overpaid me. He never told me I worked too hard. But he did encourage me. He encouraged me to get good people around me so I would be available for promotion."

The banker owned banks in other cities, including Little Rock and Paragould. He dispatched Jackson to Little Rock temporarily to resolve some problem loans. Then he sent him to Paragould, where Security Bank was floundering.

Because things were going well in Jonesboro, the owner didn't see any reason for Jackson to return. He offered Jackson a promotion and gave him a choice of going to Little Rock or staying in Paragould. "I preferred to live in Paragould. I came here in 1969 as vice-president with the assigned task of solving serious credit problems. The first week I foreclosed four used car dealers, the Honda dealer and a cotton gin. Generally, I was identified as the meanest guy in Greene County. I was looked at with great suspicion and alarm."

But Jackson straightened out the mess, and a year later he was promoted to president. In 1972 he bought the bank from his old boss by becoming the largest single stockholder. "I paid more than top dollar. He didn't loan me a dime."

Now Security Bank is Jackson's bank, a two-story gray building on the corner of Pruett and Court streets in Paragould, population 12,528, a town that provides free parking for shoppers in lots one block from the main string of stores. It's a town that has an Emerson Electric plant that employs 2,000 people and a Monroe Shock Absorber Company plant that employs 1,200. But, basically, it's a farm town, where the sidewalks are two steps above street level, where men gather on corners to talk, at Lamb's Cafeteria to drink coffee and at Percy's to shoot pool.

Jackson is in his office this morning before nine o'clock, but already he's put in a stressful day. The man and woman who lived across the street from him had been killed the day before when their private airplane crashed in a storm near Little Rock. The man was not trained in instrument flying, and in the swirling clouds that closed in, he became confused, and the airplane corkscrewed into the ground.

Jackson was up at four o'clock this morning, helping to get their affairs in order. By six he was bringing coffee and doughnuts to the gathering relatives and friends and trying to explain to his own six-year-old son what had happened to their neighbors and "who caused the storm."

It's not, Jackson says, uncommon in the life of a country banker, to advise, listen and talk about things that have nothing to do with banking. Jackson looks tired and red-eyed, but he is cordial and warm and lets me know he's glad I have come.

He is wearing a light blue patterned suit, white shirt with MDJ embroidered on the left collar, dark blue necktie, loafers with a gold ornament. "A lot of times I don't wear a suit to work," he says. "I wore a suit today because you were coming. Yesterday I had on a sport shirt."

A few years ago, when Paragould was celebrating "Pioneer Days," Jackson came to work in bib overalls. The local newspaper took a picture of him, and a St. Louis banker saw the picture. Later, when the St. Louis banker was asked to come to Paragould to speak, he accepted only on condition that Jackson provide him with bib overalls. Jackson did, and he put them on and together they posed for a picture that is displayed in Jackson's office.

The office is half the size of a basketball court, tastefully furnished with a five-foot round table, eight upholstered chairs and one couch, all of which are at the end of the room, close to the door, facing Jackson's oversized desk. Pale blue towels with the MDJ monogram hang in his private washroom. It is, by anybody's standards, a spiffy work place, and Jackson seems comfortable in it.

He is two inches above six feet, weighs 215 pounds, and appears to be in good shape. But it hasn't always been this way. Jackson, you see, once weighed—well, there's really no way to tell how much he once did weigh.

He talks about that:

"At Arkansas State I made the traveling team in football. I was a fourth-string lineman they used in lieu of equipment in practice so the equipment wouldn't get worn out. It was a good learning experience, but it interfered with my academic career, so I quit.

"I was 260 pounds then, but I had a 34-inch waist. I was accustomed to hard physical work. In the summers I'd be up at 4:30, with my dad and four brothers, and we'd get our mules and start logging, which was a sideline to our row crops. When it got too hot for the mules, we'd leave them in the shade and we'd go back into the brush. I was in good shape.

"But the penalty I paid was that, as a banker, I continued to eat

Jackson succeeded as a farmer's banker
by being out on farms almost daily.

like a logger. At one time they called me the biggest banker in Arkansas—and I was, from the standpoint of size. Most scales only weigh to 300. Above that, you have to go to a feed store or a cotton gin. You try to avoid doing that because people stare and laugh and say, 'Hey, he's as big as a bale of cotton.' Or, 'He weighs more than four sacks of feed.' ''

Jackson's largest recorded weight was 367, but "I'm sure at one time that I weighed more. When I came to Paragould, I had a 58-inch waist. But six or seven years ago I lost 150 pounds. I lost it all in about six months. I'd lost weight before, but this time I've been successful in keeping it off. It hasn't hurt me. The only time I see my doctor is when I take him duck hunting.''

How did he get the weight off and keep it off?

"When you're that fat, no matter where you sleep your wife rolls toward you. Every time I'd move, she'd roll a little more. There was no sense in flouncing around and disturbing her so one morning when I couldn't sleep, I got up early, about four o'clock, to study a loan application from a farmer who wanted to go into a hog operation. The proposal didn't make any sense to me. The feed cost he had estimated wasn't enough. I got out my copy of Morrison's *Feeds and Feeding*—it's the feeding bible, probably in its thirtieth edition—and I checked the rations, and the farmer had skipped a line when he took his figures from the chart.

"So his figures were all wrong. I sat there and thought: 'For a guy with a fair degree of sophistication and creativity, for a guy who can estimate what it takes to maintain a pregnant sow or fatten a market barrow, you sure are fat.' For me to be so grossly overweight was totally inconsistent with my professional development. It didn't make any sense. So I said: 'Beginning today, I'm going to quit having three breakfasts.' And I did. I used hypnosis and all other means known to man.''

Jackson went to a drugstore and for $2 bought a book that listed the caloric values of food and "started doing for myself what I'd been doing for hogs. I turned down the farmer's loan, the man who wanted to go into swine production. Shortly after that prices dropped, and the man was saved from bankruptcy. I remind him of that when I see him, and he reminds us that we turned him down when we solicit him for deposits.''

Jackson has what he describes as "two families but only one wife.'' He and Betty Jane are the parents of Roy Dewey, twenty, who is called "R.D.," and Janet, who is eighteen. Then there are Sam Dewey, six ("Dewey" after his big brother), and Marla Jane, fourteen months. About the baby's name, he says: "I took the 'Mar' from Marlin and just put the 'la' on the end."

Jackson recalls that he was a schoolteacher when the first two children were born and "I'd buy a can of Similac and hope I'd have enough money left at the end of the week to buy another can. The only difference now, as a bank president, is my credit rating. I call the drug store and they send a case of Similac and charge it to me. We don't have any more money to spend than when I was teaching school." He adores his "second" family, regards it as "an opportunity for us to start over. It tends to keep us very young."

Jackson and his older boy, R.D., are both pilots. Jackson owns two airplanes and sometimes flies himself around the state to meetings of the Arkansas State Board of Higher Education, of which he is vice-chairman. He is involved in "a fair amount" of other activities outside banking, including Greene County industrial efforts. He's a member of Paragould's First Methodist Church and he speaks two Sundays a month at a rural Methodist Church. "I'd speak in Baptist churches, too, if they'd let me," he says. He moved his family to Paragould from Jonesboro in the middle of an ice storm in 1970, a year after he came to Security Bank. Even though Jonesboro is only twenty-two miles away, he didn't want to commute because "I felt it was important psychologically not to be a resident of Jonesboro" and run a bank in Paragould.

When Jackson calls himself a country banker "who has never been anywhere or seen anything," he is not being totally truthful. He travels the nation to attend American Banking Association meetings, and three summers in the last ten he has attended seminars at Harvard University. He's amazed, he says, by how little understanding there is of farming outside farm areas.

"The fact is that the price the farmer gets for the wheat that goes into a loaf of bread is less than the cost of the wrapper that surrounds the bread. But in the cities, even in a heady academic atmosphere, agriculture is perceived as an industry that has a virtual guarantee of profit, prosperity and perpetuation of government farm programs. The young people, those under forty, see people driving air-conditioned farm tractors, living on elaborate farmsteads, and they regard farming as a materialistic sort of thing.

"But there is no guarantee of profit. The number of farms is decreasing substantially. They say there are 2.8 million farms, but 10 percent of them produce 80 percent of the dollar volume of farm products. Around here there are not high numbers of young farmers. The average age of farmers has substantially increased. My guess is that it now is in the middle fifties. Fewer people are coming to the farms."

It is, Jackson says, the result of "the evolution of civilization, the sociological changes in rural America." In his exaggerated way of making a point, he continues: "How do you keep 'em down on the farm after they've seen gay Paree? That's the problem. Farm kids see classmates who've gone to Detroit and now they have indoor plumbing, a fairly new car and they take vacations. That's why they're not content on the farm. They want something more than a tar paper shack to live in. I'm talking about people on the small farms. They can't make it any more. They're being squeezed out. Farms will continue to get larger because of this. Bigger farmers are buying out the little farmers who aren't making it. Economically, it's a good thing to do. It doesn't cost much more to farm another hundred acres. You already have the equipment and the manpower. You spend an additional $3,000 on fertilizer, seed and extra parts and maybe you produce an additional $15,000 gross."

Around Paragould there are a few small farms, 200 acres or so, and a few large ones, from 2,000 to 3,000 acres. But most of the farms are somewhere in between. The loans that keep them in business can range from $25,000 to $750,000, and Jackson's bank, one of two in Paragould, is where many farmers come for help.

"What is the proper role of a bank?" Jackson asks. "A bank is a quasi-public trust, with $50 million of public funds. What do you do?" What Jackson does is allot a substantial number of his bank's assets to farm production loans.

"I hold my competitors in high regard," Jackson says. "They are honest people. But their loan-to-deposit ratio is 60 percent [$60 in loans for every $100 in assets]. This bank's ratio is 70 percent, on the average. We're known as the lending bank, the agriculture bank. The competition hired a former county agent, and now they're making a fair number of agriculture loans—but still not as many as we do. They're $15 million larger than this bank, but in 1978 the dollar amount of our farm loans exceeded theirs."

How does a farm loan work? Typically, Jackson says, here's

Money may be serious business, but that doesn't prevent Jackson and bank employees from having a little fun with it. Jackson is known for a sense of humor and especially likes to poke fun at himself.

what happens with a farmer who owns most of his land:

The farmer comes to the bank right after the year begins and takes out what is called a multiple advance note. This provides him with money when he needs it throughout the year. In March, for example, he can telephone the bank to transfer $10,000 to his checking account because he's going to buy fertilizer.

For medium-size farmers, in the 800- to 900-acre range, the typical loan is from $75,000 to $100,000. Production loans generally are paid back all at once, when the crops are sold. Other loans for major farm items such as tractors, combines, cotton pickers, may have a payback in from three to five years.

Jackson's bank uses what he calls the "three Cs of lending"—character, capacity, collateral—to determine how much and under what conditions money will be loaned to farmers.

With an established farmer, the bank might ask for nothing more than a mortgage on the crop proceeds. For other farmers, a mortgage on equipment might be required. For a new farmer with mostly rented land and not much equipment, the bank might insist that he "contract forward" on most of his crop—find a buyer who will agree to pay a predetermined price when the crop is delivered. That way the bank can be more confident that the money will be there to repay the loan.

If the farmer is struggling, if the amount of his loans and his income are almost equal, the bank "becomes involved in the management decisions of that farmer, not in the day-to-day operation but in a general kind of way," Jackson says. "We might tell him: 'To finance you this year, we'll need to have an agreement that provides that you will let us help you in marketing decisions. You can't incur additional debts without our approval.' "

Who borrows most of the money? The farmers who are struggling, Jackson answers. "From top-quality, low-risk to bottom-quality, high-risk, the dollars get larger at the bottom. They borrow to produce the crops and make land payments, even payments on their houses."

Despite its liberal loan policy, Security Bank doesn't have many farmers who default, according to Jackson. In one recent year, on farm loans of $12 million, the bank lost just $200,000, and most of that was from five farmers.

When farmers have a bad year, Jackson adds, there's nothing for a banker to do except "buckle up his belt and get on the wagon with the farmer. We stay with him in good years and bad. That's

*An airborne conference on flood control with Arkansas Con-
gressman Bill Alexander is not an unusual event in the busy
business and civic life of Marlin Jackson.*

why we have a low loss ratio. There are frequent crop failures, but it's rare we can't keep a farmer alive.''

If a bank stopped lending money every time there was crop failure, Jackson says, ''we wouldn't have any farmers in this county. Every year there is too much rain, not enough rain, hail damage, and no production. So you restructure the debt. Instead of being due this year, you scatter it out over three or four years, maybe take a second mortgage on the farm.''

What happens if a farmer has two bad years in a row? That seldom happens to a good farmer, Jackson says, but if it did, the bank might go from ''we're glad to see you'' to ''oh, you're not in here wanting money again, are you?''

In the worst of years there is a nucleus of farmers who still manage to do rather well. But the bad years can be tragic for what Jackson calls the ''inadequate farmers who ignore the marketing concepts of the business.'' This is an outgrowth of twenty-five years of government-imposed farm economy, Jackson says, when farmers were told how many acres to plant and when the government was the ultimate market for many crops, through the Commodity Credit Corporation. In other words, the farmer didn't have to make marketing decisions for himself, and he tended to forget how to do it.

When the government pulled back, the economy was going full blast and the farmer, like everybody else, prospered. ''There were some great profits in the Nixon years, '73 and '74, when people who had not been out of debt in twenty years got out of debt. Some of them got indoor plumbing for the first time in their lives. Instead of the New Deal, where they killed calves and plowed up cotton and where there was a highly structured market, there was a free market. That works well if the economy is on the upswing.

''But then along came 1977, and it was a disastrous year, pricewise. Inflation was 10 percent in general and 15 to 18 percent on the farm. India exported wheat; normally it's an importer. Russia didn't need us. The Vietnam war was settled. Rice went from $8.00 [a hundredweight] in 1975 to $2.80 on the free market.''

The farmers who survived—and many didn't—finally began to learn something about marketing, Jackson says. ''But you can't learn overnight. Even with the highest IQ in the world, you can't. It would be like taking a six-week course in journalism and expecting to be a good journalist. There is a time ingredient involved in the learning process. We seem to forget this. In the change to

The adoring father with daughter Marla. Marla and her six-year-old brother, Sam Dewey, are the Jacksons' "second family." Older children are eighteen and twenty.

peace from war, the time ingredient of learning, if not lost, at least was ignored.''

What all of that means, Jackson says, is that more farmers are becoming aware of the necessity of protecting themselves by contracting in advance to sell part of their crop at a price that assures them a reasonable profit. They do this not to make Jackson's bank happy but to hedge against misfortune from the weather, the market or insects. A farmer who knows that his production cost is $5.50 for a bushel of soybeans is guaranteed a profit if he contracts to sell at $7.00 a bushel—even though the harvest price may be down to $3.75.

What if the harvest price is up to $10? Doesn't the farmer then feel cheated? No, says Jackson, not if he's held back some of his crop, as many farmers do, to sell at current market prices. The bank's influence on how much of the crop is contracted for in advance depends on where the farmer stands with the bank, whether he is considered a good risk or a bad risk, and how much money the bank has invested in the farmer.

If the bank has a bigger stake in the operation than the farmer does, then, Jackson says, the bank influences when and at what price the crop will be sold. "We try to do it diplomatically, not as a dictator. But if the farmer is in trouble and won't ask for help, then it's time for us to dissolve the relationship." If the bank and the farmer have a fifty-fifty relationship, "we'll sit together and maybe decide to sell 10,000 bushels now, put 40,000 bushels in the warehouse and see what the market does. It's a matter of talking and sifting out the risks."

Is the bank always right in its marketing decisions? Obviously it's not, Jackson says, because "we're not as well educated as our best farmers." But the bank is right more often than not, and, in the final analysis, might does make right. If the farmer disagrees, the bank always can use the weapon of cutting off the loans. To do this to a farmer who is in trouble means to liquidate him, but this, Jackson says, is extremely rare. "Most liquidations are mutually arrived at by the bank and the borrower. Both agree that it's time to get out.

"They know they can't stand another crop failure, another market failure. They're tired of floods, tired of marketing for $3 a crop that cost them $5 to produce." In most voluntary liquidations, Jackson says, the bank may find a buyer for the farm.

How much money can a good farmer earn in a year? A medium-size farmer with a $100,000 loan likely would gross $300,000 in a year, Jackson says, and from that he might net $20,000, even $30,000 "if he's lucky and prudent. But what does he have left after he's paid his living expenses for the year? He might have $12,000 in the bank if he is extremely frugal. But most don't do that well."

As farms increase in size and the number of farmers decreases, Jackson says, two things happen. One is that farmers have more control over their own destiny. "As the base gets smaller, there is greater discipline in the marketplace" and farmers have greater influence on prices through their marketing decisions. The other is that farmland becomes more expensive and the gap widens between land prices and the income from what can be produced on the land. This means that the big farmers get bigger and the little farmers may go out of business. "If you're farming 200 acres, you may need more land to make a living. If you can't afford to buy it or if you can't lease it, then you have to get out. Somebody who is very frugal might make it on 200 acres," but most don't.

Does Jackson have any regrets about not taking his banking abilities to the big city?

No, he says, a smile creasing his face. For him, rural America is where the action is, not wheeling and dealing but knowing the people with whom you do business and caring about them. It's also a lot safer.

"When we go to Washington for a banking meeting, it's not unusual to leave our home unattended and unlocked. We'll be gone, the whole family, maybe for three or four days or a week or two. The last time we were in a Washington hotel, I opened the windows to get some fresh air. In a minute a guard knocked on the door and told me that our windows were open. 'Yes, I know,' I said. 'I opened them. Is there a rule against that?'

"The guard said that, yes, there is a rule against that. The windows must remain locked. 'If you leave your room, somebody will take all of your possessions and the hotel's possessions, too,' he said. I thought he was joking with me. Here we were, 1,620 miles from home, and our house wasn't even locked. We don't even have a key to our house."

But even in rural America things aren't what they used to be. Crime is increasing, Jackson says, because people have discovered that "sin is as much fun in the country as in the city."

3 ❧ Sweet taste of America

He was not yet eighteen years old, but already he had lost count of the men he had killed. Out here in Russia, in this courage-robbing winter of 1941 and early 1942, there was no time to count. It seemed, Robert Wilhelm often thought, that there was no time for anything—except to kill, to shake in the agony and fright of it all and then to kill again.

Although nobody else in his German infantry company was as young as Wilhelm, he had learned, better than most, how to be a survivor. For that he grimly thanked the 2½ years he had lived with his parents and five of his brothers and sisters in Siberia, exiled there in 1929 by the Russian government because his German-born father owned too much land. He was only four the night his father announced that the government had taken everything, that they must leave their home in Odessa and go into exile or be imprisoned. He still remembered the frantic truck ride to the railroad station and then the journey to the northeast in the boxcar, from which his father had dropped three of the children safely into snowbanks as the train wound through towns in which friends were waiting.

The six remaining children and the parents had lived in a wooden house so far into the Siberian wilderness that, on a clear day,

---

Old Glory has special meaning for Iowa hog farmer, Robert Wilhelm, whose early life was spent in exile or in battle.

they might have seen Alaska. They ate the fish they caught and at
night they huddled together to marshal their body warmth as
winds whipped across the flatlands at fifty miles an hour and
temperatures dropped to sixty-five degrees below zero. They were
there until the gold Russian money his father had hoarded was ex-
changed for false identification papers that enabled the entire
family to return to Odessa, the Black Sea town where the masses
came on their holidays to relax, to sun and to drink their vodka.

But Robert Wilhelm never forgot two things he learned in
Siberia:

If you wrap strips of blanket around your boots and sprinkle
them with water, the ice that forms becomes an insulating barrier
against the unspeakable cold, and your feet don't freeze—even
though the feet of those around you are going numb, turning blue
and then black.

If you feel warm and comfortable, as if you'd like to sleep, you
know you're about to freeze to death, and you have to do the op-
posite of what common sense seems to dictate. You remove your
clothing and rub snow on your bare skin, on your chest, legs and
face. You rub so vigorously that you begin to sweat; that's when
you know that you're coming back to life. And then a tiny bit of
feeling returns to your skin, followed by burning pain. That pain
is good news. It means that you've made it; you're not going to
freeze to death. At least not this time.

In this Russian winter, while half of his company froze to death,
Robert Wilhelm wrapped his boots and rubbed snow on his body
and prayed: "Oh, God, forgive me for what I am doing and spare
me, if that is Your will."

Because he grew up in Russia—he was working an irrigation
pump for the Communist government when he was twelve years
old—Wilhelm knew Russian as fluently as the German that his
family spoke in hushed tones inside their house. When the Germans occupied Odessa, they drafted him into their army—after all
he was a German—and they marveled that one so young could
know two languages. In every way, Wilhelm had thought, being in
the German army was superior to being in the communist labor
force, working from 3:00 A.M. to 10:00 P.M. seven days a week, not
by choice but because those who didn't work went to prison. Even
reporting for work one hour late might mean a month behind
bars. He hated every minute of it, and his entry into the German

army seemed almost a rebirth, an opportunity to live, eat and dress as a man in a fighting machine so invincible that surely it soon would overrun the backward Russians.

He understood nothing about politics, but whatever Hitler's Germany stood for, he thought, it had to be better than the communism he was leaving, where he subsisted on vegetables and a pound of bread a day if he were lucky. The Germans sent him to Holland, where he trained for ten months, where twice every week he fixed the sinister-looking bayonet to his rifle and fought not a bag but another soldier as frightened as he was. Then they pulled the bayonets off their rifles, strapped them to their hands—like daggers—and fought some more. When the three-hour fighting sessions were over, when the officers had finished screaming their instructions, Wilhelm sometimes cried. "Why do they make us work so hard?" he asked himself. One day, near the end of the tenth month, an officer told him: "You may think you are good. But you are still not good enough. You will never be good enough."

And now, in the cold of Russia, Robert Wilhelm knew that the officer had been correct. He never would be good enough to survive this winter and the waves of Russian soldiers, the bayonet fights and the paralyzing fear that preceded every one. The night before, he had gone out to a hole in the ground to relieve a soldier who sat behind a machine gun and stared into the darkness. Wilhelm tapped him on the arm, and the man toppled over, stiff as a toy soldier whose joints had rusted. He was frozen. Wilhelm felt the soldier's face and found that his eyes were closed in the eternal sleep into which a man can be seduced by the warmth that precedes death.

Wilhelm felt anger, not because the man had died but because he had been spared the brutality of death at the end of a bayonet. And he, Wilhelm, still had that waiting for him, that awful moment when he would lose, when he would not be good enough. The Russian soldiers were not good fighters. They didn't have good officers who led them into battle, who inspired them, who died before they died—as the German officers did. They didn't have enough rifles. Those in the second and third waves ran into battle empty-handed, picking up the rifles of those who died before them. The rifles they had were almost seven feet long, and the bayonets they attached to them were three feet long. That meant that the Russian soldiers were clumsy in their movements.

In a close fight the Germans, with their shorter weapons and hand-held bayonets, were quicker and more mobile. It was said, and widely believed among the Germans, that twelve Russians died for every German.

But the Russians did have two things in their favor. They had numbers that seemed without end. And they were dressed for the Russian winter, in their heavy boots, fur caps and tan greatcoats that were so thick that sometimes a German wrist would buckle as it tried to drive a bayonet through the fabric and into the flesh. But a wrist failed only one time. In this kind of war, a soldier who made one mistake was dead. Seldom was there a second chance.

In the snow and sleet many Germans froze to death before they even had an opportunity to die in battle. They had not enough adequate clothing. There was a rumor going through the ranks that a mix-up in transportation had caused the problem. Wilhelm knew that it was no rumor. It was the truth, because he had been there that day at the railroad station when the new winter uniforms were supposed to arrive. When they opened the boxcars, they found they had been sent lightweight cotton clothing, even short pants, destined for Germans fighting in Africa. Presumably those in Africa had received the greatcoats, fur caps with ear flaps and insulated boots. The Germans angrily had burned the boxcars with the summer clothing, and in the flames Wilhelm had seen the twisted faces of those who would die in the winter, victims not of Russian bayonets but of nature.

At two o'clock one afternoon, with an icy sun overhead, the Russians started their attack. It followed their usual pattern. First there were whistles, the sounds of officers getting their troops up and ready. Then there were the screams—to Wilhelm they sounded like thousands of voices in a chorus singing "Hurrahhhhh!" The screams stretched that final H to what seemed infinity. And then more screams: "Hurrahhhhh! Hurrahhhhh! Hurrahhhhh!" Now they were coming, swarming like ants, everywhere, some falling, their greatcoats stained with crimson, others seizing the rifles from the death grips of the fallen and running ahead, almost blindly.

Wilhelm seldom saw Russian officers and he assumed that they must be somewhere in the rear, that after blowing their whistles they turned the fighting over to the sergeants and to the legions that followed the sergeants. Wilhelm sat in his hole in the ground, gripping the handles of a 9-mm machine gun that spat out death

650 times a minute. But that wasn't fast enough. He could kill 650 Russians and 650 more took their places. Wilhelm raked his shower of steel from right to left and then from left to right, but on they came. Off to his right he could see that the Russians had broken the German line. Some of them now were fighting behind him. Any moment he knew that they would be in the hole with him, hacking, trying to shoot. He hoped only that they would jump into the hole from the front, so that he could see them, so that he would have at least an instant to brace himself for death.

He continued to fire his white-hot machine gun until the Russians were almost into his hole. Then he seized a pistol in his left hand and a bayonet in his right hand and fired and stabbed, fired and stabbed. With war this close, a soldier looked straight into the eyes of those he was trying to kill and he saw reflected in their eyes the same horror of death that saturated his own body. With fear came strength Wilhelm did not know was his, strength to fight for half an hour, an hour, ninety minutes, strength to knock down a bigger man and end his life in an instant.

Because he knew Russian, Wilhelm understood what the enemy was saying, and at death the enemy was saying exactly what the Germans were saying, the universal prayer of soldiers: "Oh, God, please help me . . ."

Then the battle was over, and what lingered was the smell of death, blood and gunpowder, and the moans of the dying. Wilhelm felt mushy, as he always did after battle. His legs were like two rubber columns that folded when he tried to move them. His mouth was dry and the taste of metal was the residue of fear that lingered for hours. He tried to drink from his canteen, but he was unable to hold it on his quivering lips. The coffee, now icy cold, tumbled down the front of his coat and froze, forming a crust on top of the scum of battle. As bad as this was, it was better than the first time, when Wilhelm vomited as he tried to escape some of those he had killed.

The killing never got easier, but if he didn't kill them, they would kill him. And every battle had but one goal in mind—not to gain fifty yards or one mile but to stay alive, until the next battle. "That's all anybody was fighting for," Wilhelm would remember. "Beyond that there was no sense of purpose—for us and, I expect, for them, too."

After eighteen days at Stalingrad, the German army didn't have to order the withdrawal of Wilhelm's company. There was nothing left to withdraw. Of 320 who went into battle, only seventeen still were alive. Of the seventeen, only three were not crippled. One of the three was Robert Wilhelm, spared, somehow, by the grace of God.

As winter turned into spring and spring into summer, Wilhelm continued to fight, this time in blistering heat that reached ninety degrees and decayed the bodies of dead soldiers stacked three feet high—Germans and Russians joined together at last in common peace. The International Red Cross managed to get a truce called. Together, Germans and Russians dug holes, lined them with lime and pushed the bodies into the holes. Then the fighting resumed, Wilhelm remembered. "We were trying to kill each other minutes after we had worked side by side. It was absolutely insane, crazy. I hope to God that nobody ever has to go through that. Humans are the most cruel of all animals. What other animals would do that to each other?"

Through it all, Wilhelm prayed and Wilhelm survived, "not because I was the best fighter but because I was luckier than many." He was bayoneted once in the side and once in the hand, but neither injury was serious. As the war wound down to its con- clusion, Wilhelm, in full retreat with other soldiers, knew that he had to make a choice: Surrender to the Russians or surrender to the Americans.

"I would shoot myself before I would surrender to the Rus- sians," he told himself. So Wilhelm, now a sergeant, and another German slipped ahead, in front of their unit, and surrendered to the first American soldiers they saw. That was in France on May 5, 1945. For one year and twenty days he was imprisoned, long af- ter war's end, and as he would remember it, the treatment that he received as a prisoner was "99 percent better than in the German army." It was then that thoughts of coming to the United States first germinated in Wilhelm's mind. "The German soldier was the best fed, best dressed, best paid in Europe. But he was nothing like the American soldier. I looked at the American soldiers and I said: 'You must come from a very good country.' "

Out of prison, Wilhelm went to work on a dairy farm in upper Austria, and there he met a young woman named Clara, whose mother had died long ago and whose father had been killed in the war. She milked cows from early morning to late evening, until her hands ached. But the thing about her that Wilhelm remembered was that she never complained. She knew what hard work was, and she accepted it. He liked that, because it was an attitude that paralleled his own. The next year they fell in love and although they had nothing, they felt as if they had everything. They married in the morning and then Wilhelm went to the fields to work and his bride returned to the milking barns.

In those times Robert Wilhelm was called a "displaced person." What that meant was that he was a man without a country. Although his parents were German and although he fought in the German army for 5½ years, Germany regarded him as a foreigner because he was born in Russia. For Wilhelm, this was the greatest pain of all, "the pain inside when you are rejected by the country that you think is yours."

Robert and Clara Wilhelm grubbed out an existence on the little farm, earning the equivalent of about $10 a month. Then through their Lutheran church, they heard about a program in which American Lutheran churches brought Europeans to the United States. Would it be possible for them to get on the list and, maybe someday, come to America?

For five years they waited. Then in 1953 word came: Victor and Evelyn Stueland, cattle farmers in Calamus, Iowa, would sponsor them and give them work and a place to live until they could make it on their own. Robert and Clara Wilhelm were joyful—and frightened. With their two sons they packed their meager possessions and boarded a ship, unable to speak a sentence in English. Not only were they without money, they were also $637 in debt to the Lutheran church for paying their fare. But there was no turning back now. The great adventure was beginning.

• • •

It's a thirty-minute flight from Chicago to the Quad-Cities Airport, which serves Moline and Rock Island, in Illinois, and Davenport and Bettendorf, across the Mississippi River in Iowa. A sign proclaims the Quad-Cities as "A Welcome Change of Place. 480,000 population. $18,000 family income."

This is America's heartland, the Midwest just north of my Missouri birthplace. Although this is my first trip to the Quad-Cities, the view from the airplane reveals a landscape that is familiar to me: flat cornfields in precise, green rectangles that are cut apart by ribbons of superhighway concrete and by dusty back roads, all of which seem straight as yardsticks. The Rock River, slender, tree-lined and muddy-looking, squirms into the Mighty Mississippi at the Quad-Cities. The Mississippi looks rain-swollen and angry, its brown surface broken by ripples that rise and turn to gray before they die and disappear. It's late afternoon and the sun is an orange ball that rapidly is retreating behind the edge of the earth.

I'm inside the airport, suitcase in one hand, briefcase in the other. I look around and there they are—Robert and Clara Wilhelm, smiling, waving, pointing. "You must be . . ."

"Well, yes, I am . . ."

"Ah, we're glad you came to see us."

Clara Wilhelm, in our telephone conversation, has insisted that they will pick me up at the airport and drive me the thirty-three miles to their home in Calamus, Iowa, where, she has insisted, they will board me and feed me and even take me to play golf if I will bring my clubs.

"Ah, you don't have your clubs?" she asks. "That's too bad, but we'll take you to the golf course anyway."

Clara Wilhelm is a short, pleasant-faced woman with a quick smile and a rapid-fire way of talking that, coupled with her German accent, is somewhat difficult for me to understand. Robert Wilhelm looks about a foot taller than his wife. His face is ruddy—almost like an Indian's face—and his skin is lined from years in the sun. He wears a blue baseball-type cap with the word "Lacombe" and a hog's head on the front. He speaks more slowly than his wife, but his accent is more pronounced and he seems less comfortable with the language than she. Sometimes, when he gropes unsuccessfully to complete a sentence, he turns to her and asks, "Momma, what do I mean?"

In public, you might get the idea that Clara Wilhelm calls the shots in the family. That is my impression in the beginning, but it changes in a hurry after we are loaded into their four-year-old Chrysler Newport. Clara Wilhelm calls her shots, but not his.

As he drives through the befuddling maze of interstate highway signs around the airport, Clara tells him: "Turn here, Robert, turn here. This is the way home."

Wilhelm does not turn and, without changing expression, he says, "Ya, Momma, I'll turn where I want to turn." Then, smiling, he bends his head toward her and says, "I'm taking the back way."

It is obvious that Robert and Clara Wilhelm have been married a long time. They have that comfortable relationship that comes only after years of filing away at the rough edges of irritation, of learning what is fair to say and how to say it. She seems to know when it is proper to interrupt; he seems to know how to tell her when it's not proper. And they both can laugh about it.

All of their years together seem not to have eroded their love for each other. Rather, the years have fortified their love with a bond that seems to say: "Even if we weren't married, we'd still be best friends."

Robert Wilhelm is fifty-four and Clara is fifty-five. The sons who rode the ship with them to this new life are Alfred, thirty-two, who lives four miles away on a farm he rents, and Herbert, twenty-six, who lives next door to his parents in a seventy-five-year-old house. A daughter, Linda, is a legal secretary in Rock Island, where she lives with her husband, a carpenter. They remain a close family, and when Robert and Clara Wilhelm talk, much of what they say draws on their children's lives as reference points: "We bought this land when Fred [Alfred] was eighteen. We took that trip the year Linda graduated from high school."

Robert and Clara Wilhelm have enough money to do just about whatever they want to do these days. They've turned over to their sons much of the hard work of raising corn, soybeans and pure-bred Lacombe hogs. Free to travel, they go to Florida for a week or two every winter and back to Europe every third year to visit relatives. After these many years, Wilhelm still has trouble realizing that this good fortune belongs to him. "What we have done here we couldn't have done in Europe in 400 years. It just wouldn't have been possible. This is the greatest country on earth, and it has the greatest people on earth. Oh, how much I believe that! I wish people who were born here believed it so much."

What Robert and Clara Wilhelm have today is the result of years of backbreaking work and iron-willed commitment. When they came, they worked for the Stuelands for $125 a month, milk and a free house. "We spoke no English," Clara Wilhelm recalls, "but the people accepted us, the people around Calamus. There was the language of love, and everybody understood that. Never did I see such hospitality. People we didn't know furnished our house, put groceries on our table. They all came and brought clothes. Women brought carloads of food. It was the greatest thing there ever was. Never did I see so many kind people."

A gathering of Wilhelms. The family includes Robert (left),

wife, Clara (center), two sons, a daughter and five grandchildren.

Many of these same people still are among their closest friends because the Wilhelms have remained, essentially, the same as they always were. When you talk to people around Calamus, they likely will tell you two things: Robert and Clara Wilhelm are kind and generous and, if you needed it, they'd give you the shirt off their backs. And, their children never caused anybody any trouble because they had been taught to respect their elders.

Robert and Clara paid off their $637 debt to the church at $30 a month as he worked in the fields and she tended the garden. Then Victor Stueland bought a sow, and Wilhelm raised pigs for him, getting a bonus of $1 for each pig that went to market. After 2½ years, the Wilhelms had saved $750 and they had a car that would run more often than not. Would Victor and Evelyn Stueland feel all right if they didn't work for them any more, if they rented a place of their own? Stueland not only agreed but he also helped make arrangements for them to rent 160 acres in Miles, Iowa, forty miles to the north. They bought a sow and thirty milk cows on $5,000 they borrowed and paid back in eighteen months. They were on that farm for six years, and then they moved back to Calamus in 1962, rented the farm they now have for two years and then bought it.

Where did the money come from for a down payment? From their muscles. They worked, the two of them, from four in the morning until ten in the evening, and the children worked after school and on weekends. In Clara's words they "never went anywhere," and they had been in the United States for eight years before they ever saw the inside of a restaurant. They made their own cigarettes and they grew their own food. They sold eggs, chickens and milk in those never-ending days, and in the sweetness of freedom, they never complained that they were tired.

"The days were too short for me," Wilhelm remembers. "I always was ready to do more. I felt so happy. I can't remember that kind of happiness before, even as a child. The work might have looked hard, but for me it was easy because I knew what I was working for."

With that enthusiasm he found that he was able to do more and more, so he began to bale hay for other farmers for ten cents a bale after he finished work at his farm. Only in the winter, when night closed in early and when the howling winds drifted the snow above the door tops, did he slow down and work fewer than eight-

Wilhelm's hogs must have blood tested by veterinarian (foreground) for interstate transportation. A neighbor helps.

een hours in a day. He thought he had the world by the tail, and in many ways he did. He, Clara and the children were healthy and happy.

Today the Wilhelms own 400 acres of prime farmland on which they grow the corn and soybeans to feed the 2,000 hogs that they send to slaughterhouses and sell to breeders every year. They have a three-bedroom ranch house nestled off a country road, with a twenty-foot flagpole topped by an American flag in the front yard. "It's my way of telling people how proud I am to be an American," says Wilhelm, who, with his wife, became an American citizen in the early 1970s.

What he and Clara have done, he says, proves that success still can be manufactured through hard work and frugal living, through unswerving dedication to a dream that need not be impossible.

The problem with so many people who complain about the sad state of the nation, in Wilhelm's view, is that they aren't willing to pay the price of success. They'd rather have it handed to them, and it doesn't work that way, not even in America. "We have too many people on welfare. Can you imagine giving money to people who are able to work? America does that, and I don't know why. What's going to happen to their children? They'll grow up and all they'll know is that the government will take care of you, that you don't have to work, that you're entitled to money without earning it. That's not right. That's not what made this country great, giving away things to people who don't want to work."

But on the other hand we don't always give money to the people who really need it, Wilhelm says. "Last winter I read about an eighty-four-year-old man over in Davenport and he froze to death in his home. He didn't have money to pay the gas bill, and so the gas company turned off his gas. Why do we let that happen in this country? Couldn't the gas company sell him gas for less? Or even give him the gas? How could we allow him to die? Oh, this is how the communists create propaganda against us. They write in their newspapers that the capitalists shut off gas and allow an old man to freeze. And people believe it, and, oh, my God, it's true. What's wrong?"

Wilhelm feels fierce loyalty to the American system and he is pinched by guilt when he hears himself saying anything that seems less than totally supportive of the government. That's why, after he complains about welfare, taxes, high prices and low profits, he often will add quickly: "But this is the greatest country on the face of the earth."

Because he has seen firsthand the workings of the Communist government in Russia and the Nazi government in Germany, Wilhelm has a reality-based appreciation of democracy. "The great fear in Germany was that if you opened your mouth against Hitler, your best friend might report you. There would be a knock on your door in the night, and you'd never be seen again. That's what a dictatorship is like. They tell you what to do and what to believe. If you don't accept it, you are gone—forever.

"In a dictatorship if the dictator says the wall is black, the wall is black. If I say the wall is white, then I am against the dictator, and I am eliminated."

Communism, Wilhelm says, may be even more dangerous than a Hitler-like rule because it doesn't always look exactly like what it is, a full-blown dictatorship. "I'm not against our college students learning about communism. But what those people write in the books is not what communism really is. Maybe they write about the way communism is supposed to work. But that's not the way it really works."

How does communism really work?

"Everything they do is designed to control you," Wilhelm responds. "It's like they shut off your air and then, just before you die, they give you just a little bit of air. Then they give you a little more, just enough to keep you alive, but you never forget the power, the control that they have over you. You do what they want because, if you don't, they turn off the air."

It is simply awful, beyond belief, Wilhelm says, and the crusaders who run around and preach communism as a system of equality ought to go over and take a look for themselves. The only equality they share, he says, is "equal lack of air."

We talk into the early morning hours, the three of us, and we drink coffee at the kitchen table and consume huge squares of Clara's cherry chocolate cake, which is so sinfully delicious that I make her promise to write out the recipe so I can take it home with me. We pause only when Candy, a ten-year-old Siamese cat, wakes up and demands attention. The cat rubs against every leg in sight and won't stop, Clara predicts, until she gets what she wants.

What Candy wants is to be brushed and when Clara grasps the

brush, the cat rolls over and waits for the ecstacy that is certain to follow. The cat, Wilhelm notes solemnly, is like those people on welfare: All get more than they have coming to them.

In the morning we're going to look over the hog operation, and that's just what we do, after a breakfast of fried eggs, homemade biscuits, and bacon from their own hogs, cured at Amana, Iowa, in the Lutheran colony by some of the same folks who bring you refrigerators and microwave ovens. Wilhelm's pride and joy is the barn in which he houses, for four months, the hogs he is fattening for sale. The barn is called a "finishing house," and he and his sons built it themselves. It's a series of steel mesh pens—forty in all—and up to twenty-five pigs stay in each pen and become sort of a family. They get to know each other and they're friendly. But if you put in a stranger, a pig not part of the family, you've got trouble. At least the stranger has trouble because the other pigs pick at him and make life generally rotten.

The hogs never leave their pens until the day they are herded through a trough and onto trucks that take some to the slaughter-house but most to the farms of other hog breeders. The advantage to fattening hogs indoors: They put on weight faster since they don't exercise it off—for every three pounds of food they eat they put on one pound.

We're inside the finishing house now, and it's the first time I've ever been so close to so many pigs. These are American Lacombe, a purebred strain that originated in Canada but which has flour-ished in this country for more than twenty years. The Lacombes' advantages: They gain weight more quickly; they have broad chests that reduce the risk of respiratory disease; they have wide, flat feet.

Aw, come on now. Wide, flat feet? Since when did that become an advantage? Well, since farmers started raising pigs indoors in pens floored with wooden slats and concrete. With wide, flat feet, the Lacombes don't slip between the slats and they don't get sore feet from standing on concrete. They seem to have been designed with indoor life in mind, Wilhelm grins.

Most of each pen is plain concrete, which is uncommonly clean, I think. The pigs spend much of their time in this part of the pen. It's where they eat, sleep, drink and socialize. The rest of the pen is covered with slats, beneath which the concrete slopes toward a nine-foot-deep trench into which waste material falls. The pigs, because they are what Wilhelm calls "basically clean animals,"

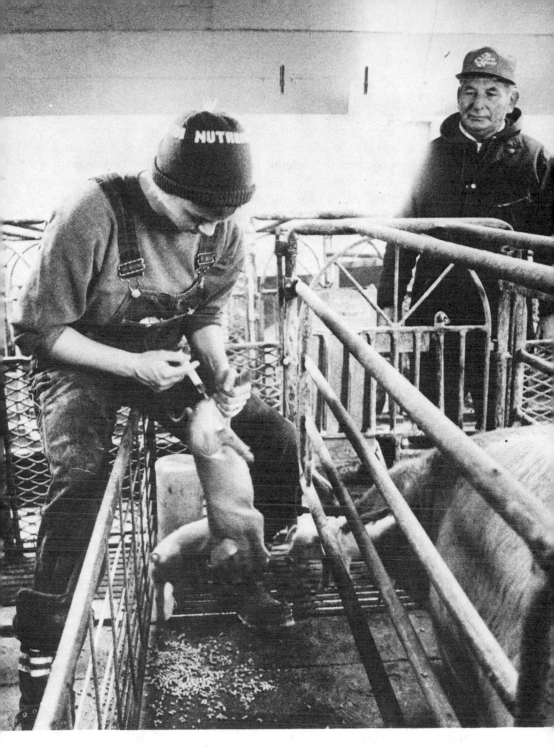

Week-old pigs receive routine medical injections from Wilhelm's daughter-in-law, Diane.

know when it's time to move toward the slats. Any pig that doesn't feel the urgency to move gets a cold shoulder from the rest of the family. I stroke some of the pigs near the edge of a pen, and their hair is coarse and so clean that I wonder if they've been run through a car wash. No, Wilhelm says, they keep themselves clean as long as there is no mud puddle around in which to wallow. They're smart, too, he says, smarter than dogs if you begin to work with them early in life, and some of those shown in 4-H by Wilhelm's grandchildren have learned to respond to their names.

They learn to suck their water out of a pipe in their pens, almost like a drinking fountain, and so their water is always fresh and clean. When they are sold to a farmer who waters from an open trough, they don't know how to drink at first, Wilhelm says. But they learn in a day or two.

Their feed is a mixture of corn and soybean meal with vitamins and minerals added, and it is augered into troughs within the pens. Wilhelm holds a handful of the food and it is clean, without any lint. "You could eat it yourself and do pretty well," he says.

This is the end product of the Wilhelm operation, 150-day-old hogs that weigh 220 pounds. The beginning product, newborn pigs the size of large kittens, are next door in another barn with their mothers in iron cages so cramped that the sows can lie only in one position. This is to keep them from rolling over and crushing their babies in the first hours of life.

What do you call a baby pig? Is it a piglet? Wilhelm laughs. "We call them little pigs."

Fifteen percent of the pigs die before they are grown, most of them in the first two weeks from illness and from mothers who, despite their tiny cages, still manage to kill, quite unintentionally, some of their babies. For a while the little pigs are permitted to run outdoors with their mothers, but when they reach sixty pounds, they go into the barn from which they don't emerge until they are to be sold or bred.

Wilhelm buys his boars, sometimes in Canada, because he is a firm believer that breeding his sows with his own boars is a fast road to hard times. "I may be wrong, but this is my opinion." Wilhelm says that the times he's tried to breed sows with his own boars, he got many little pigs that were deformed or otherwise less than ideal. So while he sells boars to other breeders, he also buys boars, often paying as much as $1,000 for an 800-pounder who "easily" can breed six or seven sows in a day. A sow, which produces two or three litters a year, is good for breeding for seven or eight years, but a boar doesn't last that long. Five years is a good span for a boar, Wilhelm says. After that the boar is shipped to a slaughterhouse, and then he's likely to turn up on the next pizza you eat, Wilhelm chuckles, because "that's what they're good for." Sows, on the other hand, may be ticketed for the prime sausage market when their breeding days are over.

How many little pigs does a sow have in each litter? Well, that's hard to say, Wilhelm answers. The average probably is eight or nine, but some sows have more, others less. It depends on the weight. A young sow delivering for the first time will have from forty to fifty pounds of pigs, an older sow from fifty to eighty pounds of pigs. The more pigs in the litter, the smaller the size of the pigs.

The births usually are without assistance, although Wilhelm and his sons ordinarily try to be present because "sometimes one gets stuck and you have to pull it out." They know that a sow will deliver in about three hours when she gets restless and begins trying to gather straw to build a nest.

Wilhelm has tried to breed through artificial insemination, but he has found it not to be as effective with pigs as with cows. He quickly gave it up and went back to boars, whose reliability is unquestioned.

Right on the farm he grinds the grain he grows on land that once was waterlogged because of poor drainage. "When I bought some of this land, people laughed at me. They asked: 'What are you going to raise on it—mallard ducks?' But I showed them. I tiled the land myself. I spent over $380 an acre on tile. And then the water ran into drainage ditches. Now I'm getting good crops on land that was all swamp. And nobody is laughing anymore."

Wilhelm has learned that he has to borrow money to make money. This concept wasn't easy for him to accept, since he always believed that borrowing was for people who didn't know how to save their own money. But so much money is required to farm that it's impossible for anybody to do it with his own money. Wilhelm remembers:

"The first time I went to a bank in America, I needed to borrow $150. The banker laughed at me. He said I had no collateral, and he gave me no money. A year later, after I had rented a farm, that same banker came out and offered me $5,000. By then I had pigs, collateral. The year before I needed the $150 about 99 percent worse than the $5,000. But I learned a lesson."

The lesson was: If a banker knows you're serious about farming and if you have something to show for it, you can get all the money you want.

"I pay a tremendous amount of interest in a year, but if I don't borrow, I don't make money. If I borrow $30,000 and pay off the interest and principal and make 10 percent for myself, that's good business. If I borrow $100,000 and make $20,000 for myself, that's great business. If I do that, I'm in good shape."

With inflation, Wilhelm figures, his land and buildings are worth more than a million dollars. In a year he handles half a million dollars and nets a $90,000 profit that is divided with his two sons. He can show a profit if he sells his slaughterhouse-bound hogs for forty cents a pound, and he can break even at thirty-six cents a pound. The big corporations that have gone into farming need forty-five cents a pound just to break even, and that's because of what he calls the clock watching that is the result of unionism. "I'm not against unions, but you can't farm and work from nine to five. You have to be there when you're needed," without the expectation of overtime pay.

"If people think meat prices are high now," Wilhelm says, "they have no idea what would happen if the family farms go out of business and the corporations take over, the way they have in the vegetable business. You know what lettuce costs now, compared to what it did cost. That's why. When the unions and the corporations get involved, prices go up. And that's why the people who live in the city should do all they can to keep the family farms going. If we don't make it, people in the city are going to be paying three or four times more for food."

That sounded like a sermon, and Wilhelm says he didn't mean it that way. Clara comes out of the house and asks Wilhelm to "get me a tomato or two." Wilhelm tells her: "You know where the garden is." But it's the same kind of exchange that I heard in the car, the way people talk when they know each other very well and when they care very much.

"She is a marvelous woman, really marvelous," Wilhelm says. "Without her none of this would have been possible. She has worked just as hard as I worked, even harder, when she was raising the little pigs. Raising them when they are small is 90 percent of the work, checking the hog house twenty times a day—and night, too—to make sure that everything is all right. By the time I got them there was only 10 percent of the work left. She has some time now to do the things she wants, and I'm glad. She deserves it." He pauses and then adds: "And I deserve it, too. I've worked hard all of my life."

The sons, Fred and Herb, come from the barns and Fred says that his father was firm with him but always fair when he was a boy. "I didn't like to work after school. It meant I couldn't play basketball like the other boys. But that was the way it was. I accepted it, because I saw how hard he and Mother worked. I'll tell you one thing: It taught me how to work hard. That's something city boys don't understand. Farm boys still do, although maybe not as much as before. I can hire two boys, one from the city and one from the farm, and in a day I can tell you which is which."

Wilhelm's relationship with his children, especially his sons, seems classically German. "I taught them right from wrong, the way my father taught me. I taught them not to do to others anything that they wouldn't do to themselves. I taught them to forgive everybody, to a certain extent. If somebody spits in my face, I wipe it off and I try to forgive them. If two days later they spit in my face again, I spit in my hand and give them one across the face. That's right, how it should be, and that's what I taught my boys."

If the boys ever came home from school and complained about the teacher, Wilhelm punished them, even if he thought the complaints were legitimate. This is because of Wilhelm's belief that the dignity and authority of the teacher must be supported at all costs. "If I think the teacher is wrong, then I go to her," he says. "I don't tell the children about it. It's between me and the teacher, not between me and the children. I see parents who tell their children that the teacher is wrong, but this is a bad mistake, because it undermines authority. This is my opinion. I may be wrong, but this is my opinion."

Clara invites us in to a lunch that is 100 percent home-grown—breaded ham, salad, pickles, tomatoes, onions, corn, potatoes and, ohhhhh, more cherry chocolate cake. Wilhelm almost brings tears to my eyes: "You know, if anybody ever told me I would eat this good, play golf, take trips, I'd have thought he was out of his mind. Everybody in America eats like a king. No king ever ate better than we're eating right now. No president eats better. It's not like this in other countries. When I grew up, until I was twenty-five, I didn't even know that lemonade existed. We are so lucky, so very, very lucky.''

Clara says, yes, she feels lucky, and busy, too—busy with the things she wants to do rather than with the things she had to do for so many years. Her schedule seldom varies, she says. On Monday she bowls. Tuesday is ladies' day at Wapsi Oaks Country Club in Calamus, and she plays golf. She mows the lawn and cleans the house on Wednesday. On Thursday she plays golf again and on Friday she bowls again.

If you think this is a good life, you're right. "We've worked so hard and now we're enjoying what we've worked for," Clara says.

We drive four miles into Calamus, a tidy hamlet of 500, and then we go to Wapsi Oaks Country Club, where the nine-hole golf course is threatened by the rampant Wapsipinnean River, which is eight feet above flood stage and closing in rapidly on the record 11.6 feet. The area in front of the first hole is under water, but this doesn't discourage the golfers, who have cut a temporary green short of the flooding, and who keep right on playing. It's a typical small-town club, like the one at which I learned to play golf, where men tee off without shirts and where a woman can play all alone and take fifteen strokes to get up a hill without anybody screaming or hitting into her. It's quiet and friendly in the club room, where drinks are seventy-five cents apiece and where Suzy, a blond college student, says she makes up to $340 a week on tips, as much as $70 on men's night alone.

"It's the best job anybody could find in the summertime," she says. The people in the club room all know her by name and they are polite and understanding when they have to wait for their drinks, since Suzy is working alone.

Robert and Clara Wilhelm have been members of Wapsi Oaks Country Club for three years. It carries a $300 entry fee and annual dues of $206, and some not as fortunate as the Wilhelms have been on the waiting list for five years. The Wilhelms eat here at least once a week—the Friday night seafood dinner is their favorite—and perhaps one other night.

This, Wilhelm says, "is a long way from where I came from." Most of the people in the club room know Wilhelm by name, but few are aware of his life before he came to Calamus. One man says he thinks that Wilhelm was in the army during the war.

We leave to drive to the airport. From there Robert and Clara Wilhelm are going to a friend's house to play cards. "That's fun for us," she says, "a chance to be with good people for a good evening."

At the airport we say our good-byes and Clara Wilhelm, true to her word, produces for me the recipe for her cherry chocolate cake. The ingredients: One box of chocolate cake mix, one three-ounce package of cherry JELL-O, one small package of marsh-mallows, one can of cherry pie filling.

The directions, in her handwriting on lined notebook paper: "Grease cake pan good. Put marshmallows in bottom of pan. Mix JELL-O real good with cherry pie filling. Put on top of marshmal-lows. Mix cake mix according to directions. Put on top of cherry mixture and bake twenty-five minutes in 350-degree oven."

After that all you have to do is eat—and enjoy. And then eat some more.

The jetliner is in the air in a few moments, on the half-hour jaunt to Chicago. I sit next to a man who is an executive at a Quad-Cities foundry and who is on his way to Detroit to try to get a bid to manufacture a part for a new automobile. He tells me that he wouldn't want to live anywhere else in the world.

"We have the friendliest people right here," he says.

Yes, I know, I tell him. I just left two of them.

4 ⇜ From Wall Street to cornfields

Have you ever limped home at the end of a soul-bending day, your mind as pulpy as your body, and concluded that what you were putting into your career was out of proportion to what your career was giving back?

Have you ever wanted to chuck it all and get a fresh start in something new and different?

If you have, then welcome to the club. It's happened to a lot of us. Yet something held you back. Perhaps it was the promise that tomorrow would be better. Or perhaps it was the fear that something new would be worse. At any rate you didn't make a change, but you always wondered: What if . . . ?

I'm in southwest Minnesota, so far into the country that the road signs point to Sioux Falls rather than to Minneapolis, and I'm driving through farmland that is as black as coal, like potting soil. I'm on my way to visit Peter Thompson, who grows corn and soybeans on 400 acres in Jackson County, near the towns of Windom and Mountain Lake. Thompson is one of the few among us who never asked, "What if . . . ?" Without looking back, he went ahead and did it—chucked his big-city career and moved to the country.

Five years ago Thompson was wearing a gray flannel suit on

Peter Thompson left a lucrative business career in
New York City to grow corn in Minnesota.

Wall Street, where he was corporate senior vice-president and national sales manager for Paine, Webber, Jackson and Curtis, one of the nation's biggest brokerage houses. But one evening he trudged home to the suburbs to lick his battle wounds, and he asked himself: "Am I going to be doing this for the next twenty years?" Not long after that, he resigned and began to look for the best farmland he could buy. After twenty years in New York City, he was going to become a farmer. Why a farmer? "For a long time I had had a desire to put seeds in the ground and watch them grow."

Would Thompson, forty-eight, married and the father of two grown children, share his story with me? On the telephone he had not encouraged me to come. He was a private person, he had said. He did not seek publicity and he did not want publicity. Yet he didn't tell me not to come. I wanted to meet him because I thought we had a lot in common—not just age but the reality that we both had dared to do it, to stop climbing our ladders, to abandon the corporate games, to try something that promised to be fun.

I had surrendered a newspaper editorship. He had walked away from the world of high finance, declaring: "After you cross a certain threshold, you begin to realize that other people's opinions really don't matter as much as your own."

I could identify with that. Thompson was saying that the time comes for some of us to do what we want to do and need to do, just for ourselves, for our own private reasons. Pete Thompson and I had bitten the same bullet, and I wanted to meet him.

Through the haze of my thoughts, a sign announces that I have entered Le Sueur County. Boy, that's a name I know—Le Sueur—but where have I heard . . . ? I pop over the crest of a hill, and right there in front of me, atop a signboard, stands a familiar figure, the Jolly Green Giant. He's at least fifteen feet tall, and he's welcoming me to his valley, the Valley of the Jolly Green Giant. This is the home of Le Sueur Packing Company, which ships vegetables all over the country in cans labeled with the Giant's picture. For all of these years I thought the Valley was a make-believe place, something they brainstormed in an advertising meeting. But here it is, the real Valley, and it's as lush and fertile-looking as the Giant says it is in his television commercials.

I'm still thinking about that when it's time to leave the highway and turn south on an unmarked road. Twelve minutes later I'm nosing into the driveway in front of a two-story, snow-white house in the middle of an ocean of mowed grass and towering cottonwood trees. Silver-colored grain storage bins stand guard beside the house and in front of outbuildings that are painted classic barn red and trimmed in white.

This is where Pete Thompson and his wife, Polly, live, so very far in miles and life style from Rye, New York, cocktail parties and gray flannel suits.

Thompson is startled to see me because, even though he has scrawled my name on the kitchen calendar, he has forgotten that this is the day of my visit. But he recovers quickly, and when he says, "I believe I have some time for you," he sounds not like a Midwestern farmer but like an eastern businessman, his words crisp and precise. I can't help thinking of the story about how you can take the boy out of the country, but you can't take the country out of the boy. It must work the other way, too: You can take the businessman out of business, but you can't . . . .

Thompson is hatless, his dark hair parted neatly on the left side. His tan work pants and white sport shirt are fresh looking, almost as if they have been starched, but this is not because he is a gentleman farmer who pays others to do the work. Thompson farms his 400 acres by himself, except during harvesting when he and those he hires push themselves day and night to beat the crop-killing frosts that come early in this part of the country. For him farming is bone-tiring work, yet it is seldom that he is as fatigued as he was when he worked late in the city, rode the train home to Rye and swallowed his food without tasting it.

He is chunky, like a football blocking back, and his body appears hard. He has lost thirty pounds since he started farming. "I was soft and blubbery when I did office work. But I'm not soft and blubbery now. I work pretty damned hard. There is no automatic way to pick rocks and to clean bins. You have to bend down and you have to shovel. There still is a lot of manual labor on the farm. There is no way to get out of hard physical labor."

Thompson's face is lined—across the forehead and around the eyes—yet the lines seem to appear more as residue of what was than as announcements of what is. When he first came to the farm, neighbors said that he looked nervous and haggard. They were quite correct, he says. "My nerve endings were raw. I wasn't exactly hyper, but I always had to be on the go." But now the nervous system has repaired itself, a five-year healing process that

Thompson says occurred only because he became his own man, free of the corporate chains that forced him to walk when he wanted to run. "Now I can tolerate disappointments and breakdowns. Something goes wrong, and my philosophical attitude is: 'Oh, well, it's busted; let's fix it.' Ten years ago I would have screamed: 'Dammit, why did this happen?' "

Another mark of his tranquility is that he has freed himself of the urgency that once connected him to what he thought was the real world. When he first came to the farm, he was almost rabid in his desire to keep up with the stock market, to know where it stood not only at closing but also at opening and at noon. "For an extended period, I was uncomfortable if I didn't know what was going on. Five years later I wonder if the market is up or down, but I wait to read about it in the newspaper tomorrow."

Thompson has found his real world out here in the quiet of the country, where everybody knows everybody else, where maybe one car will come down the gravel road in front of his house in a whole day and where both Thompson and the driver of that car will wave, because they are neighbors. It's been a long trip for Thompson, from there to here, and he is not eager or willing to spend much time discussing how his life used to be.

The son of a stockbroker, he grew up on Long Island, went away to a private boarding school in Connecticut, then to Cornell University, where he played freshman football, became a member of the varsity rowing crew and earned a liberal arts degree. After graduation he went into the army as an airborne artillery officer. When his time was served, he returned to New York and, without his father's opening any doors for him, he went to work for Paine, Webber, Jackson and Curtis.

His father never influenced his decision, and Thompson decided to enter the brokerage business less because that was what he wanted than because he didn't want anything else any more. He applied through the personnel office, "just like everybody else," and the company started him at the bottom of the ladder, at $325 a month.

In the years that followed, Pete Thompson clawed his way up that ladder, "not out of any special genius," he says, "but out of sheer, brutal hard work and long hours. I worked like a slob. That's the best way I can describe it." People who saw Thompson at work were amazed that anybody would—or could—put so much time and energy into a job. He entered management in the early 1960s and he was invited to become a partner in the late 1960s. In the early days it was enjoyable, making changes that produced results and inhaling the excitement. But when he reached senior management, even though his salary hit six figures, "it wasn't nearly so much fun."

Changes that he felt were needed became more difficult to implement. He describes himself as "always controversial, a maverick, the creative guy in the company. They sort of tolerated me." But it seemed to Thompson that he consistently was crashing head-on with "various interests that were at odds with what I wanted to do. It didn't bother me, but it did wear me down."

When he resigned from the firm, all of his colleagues were surprised. Some were stunned, and they asked questions like: "How can you be dumb enough to give it all up?" "How can you walk away from what you've worked so hard to achieve?" The chairman of the board, in Thompson's words, "did everything but beg me to remain with the firm. But by then I'd made up my mind. I went out quietly, and I left it all on the table, including what I'd put into my pension fund."

By now Thompson and I are inside the 100-year-old farmhouse, past a sleeping cat and into the kitchen, where Thompson heats water for instant coffee. Here is a man who was only one short step from the top of his profession. As national sales manager, he was at a level equaled by only a handful of other executives. Now here he is, a farmer who at first knew so little about farming that he carried manuals with him to the fields for guidance. Why did he give it all up and start over from scratch?

For him, it came down to asking, "Is this all there is?"—and to wanting to do "what God has created me to do." Pete Thompson simply felt that the desire for the Wall Street job wasn't there anymore. It's something that many of us realize at some time about our jobs, he says, but most of us don't do anything about it.

"I believe that everybody has subliminal aspirations. I hear people say, 'Gee, I should go into politics. I'm smarter than those jerks in Washington.' Somebody else says, 'I'd like to run a sailing boat.' I believe we all get fed up with what we do."

The difference with Pete Thompson—and with me, too, he reminds me—is that "we pulled the trigger. This is the only thing that differentiates me from others on Wall Street. I didn't just *talk* about getting out; I *got* out."

There are no two ways about it—Pete Thompson's story is exceptional. That doesn't surprise me. But what does surprise me is that now he seems less hesitant to tell that story than I expected, because of his earlier reluctance. He empties one coffee cup after another, smokes one filter cigarette after another, appears to be as engrossed in what he is saying as I am. Later in the day we will drive out to his fields and park beside corn that is almost as high as an elephant's eye and Thompson will say: "This is my best. There is real satisfaction in being able to touch my corn and walk on my ground. I never felt that kind of satisfaction in all those years in New York.

"When I grew up on Long Island, in Great Neck, it was country, kind of like this. Then the asphalt came and the Pizza Huts, and I thought all of this was gone forever"— the wide-open expanses of green, the reassurance of a light in a neighbor's window so very far away.

Thompson can stand alone in the silence of his farm and feel that he has turned back time sixty or eighty years. And it may be, he suggests, that he is cut out to be a man of that generation more than this generation. Perhaps this is the real reason that Thompson has found peace here on the farm. He is where he belongs.

How did his family react to his decision to leave the bright lights of the city?

Polly Thompson was in many ways a typical suburban housewife and mother. She drove a station wagon, rode a horse, played bridge in three clubs, helped her favorite hospital raise money, held the presidency of the Junior Guild in her church. But, perhaps unlike many other women in the suburbs, she was, in her words, "at loose ends" much of the time and concerned that she and her husband did so little together. Thompson's commitment to work, while bringing professional rewards, left little time for the two of them to be together, even to talk.

Her reaction to moving to the country was to regard it as the answer to a prayer, as a way that she and her husband might get back on the same track. So she was ready and eager to start their new adventure.

The children were not so enthusiastic. Their son, Jim, then sixteen and a junior in high school, was insistent in making his parents understand that he didn't want to leave his friends and that it wasn't fair to take him away from his roots. Their daughter, Sally, then eighteen and a freshman at Wellesley College, was "very un-

Polly Thompson with two of her six thoroughbred horses.
She teaches riding.

derstanding and gracious'' about it, although not overwhelmed by her desire to come to Minnesota.

How have things worked out for the three of them?

Sally, now married, is a graduate of the University of Minnesota with a degree in agricultural economics. She teaches at Montana State University. Once she called home to say, ''I wanted to say thanks for bringing the family to Minnesota.''

Jim, working beside his father on the farm one summer, remarked, ''For the first time I feel I really know you.'' He is a student at the University of Minnesota, where, his mother says, he plays tennis and hopes to go into communication.

And Polly Thompson? She has not been disappointed in her hopes that she would find greater purpose in life and that her husband would be reborn, far from the corporate treadmills. Thompson, she says, still is ''the same basic workaholic he always was. But now it's a much more healthy existence for him, better than being a workaholic on Wall Street with the bad air and personality clashes. It's been a challenge for him to learn farming. He's never been bored. And we have so much to talk about.''

When they first came to the country, Polly worked at a supermarket, marking prices on cans. She never felt that was a step down, she says, but rather a step toward getting the family settled in a new life. While she was doing that, Thompson, eager to learn all he could about farming, was working in the bins for a seed company.

Polly Thompson now sells advertising for a 250-watt radio station in Windom, KDOM, and she has six thoroughbred horses that she trains. She also teaches riding to the young people who come to her for lessons. She is tall and slender and, as a matter of fact, she still looks like the picture of a suburban woman, especially when she's out back at the barn, tending her horses. She and Thompson seem to have a relationship in which both are comfortable. They're social loners to an extent but they disagree on the reason why.

Pete Thompson: ''In the main the people around here are German, Norwegian, Swedish, Danish—people who generally have a slow take to newcomers.'' Their immediate neighbors gave them the benefit of every doubt. But, Thompson continues, ''On the overall picture I'd say that it's taken five years to be made to feel welcome in many areas. Last week I went into Mountain Lake on an errand, and I noticed that several of the tradesmen and others stuck their necks out and said, 'Hi, Pete . . . .' I realize that this is now my hometown.''

Polly Thompson: "Oh, Pete, people have been more friendly than that. When we came here from New York, everybody wanted to hear why we'd come. They were all willing to talk to me. The neighbors were wonderful. They tried to involve us socially, but we declined a lot of invitations, because you were so busy on the farm and I was busy with my job, the house and the horses. We could have had more friends if we had had more time.''

But there is no disagreement on their mutual satisfaction with what Polly Thompson calls the "very simple, unsophisticated but happy" life that they lead. Friends from New York seem as amazed by that as by Thompson's decision to come here. Not long ago a former business associate stopped by on his way to somewhere, surveyed the solitude and asked, not totally as a joke: "What do you do on Saturday night—go to Sioux Falls and watch the Indians get their hair cut?''

The truth of the matter, Polly Thompson says, is that she and Pete don't much miss the excitement of the big city. "We never went to the theater much, only occasionally, for some fund-raising event. We didn't go to the galleries much. We don't mind what we miss. We're busier than I ever thought we would be. I kind of thought we could come and sit and watch the corn grow. In Rye we'd sit in the sun. But we can't do that here. I have a picture of Pete in the hammock out in the yard. It's the only time he's ever been in it—to have his picture taken. He's just too busy.''

What attracted Pete Thompson to this faraway corner of Minnesota? That's a long story. Let's start at the beginning.

He looked at farmland in several parts of the country, and in one state he even went to a luncheon set up by a friend who wanted him to meet other farmers. But the other farmers turned out to be a judge, a merchant, a police officer and several lawyers, "who worked in town to keep their farms going. They were gentleman farmers and their idea of farming was to own the land and hire other people to do the work. But I wanted to work where I could do it all, plant, harvest, pick rocks, where I could see the effect of my work, the product of my work.''

He went to his alma mater, Cornell University, where Stanley Warren, the retired dean of the College of Agriculture, urged him to think not just about land but about "the whole picture," including people and politics.

Thompson, as befits a businessman, didn't think in a narrow vein. He asked Warren's opinion about Brazil. That's a wonderful area, Warren said, "but what about the political environment?" What about the southeastern states? Well, they tended to have a "people problem, for want of a better description." Illinois? No, land costs were too high when compared with the rate of return from the crops.

Finally Thompson asked Warren: "If you had your choice of farming anywhere in the world, where would you choose?" Warren's answer: southwestern Minnesota.

So he came in the spring to look around and he liked what he saw. There was just enough ground exposed through the melting snow for him to see the dark, rich soil. Even in the mud and the chilling wind, he was impressed. This was what he was looking for, and he was fortunate to find 400 acres of contiguous prime land that was coming on the market.

Land prices have more than doubled in the years since, but back then the price Thompson paid was the highest in the area. He went into the Federal Land Bank office in Windom to fill out some forms, and another farmer came in and asked manager Grant Johnson: "Hey, Grant, did you hear about that fellow from New York who paid that enormous price? Ain't no farmland worth that much."

The story that went around town was that Thompson was going to start a horse farm. But instead, he started planting corn and soybeans, learning as he went, and when neighbors saw that, they began to view the Thompson family as one of their own. Polly Thompson remembers a telephone call from a neighbor asking if she and Pete would be home the next night. Yes, she said, expecting that the neighbor would visit. Instead, dozens of people showed up and brought chairs, tables, beer and food to welcome the Thompsons. It was, Pete says, a kind of modern-day barn raising and a show of kindness that touched his soul.

It was back in those early days that his first misconception about farming was straightened out. He thought that farmers worked from sunup to sundown. But at midnight, when he was driving back from signing the papers to buy his land, he saw winking lights in the fields, tiny specks that moved, almost as if they were attached to tractors. But at midnight?

He asked a farm friend who was with him, and, yes, those were lights on tractors, and they seemed to be everywhere, almost in every field. That was his introduction to the reality that during planting and harvesting, Minnesota farming continues around the clock. This is because this corner of Minnesota is on the frontier of corn production, with a shorter growing season than Iowa or Illinois. As a result, farmers, in Thompson's words, "have to go like hell" to get the crops in as soon as conditions in the spring permit so that not a single day of the growing season will be wasted. When the crops mature in the fall, frosts are not uncommon, and harvesting becomes a twenty-four-hour operation. After that the rush comes to get the ground plowed before the heavy freezes, so that it will be workable when spring comes again.

From the middle of September to early November, a farmer around here "can forget about eight hours' sleep," Thompson says. "When the weather is bad, when it's raining, that's when you get a good night's sleep."

Farmers' wives have been known to pray for bad weather, just so their men could get some rest. With fatigue, the level of accidents rises, and a reliable farmer can drive a combine through a fence, because he is so sleep-starved that he loses touch with what he is doing.

Thompson once plowed for forty-two straight hours, stopping his tractor only to refuel. When he finally tried to climb down, he fell headfirst to the field because his legs, which were without feeling, gave way under him.

Another of Thompson's misconceptions was that farmers always had plenty of free time when they were not in the fields. "But if a man is serious about farming, he always can find something to do. You can drive past a farm and say, 'My, it looks peaceful,' but what you don't see is the farmer who is behind the buildings working on his machinery."

Thompson has learned, through adult extension courses, to do his own electrical wiring, plumbing and welding. "For people who've always farmed, a lot of this is passed down from father to son. But nobody passed it down to me. I've had to learn on my own. When you're out here ten or fifteen miles from town, you can't pick up the telephone every time you have a problem. You have to fix it yourself."

After farming for five years, Thompson estimates that he is

He has been farming five years, but Thompson thinks it will be

another ten before he has earned the name of "farmer."

one-third of the way "up the learning curve. In fifteen years maybe I can call myself a farmer. This is not humble pie. But there's so much to do and so much to learn that I don't think anybody could begin to call himself a farmer until he's been at it fifteen years and has been reasonably successful.

"I had no apprenticeship. I had to collapse my apprenticeship, try to knock it down to nothing. I read the manuals and I looked for help where I could get it. Neighbors help, but you don't lean on neighbors for help. You take great pride in independence. This is what it takes to survive."

One thing that hasn't surprised him is the reality that farm people are different from city people. He already knew that because, as an army officer, he found that during training the most competent and most physically fit men seemed to be those who came from rural areas. They knew how to handle machinery, trucks, tools and weapons, and they were easy to pick out. Thompson trained close to 1,800 soldiers and "within a short span of time I could tell if a boy was from the farm or the city. The farm boys had a singular competence about them." Later, as a businessman, he would meet men who grew up on farms and "I always seemed to like their manner. They were direct and hardworking, and many of them became my friends."

What makes rural people stand out this way? There are at least three factors, Thompson says, and one is their early assumption of responsibility. "Farm kids are not sheltered. It's not unusual to see a kid of eight or ten driving a tractor, baling hay, picking rocks." The second factor is the continual presence of the parents. The urban boy sees his father go off to work in the morning, not to reappear until late. "But this doesn't happen on the farm. The boy watches his dad get up, hook up the machinery and go to the fields. The father is there for discipline and encouragement; and city people don't have this."

Thompson knows the truth of this firsthand. "I never got to know my son until we moved to the farm."

The third factor that helps mold the unique qualities of the farmer is religion, Thompson says. "To a large degree we're able to see God's handiwork on the farm. The church is the center of social life. It's not a mixed congregation as in the city, where you have a plumber, Wall Street executive and shopkeeper sitting side by side. Out here we're a homogeneous body. Ninety-five percent of us are farmers. When the minister talks about sowing and reaping, about pestilence and other things, we can zero in as a group that really understands. Somehow, the Bible takes on more clarity when you're a farmer." Religion becomes not one hour on Sunday but a strong influence on daily life, says Thompson, who is Lutheran and an officer in his church.

If Thompson came into farming with the idea that government programs would prop him up or bail him out, he quickly discovered that he was wrong. The people who stayed on the farm during the exodus to the city from the late 1920s to the 1960s are hardy, and they know how to take care of themselves, he says.

"Contrary to the garbage you read in newspapers and magazines," he feels that farmers are making it pretty much on their own. In five years, he says, he has not "received one dime" of help from the government, not even a visit from a county agent. "I'm not complaining, but I'm saying that it's a myth that the government does everything for farmers. I didn't come here looking for government help. But I was under the impression that farmers always were on the dole. Now I can tell you that at least corn and soybean farming is totally at variance with that idea."

The winters in Minnesota are long and brutal, but Thompson says he has been bothered less by the weather than he expected.

"I'm less cold in Minnesota than on certain days in New York. In New York people dress for show. You wear fancy gloves and a light topcoat. Then you freeze to death. I put on thermal underwear here in October and take it off in May. It's amazing how the body adapts to this. If you tapped a Minnesota farmer's blood, it would pour like molasses. You see farmers walking around at thirty degrees like it's eighty, bareheaded, with only a light shirt on."

Thompson has come close to getting lost in blizzards. He has suffered frostbite on his face. He has walked up a roof-high snowdrift packed so hard that he left not a track—it was "just like a bloody rock." He doesn't enjoy winter in Minnesota, "but I refuse to dwell on how bad it is."

Since he's been on the farm, Thompson has had what he regards as two problem years out of five, one caused by drought, the other by an early freeze. "There are no real crop failures. But hail can come and blitz you," and hail is more common in this area than Thompson had expected. He figures it costs $80,000 to put in his crops, and his hail insurance covers most of that.

The land that Thompson farms now brings $3,000 an acre, but

"On a farm, there is no way to get out of hard physical labor,"
Thompson says.

land just ten miles to the west is selling for less than $1,000 an acre. The variation in the quality of the land within the county is enormous. Mother Nature herself must have blessed Thompson's land and land like it. The higher yield this prime land returns is the reason that he is able to live off his 400 acres at a time when many farmers his size are either trying to acquire more land or going out of business. "If we're talking about a difference of thirty and fifty bushels an acre at a $5 price, that's a difference of $100 an acre. On 400 acres that is a difference of $40,000. I can't explain it. We all basically do the same things. We go over the ground the same number of times, planting, cultivating, harvesting. But the results are vastly different."

Thompson is not what he calls "a bold contractor" on the futures market. He commits to sell at a predetermined price only modest amounts of corn and soybeans. But "how you market your crop can be the difference between a good and poor year." He calculates a price at which he can sell and make a reasonable profit, and he tries to keep his cash flow six months ahead, so that he will not be forced to sell if prices suddenly dip. "As a general rule, I sell once the grain is in the bins. But the selling may be spread out over an entire year."

Thompson doesn't get excited about the temporary ups and downs of grain prices. "I spent most of my life in the trading part of Wall Street. I think I have fairly cool nerves. I have watched precipitous declines and remarkable rallies. I try not to be swayed by either. I know I have a valuable product. I have a firm belief that my product will not drop off the page. It isn't the same on Wall Street. I've watched companies enjoy marvelous success and then turn to ashes overnight."

If you ask folks around Jackson County if they know Thompson, they may say: "Yeah, he's that feller who's been working with the farmers." They're talking about Thompson's efforts to unite farmers to find new markets for their crops, markets that can mean more jobs in the area.

Thompson views rural America as being treated as a colony by urban America. The raw materials produced on the farm are shipped out to be processed, to have value added and then to be sold. As a result, farmers get no benefit from what happens after they market their crops. Thompson's hope is that some of this benefit eventually can be kept at home.

"I'm talking about something like converting corn to a sweetener, crop residue to alcohol, adding some value," he explains. "This is where the raw materials are, and it makes no sense that they are shipped to other places to be processed." But because it is happening, rural America is losing high-grade people to the cities. "Some farms are too small for sons and daughters to remain on them after they're grown. These people are educated, responsible, and I'd like to have job opportunities for them on high-skill levels, so they wouldn't have to leave and go to the cities."

So far he has spent months exploring the possibilities of processing a corn sweetener in this area, "trying to find the right value-added deal that would interest farmers. This is not from a selfish viewpoint. It's altruistic, about as much as anybody possibly could be." He hopes that, as time passes, more farmers will come to this awareness of potential new markets for their products.

Polly Thompson comes in from the barn, where her horses are stabled, and tells her husband that it's time for her to be off to call on some of her accounts. After she leaves, we walk out to the barn and Thompson says that the horses "are primarily hers." Yet when he brings them gently into their stalls, feeds them, strokes them, talks to them, he is a different man, I imagine, than the man who huffed and puffed on Wall Street for so many years.

Thompson seems as proud as a new father as he shows me through his other outbuildings, including one that has an incredible assortment of nuts and bolts, all precisely boxed by size. "You can't run to town every time you need something. You have to keep it right here, and you have to be able to find it."

I climb into the cab of his $41,000 tractor, a green monster with a 464-cubic-inch engine, bucket seat, sixteen gears, air conditioner and radio. "It's quiet and it's comfortable," Thompson says. "It needs to be—because I spend a thousand hours a year in it."

We're back at the house, which has four bedrooms, a full attic and full basement. Thompson has painted it twice in five years, trying to compensate for the lack of care that was apparent when he bought it. The outbuildings were run down, too, and he counted forty-seven broken windows when he came. The first years here were not the easiest, as he struggled to lift what he had purchased up to standard and as he tried to figure out the riddles of farming. He's more comfortable now, and the moments are rare when he asks, "What am I doing here?" It isn't easy and it never will be, but it is rewarding and it is his. He can see the results of his efforts. Even some of his mistakes have been forgiven by the fertile ground and by the growing-season weather, which seems to offer rain when rain is needed.

We go inside for lunch, which Thompson prepares—as he always does when his wife is at work. He pulls a restaurant-size can of lasagne from the cupboard, spoons it into a pan that he puts on the stove. He slips bread into a toaster and pours milk into pint-size glasses. We eat, and Thompson wonders if it is unusual for me to come to a farm and have a meal straight from a can. Before I can answer, he continues: "The way I do things is relatively uncivilized in some ways. I don't apologize for it; I recognize it."

Not long after that I drive off, and Pete Thompson stands in the yard and waves good-by.

As I retrace my path through the Jolly Green Giant's valley, I think about what Thompson has said, that perhaps he is more suited to the generations of sixty or eighty years ago to this generation. I'm not at all sure that I agree with him. Maybe he's more suited to the generations that are yet to come, generations in which people, hopefully, will bite their bullets or pull their triggers and then crawl out of their ruts and fix their lives.

Maybe Pete Thompson is so far out in front that he thinks he is behind.

5 ɞ In cotton country, family comes first

The fracture in the earth's crust begins at New Madrid, in the southeast Missouri bootheel, and runs ninety miles southwest to Marked Tree, Arkansas. It is called the New Madrid Fault and all along it—and for 30,000 square miles around it—the earth heaved in late 1811 and again, from aftershocks, in early 1812.

It was the New Madrid earthquake and it was one of the largest ever recorded, not in terms of damage and death—because the area was sparsely settled—but in terms of changing forever part of the earth's face. In stories handed down from generation to generation, people say that the ground rose in gigantic waves and rippled across the countryside, much like tide at the seashore. Giant cypress trees, some of them more than 100 feet tall, toppled like matchsticks and were swallowed up by the earth, never to be seen again. They say that for days the rivers ran backward, even the Mighty Mississippi, which today roughly parallels the fault line thirty miles to the east.

What is known beyond doubt is that the Mississippi River did change its course in some places. Throughout the 30,000-square-mile area, some land sank from five to fifteen feet; other land rose as much as fifteen feet. Then the rains came and the rivers overflowed and there was no place for the water to go. Much of the

Larry Sanders, a friend says, "has more love in his heart for his fellow-man than anybody you'll ever see again."

northeast part of what in 1836 became the state of Arkansas turned to swampland as water drained down from the higher ground in Missouri. As late as 1920 it still was swampland, considered virtually unusable for anything. You could buy all the land you wanted, the natives say, for $1 an acre, but few people wanted it at any price.

Then the federal government began cutting a pattern of drainage ditches into the Arkansas countryside, with the smaller ditches emptying into those that were larger. The biggest ditches of them all, up to thirty feet wide and twenty feet deep, eventually flowed into the Mississippi River, carrying away the water of a century and transforming the swampland into what would become a farming paradise, a mixture of thick black dirt in some places, sandy loam in others.

Still, people didn't flock into the area, and one reason was that it was overgrown with trees. Much of the land never had been cleared. Roads were poor and few in number. Mostly they were dirt paths that turned to mud when the rains came and mired down the horse-pulled wagons. The biggest business in the area was brewing moonshine liquor in homemade stills that were carefully hidden in the trees, far enough from the roads, moonshiners hoped, so that federal revenue agents couldn't see the blue smoke that curled up when they ignited their wood fires to fuel the stills.

One of the first families to move into the area from the outside, for the purpose of farming, was Walter Jackson Sanders, his wife, Bessie, and their first-born son, Henry Dean Sanders. They came in 1921, tired of the meager existence that Walter Sanders grubbed out as a sawmill worker and cotton picker in the Arkansas Ozark country to the northwest. They bought 160 acres almost in the middle of a triangle formed by the towns of Monette, Leachville and Caraway. They cleared the land, marveling at the rich black soil brought to some of the ridgetops by the earthquake, and then they started growing cotton.

Walter and Bessie Sanders farmed their land for twenty-five years, gradually giving way to their son, Henry Dean, who bought more land and who became widely known throughout the area for his quickness to embrace mechanized farming—he had the area's first mechanical cotton picker in 1948—and to use chemicals to keep down weeds that for years had been chopped out by laborers using hoes.

His only son, Larry Sanders, farmed with him, side by side, and

Henry Dean remembers that "farming was the only thing Larry wanted to do. When he got out of high school, I tried to get him to go to college. He went for one semester, but he didn't like it and he quit. He told me that the only way he'd ever go back was if I made him go back. I told him I wouldn't make him go back, but I'd make him wish he had. So we started building fences, and that's really hard work. One day Larry looked at me and said: 'I guess you meant what you said. I wish I had gone back to school.' "

Nevertheless, Larry kept farming with his father until he married in 1964, and then he and his bride bought land of their own eighty miles away. But three years later, after three bad crops, they came back to what had been home for Larry. Larry took much of the land assembled by his grandfather and by his father, bought more, rented some and became one of the biggest farmers in the whole area. Today, at age thirty-six, he farms about 1,600 acres in the Monette, Leachville, Caraway triangle, and he uses another 1,700 acres for pasture for his cattle in Batesville, 100 miles to the west, and in Ash Flat, forty-five miles north of Batesville.

Larry Sanders is back home and a dream has been realized—a dream that he one day would farm for himself the land on which he had worked as a boy. It is a dream that will be passed along eventually to one, two or all three of his sons.

• • •

I'm on my way to visit Larry Sanders, whose mailing address is Caraway, Arkansas, but who actually lives closer to Monette. It is not the country's most accessible spot. From St. Louis I drive south 213 miles on Interstate 55, and I'm in Mississippi County, Arkansas, which calls itself the biggest rain-grown cotton- producing county in America. What that means is that farmers rely on nature, not irrigation, to water their cotton fields.

As I drive through the county, I pass liquor store after liquor store, all identified by signs that carry a single word: "Whiskey." Many of the stores feature drive-up windows, where you can buy your liquor without getting out of your car. It's advertised "for your convenience," but some natives tell me that it's also to keep people from seeing you walking into a whiskey store. I marvel at what I'm seeing as I drive. On the left, in somebody's front yard, is a hand-lettered sign, that advertises: "Big worms, $1.25 a box."

On the right is Gable's Club, where a yellow sign announces beer, pool and dancing. Then I go past the Farmers' Flying Service, where two crop-dusting airplanes are parked near the highway.

And then I'm out of Mississippi County and into Craighead County. Suddenly there are no more whiskey stores. I'm in a dry county—a county, I will find out later, that fights like a tiger on those rare occasions when somebody starts a movement to legalize the sale of liquor.

This is the county in which Larry Sanders lives with his thirty-four-year-old wife, Diana, and their three sons, a family that later in the summer will be named Craighead County's Farm Family of the Year. I've never met any of them, but I have telephoned Mrs. Sanders a number of times to arrange this meeting. The last time we talked, about a week earlier, she expressed amazement that anybody would come all the way from Philadelphia to see her and Larry. "We're just ordinary people," she said. "This whole county is filled with people just like us." When I told her that was why I was coming to see them, I got an earful of silence and then: "Really?"

Two miles before Monette, I turn south on an asphalt road and drive toward Caraway. I can't miss the Sanders home, she has told me, because it's made out of stone and "looks like it was designed in Mexico."

The fields of cotton and soybeans, planted in rows as straight as plumb lines, fan out in every direction. Off to the left a tractor kicks up dust. As I get closer, I see that the tractor driver has long, blond hair, ponytailed down the back of bib overalls. I'm surprised to see a boy in this part of the country with such long hair. In Philadelphia, yes. But in Caraway? How can it be? As I drive past the tractor I find that, indeed, it can't be. Or at least it isn't. The tractor driver is a young woman, and a good-looking woman, too. She smiles and waves at me.

Then I'm at the Sanders house, five miles outside Caraway, and it truly is a house that I couldn't miss. It is built from fieldstone that Larry Sanders trucked from his pasture near Ash Flat. It is trimmed with timber sawed from his land near Batesville. The roof is made of cypress shingles that Larry Sanders cut himself. The house is big, 4,100 square feet, and it is sprawling, since it's all on one floor. I realize that it is almost five times the size of my condominium unit.

It looks decidedly Mexican, with arches at the end of the front porch, the low, almost flat, slope of the roof, the wagon wheel that has been planted into the ground near the porch for decoration. Larry and Diana picked the house plan out of a book one evening as they were lying in bed and thinking about their dream house. "It was influenced by the only trip we ever took—to Texas and Mexico," Diana Sanders will say. "We fell in love with the architecture. We both like things that are rustic and western. We're not fancy folks, and there's nothing fancy about this house. It's livable. But it's not fancy."

I turn into the driveway and pull up beside a rusting Phillips 66 gasoline pump from which Larry fuels his two-year-old pickup and his wife's eight-year-old station wagon, the family car with 110,000 miles on it. Diana Sanders is standing outside the house, talking with a contractor who is installing a storm door. She is wearing sandals, a denim skirt and a yellow print blouse, a slender woman with light brown hair and eyes that shine as she welcomes me and calls me by my first name.

"Why, you must be Darrell. Come on in and have something to drink. Larry's not here now, but I'll call him. We're really glad you're here, and we want to get to know you. I hope we find out as much about you as you do about us."

We're inside the house now and I find that it is as spectacular as the outside. The kitchen cabinets are made from oak lumber that Larry Sanders tore out of an old barn. Some walls are paneled with homegrown cypress. Other walls are faced with fieldstones, some of which still have moss growing on them. The family room looks big enough to play basketball in. It's twenty-eight by twenty-four feet, and the fireplace built into a stone wall stretches from floor to vaulted, beamed ceiling. It's a fireplace that burns constantly in the winter, with oak they chop themselves, and sometimes, when it's really cold, they bring in the newborn calves, wrap them in blankets and let them sleep and soak up the heat. "That works all right until they get adventurous and start walking around," Diana Sanders says. "Then they go outside."

Through sliding glass doors, we walk from the family room to a concrete patio, the centerpiece of which is a giant tree stump, four feet in diameter, shaped into a picnic table. It is, yes, you guessed it, part of a 100-foot-long cypress tree that was unearthed by plow on the property three years ago, buried in last century's thunderous earthquake. It's still hard and firm as it must have been in 1811 because cypress, like cedar and fir, doesn't rot. Ever.

Diana Sanders calls her husband on their citizens band radio: "KMR 22-71. Hey, Larry, Darrell's here. Can you come home now?" Larry Sanders has no radio name—only call letters. "We tried to get him to pick a name," says his wife, "but he just wouldn't do it."

I'm offered a glass of lemonade, which I eagerly accept, and then the house tour continues, while we wait for Larry Sanders:

• Through the bedrooms, one for each of the three boys, one for Diana and Larry. Each bedroom, except theirs, is wallpapered, and Diana Sanders and a friend did it all by themselves. The master room, with adjoining bathroom, is paneled in rough-sawn cypress.

• Into Larry's den, where he does his bookkeeping at a tiny desk and where the walls are adorned with heads of animals he has killed, not with a rifle but with bow and arrow. The biggest head belongs to a moose that Larry fatally wounded with an eighty-five-yard shot to the kidneys in 1972 while he and friends were hunting in Montana.

• Into "Diana's room," where she does the laundry, irons on a board that folds out of the wall, cuts patterns for the clothes that she makes for herself and sometimes for her sons and her mother.

• Out into the garage, which is big enough to accommodate four vehicles and which has a vaulted ceiling so high that when the boys play basketball at a goal screwed into the wall, they never have to be concerned that an arching shot will rebound off the ceiling.

Mrs. Sanders was born Diana Bunting in Paragould, Arkansas, about forty-five minutes up the road, northwest of Monette. Her mother was from the area but her father, an ironworker, was from Illinois and "he couldn't wait to rush me back to Illinois. He said he hoped he'd never have to come back again. He didn't like Arkansas and what he considered the poverty in which the people lived. And there was a lot of poverty then. This area hadn't even scratched the surface of being progressive. Most of the land was not even settled, still in timber.

"Daddy used to look at the slogan on the Arkansas license plates—'Land of Opportunity'—and he'd laugh and say, 'Yeah, take the first opportunity to get out.' But he doesn't feel that way anymore. He loves to come and visit us."

She grew up in Bloomington, Illinois, a college town of 50,000, attended high school there and began her studies to become a registered nurse. But those plans went out the window in 1964, six years after she first met Larry Sanders while she was visiting a friend in Paragould during the summer.

After off-and-on summertime dating for six years, she and Larry decided to get married and "Larry went with me back to Bloomington to give back the ring this other fellow I was dating had given me. It was a sticky situation."

They married and Diana left nursing school ("You couldn't be in nursing school back then if you were married.") and Larry left the farmland he had worked with his father since boyhood. He and Diana bought 560 acres at Forest City, Arkansas, sixty miles west of Memphis and about eighty miles southwest of where they now live. They lived there for three years in a log cabin and, Diana says, while the marriage prospered, their farming did not. They moved back onto Larry's father's land in 1967 and lived for ten years in a brick house that now is occupied by one of their hired hands. Then in 1977 they built their dream house, for $55,000. They kept down the cost because they subcontracted the work themselves and furnished fieldstone and timber. It's a house that, if you put it in the Philadelphia suburbs, would cost $175,000—and the people who'd buy it at that price would think they'd stolen it.

Does Diana ever have any regrets about giving up a nursing career in the city for the life of a farm wife and mother?

"I've never missed it," she answers. "I'm busy with the boys and with Larry. It was a great experience—that year in nurse's training—but this, what I have now, is my career. I have the boys and a husband and they love, respect and honor me. The boys think Mommy can do just about anything. I like to be with my family. My career will change as my family changes."

What does she mean by that?

"It's important to keep a wonderful working relationship with your husband while the children are small. The children are going to be gone someday, but you'll still have the same husband. And if you've neglected him all those years, while you were caring for the children, then it's awfully hard to catch up for what you've missed."

Children, she says, "need to know that their parents have a life apart from them and that they don't control your life. In the winter our boys are in bed by nine and Larry and I have a good hour to ourselves. We turn off the television, sit and listen to each other, talk about our plans for the future, things we hope we can do. In the summer the boys stay up later, so Larry and I have our time together at breakfast, early, before the boys get up.''

What she and Larry have, she says, is an inner happiness rooted in their belief in God, nourished by going to Milligan Ridge Missionary Baptist Church, six miles away, sometimes two or three times a week. ''Things happen that frustrate us, but if you have inner happiness, then that can't be taken away just because something goes wrong—''

There's a thumping on the door and Diana knows that her husband is home. The door from the garage pops open and Larry walks briskly into the kitchen, smiling, extending his right hand toward me. He is short, five feet, seven inches, but in his ten-gallon-type hat, he looks six-and-a-half feet tall. He wears cowboy boots, dusty blue jeans, a bright green cotton shirt with short sleeves and a tan leather belt with ''LARRY'' burned in capital letters across the back.

Larry Sanders is massively put together in his upper body, which tapers sharply at the waist and gives him the V-like appearance that you tend to associate with weight lifters and men who pose for muscle-building-course advertisements. At 170 pounds he looks at if he could play cornerback for the National Football League team of his choice. He is simply all muscle and hard as a brick wall—the result, he will tell me later, of years of working in the fields and shooting his bow and arrow.

He is deeply tanned on the arms, face and neck and, when he smiles, his straight white teeth flash like ivory against a background of brown velvet. Black, curly hair, matted with perspiration, sticks out from beneath his hat.

Before we can say more than ''Hello, good to see you,'' there is another thump at the same door and into the kitchen march— well, this is something that has to be seen to be believed: three boys—Shannon, twelve; Nathan, ten; Heath, seven—and each of them is wearing a ten-gallon hat and looking so much like their father that I'm blinking and trying to figure out if it's really happening. They, too, wear dusty jeans and cowboy boots and short-sleeve shirts and they are tanned by the sun because they, too, work in the fields, alongside their father and the five hired hands who live year-round on the property.

What really amazes me, aside from their appearance, is how easily they meet a stranger. These obviously are boys who are ac-

Nathan at the piano . . .

Shannon at the wheel of a $30,000 tractor . . .

and Heath, in a boy's special world.

customed to being around adults they don't know. They shake my hand and smile, and Heath, whose hat is almost as tall as he is, asks me if I know that he drives a pickup truck.

Yes, that's right. At age seven Heath Sanders really does drive a pickup—not on roads but in soybean fields. They call it "the bean truck" and it carries the fertilizer and chemicals that go into the soybean fields. "I'll tell you something," Larry Sanders says. "Heath will sit in that hot truck all day to drive it ten feet. It's his first job in the field and he loves it."

At twelve, Shannon long since has graduated from the bean truck. He's paid by his father as a full-time tractor hand and on payday he beats a path to the bank in Monette to deposit his check. What kind of work does a twelve-year-old kid do on a tractor? What does he really do? Well, I find out the next day. Larry and I go to the soybean fields and there is Shannon, all by himself, driving a $30,000 tractor rigged to spray weed-killer on twelve rows at once. This is not an easy job and I wouldn't want to try to do it myself—not because it's so hard physically but because it's very exacting. The sprays are set to curl the chemicals right around the stalks and if the tractor isn't driven at precisely the right spot between the rows, the chemicals will douse not weeds but soybean plants—and kill them. So Shannon sits in the glass-enclosed cockpit of the tractor, eight feet off the ground, and keeps his eyes fixed on the notch of the tractor's hood that he lines up on the rows that he's spraying.

I encourage you to think about doing that for eight or ten hours a day—as Shannon does—the next time you feel like complaining because you have to mow the grass in your front yard. This is big-time work, what Shannon is doing, and he does it like a man, his hands, shoes and bottoms of his jeans stained bright yellow from the chemicals, just like his father's.

And Nathan, the ten-year-old son? Well, he's a tractor driver, too, not so much to plow and spread chemicals in the field as to cut weeds and mow the lawns around the homes where the hired hands live with their families. Nathan, the best student of the three, paints pictures, plays the piano and writes some of his own music. He plays one of his songs for me—entitled "Ridin' Horseback." His comment about it: "Mom says I wrote it, I say I made it up and my piano teacher says I composed it. What do you think I did?"

Nathan, his father says, probably will be the one of the sons who goes to college and does not go into farming. Nathan has a variety of interests, including baseball. He catches for the Little League team that his father coaches. Shannon plays third base on the same team and the night before, in the league's all-star game, their team has won, 11-10, and Shannon has hit a double, Nathan, a single, and together they have engineered a double play.

These are three remarkable kids and over and over again, during the two days I spend with Larry and Diana Sanders, I find myself telling them: "You must really be proud of your boys."

Larry smiles and says that, yes, they are proud, and that growing up on a farm is a great experience for a boy. "They learn how to respect equipment—so they don't fear it. They learn where life comes from and where food comes from. They know it's not just something that comes from the grocery store. They know what goes into feeding and clothing the country."

The people around Caraway and Monette will tell you that Larry Sanders is widely known and universally respected, a man who has carved a good living for himself and his family out of the soil he loves, a man whose word is his bond and who believes ill about nobody until ill is proven beyond a shadow of a doubt.

"I've never seen anybody like him," says Woody Wicker, part-time Baptist preacher and part-time field hand and welder for the Sanders family. "Larry has more love in his heart for his fellow-man than anybody you'll ever see again. He finds good in everybody. The charity work he does . . . well, let me tell you: A hired hand will bring his whole family over here to work. And Larry will put every one of them to work and pay them—whether there is work that needs to be done or not.

"He never gives anybody something for nothing, but what he does is a form of charity, in my opinion. In my church I preach on love, the love of God to people, loving your brother as Jesus loved. We used to harp on the salvation of sinners. We still preach on that, on repentance, but in a different way, through the voice of love for your fellow-man.

"A few years ago a man would buy a cow and tell the owner that he'd pay him in the fall. And that would be OK, go ahead and take the cow. You took a man at his word. But we've gotten away from that. We don't trust people anymore. It's because of greed. That's what has caused us to be this way. Just look at our courts. You fall down and you sue somebody for damages. What it boils down to is that I try to do it to you before you do it to me. We've reversed the golden rule. But that's not true at this house, with Larry Sanders. I could say, 'Larry, I need $8,000,' and he'd give it to me, if he had it, without asking a single question. He's that kind of man.''

How did Larry Sanders get to be that kind of man? He's embarrassed when I ask him about it. Finally, after his second glass of lemonade, he begins to talk:

"The church is a very important part of our lives. It's more than just going to church. It's what is in our hearts—happiness and peace. If you know the Lord Jesus Christ as your personal savior, if you conduct yourself as He wants you to, then everything else in your life will fall into place.

"Yeah, things get out of hand sometimes, and we have too much rain or not enough rain, or I feel the farm is running me instead of me running the farm. I wonder what's going on when the problems seem to close in on me. But I open up the word of God and I find promises, promises that everything will work out. And it's like planting a seed within a person, a daily seed of hope. And then the problems don't seem so big.''

Other people around the area tell you that Larry Sanders has been financially successful because, like his father before him, he's been willing to expand, buy modern equipment, hire people to work for him. In short, they say, he's willing to spend money almost as fast as he borrows it from the bank, because he knows this is what it takes to make money.

"It's not easy to get to the point where you're comfortable doing that, borrowing money, I mean," Larry says. "We've all been taught not to spend money we don't have, not to buy anything we can't afford, can't pay cash for. But it doesn't work that way in farming. You have to buy it with the bank's money. It takes a while to figure that out, but that's how it works.''

How much does Larry Sanders borrow in a year? How much does he have left after he's paid back the bank and settled all of his expenses? "Well, you can look at him and tell he's making money," a Monette businessman told me. "He knows what he's doing.''

Larry wouldn't discuss finances with me, smiling and saying that there are some things you don't tell "even to somebody who's come all the way from Philadelphia.'' He's doing better than some farmers, not so good as others, he says, as the cost of farming con-

Like every farmer, Larry Sanders has a deep familiarity with machinery, in this case, a combine.

tinues to go up, regardless of what happens to the market price his cotton and soybeans command. His bills from Farmers' Flying Service—for spraying chemicals and seeding his fields with rye-grass and winter wheat—come to about $10,000 a year. And just the other day he asked the people at the fertilizer-chemical store how much he owes them and the answer was: $20,000.

Larry farms 1,000 acres of soybeans and the other 600 acres in cotton and wheat. This year he has planted less cotton than ever before—because the spring was too wet, because cotton prices are down and because the cost of growing cotton is much higher than the cost of growing soybeans. Lots of other farmers in the area are cutting back on cotton, too, he says. "Some people who used to be cotton farmers don't have a stalk this year. They've all gone to soybeans."

The problem, he says, is that it takes a market price of at least sixty-five cents a pound to make it as a cotton farmer. "Last year we got about sixty-seven cents and that was all right. This year it's sixty cents and that's not good." Each acre produces about 1,500 pounds of cotton, which converts to a single 500-pound bale after it's ginned and the seeds and lint removed. At sixty cents a pound, that comes to $300 gross for each acre. But the government figures the cost of growing an acre of cotton is about $150. That leaves $150, minus other expenses. And that's less than soybeans, he says.

A good portion of his income comes from buying and selling cattle. A neighbor, Elihue Price, buys the cattle for him on com-mission—"thin cattle with a good frame" is the way he describes the cattle he wants. Price, who has a metal sign near his barn that proclaims "The Price Is Right," is sleepy eyed. And it's no wonder. When we arrived at his house about 2:00 P.M., Larry got no response after ringing the doorbell and then knocking for a full minute. So he opened the door and went inside and there was Price, napping in a chair.

Price, who owns some of the land that Larry Sanders rents for soybeans, buys cattle in the fall and Larry keeps them on the home place over the winter, letting them fatten up off the ryegrass, wheat and milo. Then he trucks them up to the pastures in the hills, near Batesville and Ash Flat.

The cattle—from 300 to 500 head—eat through the summer and into the fall and gain 200 pounds or more each. Since they are sold by the pound—from fifty to sixty cents is a good average, Price says—you can figure out that 200 pounds amounts to a reasonable profit on each head when the cattle are sold in the fall, about the time of the first frost. Then Price buys more cattle and the cycle starts over again.

While Larry works in the fields, Diana works around the house—sewing, preparing meals for the hired hands during the busy harvesttimes, canning vegetables and working in the garden. The garden, she says, is not her favorite task and "I do it only because I have to. Everybody else is busy doing something else." She also does the family marketing, and there's more of that than you might expect. It's true that they raise many of their vegetables and almost all of the meat they eat. They swap some beef every year for pork from a hog farmer near Batesville. But, Diana says, "We still spend $50 a week at the grocery store—for paper products, ice cream, milk, chocolate syrup, potato chips and bread."

While the Sanderses borrow money from the bank for their big farm equipment purchases and to finance putting in the year's crops, they shy away from buying things on time payment plans, "farmer's terms," in Diana's words. "That's the way they sell furniture in a lot of small towns. You get the furniture, but you pay nothing until the crop is sold in the fall. Then you pay it all at once. That's the only way a lot of people can buy the things they need. But on furniture and things, we try to save until we can afford to pay for what we want," she says.

Diana says their social life—"what there is of it"—is centered on their children and their church. They go to an occasional party ("We don't drink and we'd never be invited to a party where drinks were served.") but mostly they stay at home. "I often tell Larry to put the car and truck behind the house and let's stay here with each other and the boys."

Larry enjoys his work with the baseball team, despite occasional hassling from parents who wonder why their boys aren't playing more. He handles these parents by inviting them to come to practice and watch. "That usually answers all their questions."

Diana is a county 4-H leader and, during the time I spend at the Sanders home, it becomes obvious that this amounts to far more than running the monthly meetings. The telephone rings six or eight times a day; 4-H children ask questions about their projects, the records they must keep, the things they must do to win a coveted project prize. She worries, she says, not so much about the 4-H kids as about the others who "get into the kinds of problems that so many children have''—drugs, drinking, out-of-wedlock pregnancy.

"Most city folks come to a little town and expect to find things perfect, no serious problems. But we have them. Pregnancy is hardly looked on as anything out of the ordinary. The high school had to go to a closed lunch hour because when the children were free to go to town for lunch, they were coming back high on drugs. The school board called a town meeting and a narcotics agent came to talk to parents about what to look for and what to do if they suspected their children were on drugs. No, I'll tell you, drugs are no respecter of any town.''

While I spend hours talking with Diana, across the kitchen table, alternately drinking coffee and lemonade, much of my time with Larry is in his pickup, which he wheels like a race driver through the narrow back roads, leaving a trail of white dust. He honks and waves at drivers of other trucks, tractors and combines. Everybody waves. Most of them honk. All of them smile.

We drive to a cotton field where Woody Wicker is trying to coax a balky tractor into starting. Wicker, the part-time preacher and part-time hired hand, is a candidate for anybody's list of all-time unforgettable characters. Brother Woody, as he's called by members of Rowe's Chapel Baptist Church where he has preached for a year and a half, is forty-two, a huge man, well in excess of 250 pounds. He didn't become a minister necessarily because he wanted to, he says, but because God wanted him to.

"I was 'called' at an early age, but I tried to run away from it,'' he tells me. "I had a lot of different jobs. I was vice president of a dry cleaning equipment company, and I traveled all over the United States and Europe. And I made good money, too, maybe $65,000 or $80,000 a year. I've seen everything there is to see—like going into Greenwich Village and seeing seventy beautiful women who aren't really women. They're men dressed up like women. Nobody around here believes that happens. But it does. I saw it myself.''

But for all those years he worked and traveled, he says, he never was happy. "When the Lord wants you, He gets you—eventually. I never had peace of mind, although I had money. Now I have peace of mind, but I don't have any money." He's smiling broadly as he says that, standing at the edge of the cotton field, wearing bib overalls, boots, a multi-colored Hawaiian shirt and a baseball

Larry with Woody Wicker, part-time preacher, part-time hired hand.

umpire's black cap. He hands me a green-colored business card that introduces him as "Woodie C. Wicker, pastor" and tells me this is something to remember him by. "The guy who made up them cards didn't know how to spell my first name," he says. "It's Woody, W-O-O-D-Y. That's a funny way to spell it, but my mother named me after Woody Herman, the bandleader. She really liked him."

Woody Wicker gets paid $110 a week by "my little church," which has fifty members. In addition he is provided with a house and some other benefits. Rowe's Chapel Baptist Church is one of many small churches in Craighead County, and these churches always have been active, although once their memberships were larger.

"There are forty Southern Baptist Churches in this county and forty or fifty Missionary Baptist Churches," Brother Woody says. "This started when there was one farmhouse on every 200 acres, and people wanted their own community church. Now there is one house to every 1,000 acres, because farms have gotten bigger, and people have moved out. But they're starting to come back now. They're moving back from the cities, from Jonesboro, Paragould, Osceola, back to where they can grow gardens and exist. They're going back to basics."

Brother Woody, who ate a whole chicken at lunch one day while I gawked in disbelief, was a leader back in the spring in the banding together of churches to defeat, by a three-to-one margin, a proposal to allow the sale of liquor in Craighead County, which has been dry since World War II.

"They—the businessmen in Jonesboro—spent $400,000 to try to get whiskey in and we spent $35,000 to keep it out."

Why did the churches fight whiskey? The basic reason, says Brother Woody, is the feeling that there's more drinking, more drunkenness, more alcoholism when whiskey is more readily available. You can go into neighboring Mississippi County, he says, and see drunks all over the place. The churches' next target, he says, will be the private clubs, where members are able to buy whiskey by the drink. "Most of them are nothing but glorified bars," Brother Woody says.

Brother Woody is from Hornersville, in the Missouri boot heel. How far away is that? "Well, as the crow flies it's seventeen or eighteen miles. If you're walking and carrying a can of gasoline, it's like thirty miles." His father, Peck Wicker, is the founder and

Life in the Sanders family is nourished by worship at Milligan Ridge Missionary Baptist Church. Diana, center, admires a newcomer, while Larry, Bible tucked under his arm at left, is greeted by a fellow parishioner.

originator of what Woody calls "that incredible" Wicker's Barbecuing Sauce, which you can find on any grocery store shelf in the
area, he says, and in parts of thirty-eight states. "We even sell it
up in Flint, Michigan, because that's where people from here went
when they left the farms to get jobs in the auto plants." That's
right, Diana Sanders has said. There's a standing joke that nobody from Arkansas needs a road map to get to Flint. You can
just follow the bologna skins left by those who went before you.

How does Wicker's Barbecuing Sauce rate with me? Well, I
tried a bottle and I must tell you that it's not bad. Spicy, hot, lots
of vinegar. It was, Woody says, the reason why his father's barbe-
cue stand in Hornersville became a legend years ago. Woody insists that Craig Claiborne, fabled food editor of the *New York
Times,* ate there three times, wrote that it was one of a handful of
places in the country worth going back to for more.

Judging from Brother Woody's girth, I believe he took Claiborne's advice.

Late one afternoon I go down to the Monette cotton gin, where
I meet Norman Bailey, who's been in the area for almost fifty
years and who farmed full-time until ten years ago, when he leased
his acreage and devoted all his time to the L.G. Carter Gin Co.
"We don't have any titles, but if you have to call me something,
call me the bookkeeper," he says.

His observations of farming changes over the years are incisive.
"We used to have 175 to 200 customers here at the gin. Now we
have thirty-five. What happened? Well, the children who would
have gone into farming didn't have any place to go. So they left
the farm and went to work in factories, doing whatever they could
find. There was a time when a father would give his son 50 or 100
acres off his farm, and the son could live off that and raise a family. But that can't be done anymore. Today the farmer needs all the
land he's got—300 or 400 acres—just to make a living for himself."

The difference in the farm people themselves, Bailey says, is
that forty years ago they lived on what they made. "It was a poor,
meager way of life, sometimes, but they accepted that. Today people aren't like that. They want the luxuries everybody else has and
if they can't get them on the farm, they leave." The result of this
movement, Bailey says, is that the farmers who remain—like
Larry Sanders—are making a good living, enjoying some of life's
luxuries and sending their children to college. Forty years ago,

Bailey says, nobody went to college and "only maybe half got out of high school."

It is early the next morning—before nine o'clock—when I pull off State Highway 18 at the Farmers' Flying Service and ask if Randy Speidel, the owner, has time to talk to me. I think the likelihood is very small, considering that Speidel is in his crop-dusting airplane with the motor running. But he shuts off the motor, invites me into his concrete-block office building and spends forty minutes giving me the ABC's of what he does for a living. It is a real education.

A former helicopter pilot in Vietnam, Speidel, thirty-three, flew corporate planes and air freight before starting this business three years ago. He has three airplanes, specially built Grumman Ag-Cats that cost $90,000 when they are new. His are used, built in 1961, 1964 and 1965. These Ag-Cats "last almost indefinitely" if you take care of them, he says. The first of them, bearing serial number 1, was made in 1958 and still is in service in Walnut Ridge, Arkansas.

The Ag-Cats have stubby bodies, two wings and huge engines—up to 600 horsepower—because of the enormous loads of fertilizer and chemicals they must carry, as much as 2,000 pounds. When you consider that an Ag-Cat, empty, weighs only 3,500 pounds, you get an idea of just how much load it's capable of getting into the sky. But in Speidel's business there's something more important than getting it into the sky; it's keeping it in the sky.

"A lot of times, in hot weather, when the air is dense, you can get off the ground with more than you can fly with. You go into a turn and you start to fall—because the plane is too heavy. And you have to drop some of what you're carrying."

That doesn't happen to him often, he says, because he's learned that on the hot, humid days you fly with 250 gallons of chemicals, not with a full 300 gallons. So far he's been able to avoid the obstacles that pose a daily threat to his life and limb: fence posts, trees, irrigation systems. He flies low—right on top of the crops when he's spraying on liquid chemical, about twenty feet when he's unloading solid matter. How low is "right on top" of the crops? "Well," he says, a smile creasing his tanned face, "if I land with cotton bolls tangled in my wheels, I know it's been a good flight."

Speidel has a customer list of 115 farmers, more than double what he had after his first year. At the busiest time of the season—from late July through September, when he's spraying cotton for worms and then defoliating it to expose the cotton bolls for harvest—he often flies twelve hours a day. At other times of the year, he's "lucky to get two or three hours a day."

Because competition is keen—there are six crop-dusters within a ten-mile radius—prices are kept quite low, Speidel says. He charges $2.00 an acre for laying on herbicides, $1.75 for insecticides, and 2½ cents a pound for spreading fertilizer and seeding. How long does it take to cover an acre? An acre, Speidel says, "can be done just like that"—and he snaps a finger to show what he means. "Some years you make a good living and other years not so good."

There is one other person I should see before I leave town, I'm told. He's a retired cotton breeder. Yes, that's right. He has devoted much of his life to trying to improve the varieties of cotton through inbreeding and cross-pollination. What is it that he wants to improve? Increased yield per acre is the biggest item. Some others are greater wilt resistance, higher breaking strength, more uniformity.

Once he owned a cotton gin, which he sold for a few million dollars, but even today he still has an office near the gin and he and his wife go to the office almost every day, sometimes to do nothing but read magazines and talk. He is, I am told, somebody with a wealth of stories to tell, somebody I will find extraordinary.

Larry Sanders's father, Henry Dean, who is semiretired now, goes along to introduce me to this man "because he is not very anxious, sometimes, to talk to people he doesn't know." So Henry Dean tells the man who I am and why I'm here. He looks at me and asks: "Why do you want to see me? There isn't anything I could tell you that you couldn't find out someplace else."

He tells me that he's wary of all writers, especially people "who say they're working on a book. I'll tell you one thing. If you write anything about me, don't use my name. I don't want my name to appear in any book. Do you understand that?"

That's about as plain as anybody has put it to me recently and I tell him that's fine with me. Then a strange thing happens. While he tells me that he has nothing to say, he spins fascinating tales of yesteryear:

"The whole area, a long time ago, was infested by swamp rattlesnakes, mean critters maybe thirty inches long and as big around

Diana has no regrets about giving up a nursing career to be a
farm wife. She has sons and a husband who "love, respect and
honor me."

as my arm. When they got mad, they gave off a scent. And they got mad easily. You could smell when they were around. They had jaws full of venom, and they were mean. They drowned in the flood of '37 because that turned all the land into a giant lake and killed everything except the water snakes. You won't find any snakes around now, except for a water moccasin or two around the drainage ditches.''

When he has finished with snakes, he takes up the "incredible" price of farmland today, from $1,500 to $2,000 an acre. "That doesn't mean that the people who own it are rich. You have a big book value, but a day of reckoning comes sometime, if you sell, and when the government gets through with you, then you're certainly not rich.'' People who live on this $2,000 land aren't living as well as they did when it was $200 land. "So how can anybody figure that the land is worth more?''

By now it's getting on into late afternoon. I still have two things to do on this day, my last with Larry and Diana Sanders. At my request they are treating me to a genuine Arkansas fried catfish dinner, and they're taking me with them to the Wednesday night prayer-song service at Milligan Ridge Baptist Church.

Why would I ask them to treat me to fried catfish? Because it's been forty years since I've eaten catfish and the ones I remember—the ones I caught in the Osage River near my home in Missouri—had so many bones that I vowed I'd never eat one again. But things are different now, Larry tells me. They don't pull catfish out of the rivers anymore. They breed them in commercial ponds and, over the years, they've bred the little bones right out of their bodies. Now they have just a backbone and a few rib-like bones—and that's it. They are marvelous eating, Diana says, when they're rolled in cornmeal, deep-fried and served with hush puppies, baked potato, tartar sauce, quartered onions and coleslaw.

We drive ten minutes up the road to Leachville, at the northern end of the triangle, and at Kirby's Malt Shop we have our catfish and guess what? Larry Sanders is correct. The little bones of yesteryear are gone. The catfish is excellent. Our bill for six, including the three children, is a whopping $22.54. Can you believe that? I thought it was a typographical error.

Now we head out in the two-seat, four-door pickup for Milligan Ridge and the church meeting, which starts at 7:30. We bump

For some, fun means diving into a wagonload of cotton.

along the dirt road, past flooded rice fields—that's how rice is grown—and thirsty-looking soybeans and cotton. Finally, at 7:30 sharp, we arrive at the church, a neat-looking building with white asbestos shingles. Brother Waymon Holt, who has been full-time minister for fourteen years, is leading thirty-five people in singing.

"Blessed assurance, Jesus is mine, oh, what a foretaste of glory divine . . . "

The song is finished and Brother Waymon—everybody is on a first-name basis—says, "Oh, blessed assurance. What a wonderful message. You can do many things if you have assurance." His Bible study is an examination of Second Peter and it goes to this point: God never bends the rules; God does things right. The way He did things right was to have Jesus bear our sins in His body. God has paid for our sins. There are no shortcuts for us to take in showing our appreciation. The right way is to be born again, acknowledge our sins, repent, "receive Jesus Christ by faith as our own personal savior. This is the only way to escape the corruption that has been bred into the world through lust. Until you know Jesus as your personal savior, there will be no new day dawning . . . and your heart always will be in a dark place, the squalid dark of the whole world system."

It's the best system man has been able to work out, Brother Waymon says, but without the Lord it's nothing to write home about.

We're on our way home now, back to the Sanders house of fieldstone and cypress wood, of warmth and closeness, of, yes, love—even love for somebody who forty-eight hours ago was not a face but a name and a voice on the telephone.

We share watermelon, lemonade and chocolate chip cookies and I show them pictures of my wife and my two sons. They get out their family album and show me pictures of life on the pasture-land at Ash Flat. We promise to write each other. The kids, Shannon, Nathan and Heath, tell me good-by and ask when I'm coming back.

This has been a good two days. I'd like to come back. Real soon.

Going home.

6 ⊷§ The grapes of joy

This is like a dream. You think it's happening, but you're not quite sure. Here we are, eight of us, two men and six women, and we have shed the clothes we came in and now we are wearing Bermuda shorts, cut-offs, rolled-up jeans or whatever we regard as our wardrobe dregs.

This outrageous exposure of skin has not gone unnoticed by a thirteen-piece German band, which overrides the swelling laughter with a brassy delivery of "The Stripper." We pretend not to notice as, one after another, we climb a five-foot ladder into a round wooden vat that is almost waist high and filled above the ankles with a pulpy, sticky mess that oozes between the toes and ignites screams of dismay before it swallows the feet.

The eight of us fit together snugly around the perimeter of the vat, stomachs to backs, our circle facing counterclockwise. When the band switches to "Pennsylvania Polka," we push and shove, slip and slide, and our circle begins to move. At first my feet are cold and uncomfortable, but now they are warm, almost hot, as if I'm wading in witches' brew. Nobody is worried about falling down, because there is no place to fall. Others have climbed the ladder and invaded the center of our circle so that the vat now is a solid hunk of people.

Jerry Fry spends more time at the computer terminal than in the fields, but he feels there is still romance in growing grapes.

Suddenly it's impossible for our circle to go around any more, so we stand and jiggle our feet up and down, as if we're exercising, running in place. Outside the vat people mill around impatiently and tell us: "Hey, your time's up. It's our turn."

I struggle out of the vat and my feet and legs are the color of caramel apples and just about as sticky. Somebody turns a hose on me, and through the spray I hear: "Well, whadda you think?"

Well, what do you think? Can you imagine where I am and what I've been doing? Let me tell you. I'm with Jerry Fry at his grape ranch in Lodi, California, and this party tonight is the highlight of the harvest, that once-a-year time when Jerry and Peggy Fry bring their friends and other growers to their house for food, wine and an opportunity to slosh around in the vat and crush the grapes that will become Jerry Fry's homemade wine for the next year.

They started in 1965, these parties, not long after the Frys came here from the San Francisco Bay area, two hours to the west. First there were twelve guests, then twenty-five, then fifty. Now there are eighty, and they're dancing and urging Fry to hurry and dig up the side of beef, wrapped in wet burlap, that he buried early in the morning and cooked on top of a smoldering underground fire.

It's a party to end all parties, and it's fitting that it should take place here, in the San Joaquin Valley, which seems to me a place to end all places. Lodi is at the north end of the valley, which stretches 280 miles south to Bakersfield and which is walled by the Sierra Nevada on the east and the Coast ranges on the west. The valley is the heart of California's wine industry, with an annual crush of wine grapes that is estimated at a million and a half tons—ten times the crush from all the coastal counties combined. The valley is dotted with towns that have names as familiar as the wine labels on which they appear: Modesto, Madera, Fresno, Lodi.

You enter Lodi off State Highway 99, and the first street you hit is Cherokee Lane, which is crowded with motels and restaurants, one of which is the Hollywood Cafe, where with lunch or dinner you can buy for fifty cents a half bottle of *vin rosé* that has a taste worth three times the price. Even as you approach this community of 31,000, you are served notice that this is the start of something good, a sign that greets you with: "Welcome to Lodi, Romantic Wine Country."

And that's really how it is. You walk into a vineyard at seven o'clock in the morning, when the vines are dew coated and the sun is struggling to shake out of sleep, and you feel the romance. Jerry Fry feels it, too, after these many years: "This is a special way to make a living."

He has 500 acres of vineyards, and 85 percent of the grapes they yield go into wine even though most are table grapes, grown to be eaten rather than to be sipped. These are Tokay grapes, pinball-size, plump and pinkish-purple, excellent for making champagne, sherry, even brandy, because they have no distinctive taste of their own and blend easily with the juices of more flavorful grapes.

The vines are heavy with grapes, but you have to search for them because most of the clusters are hidden beneath the heavy leaves of the vines. The leaves are the only protection the grapes have from the sun, which by midafternoon becomes so torrid that the pickers retreat and don't return until 6:30 the next morning, when the temperature is down thirty degrees.

Fry drives his Jeep into the vineyard, and we walk among the rows of vines, some more than 75 years old, and from time to time he stops, reaches in and palms a cluster of grapes, inspecting them meticulously, as if to reinforce his belief that indeed this is a very good year. Where they emerge from the sandy, weedless soil, some of the vines have trunks the size of small trees, four to six inches in diameter. Their gnarled branches twist upward, shoulder high, some supported by wooden stakes, others left to bear the full burden of their own weight. This is a vineyard—like all of Fry's—that is old style, that can be harvested only by hand because no mechanical picker has yet been invented to get inside the branches and claw loose the juicy clumps of grapes. Around here you find none of the wires, none of the lattices on which some of the new vineyards spread out their vines to welcome the machines that do the work of many sweating pickers.

The Mexicans who pick for Fry are migrants who follow the ripening of the crops up from the south, arriving at his ranch about the middle of August to begin a harvest that for many of them will continue until late October.

Some of them have worked for Fry for ten years, coming back each season, he says, because "they know I treat them right." I'm amazed at how many he calls by name. There is José and Pascuale and Pablo and Rivera, all of whom smile their greetings as they hurry about their business of filling their boxes, bringing them to the wagon, where they are credited for each box, and then returning to the vines.

Each box contains about fourteen bunches of grapes and weighs twenty-three pounds. Pickers are paid eighty-five cents for each box they fill, and a really good picker can load 90 to 100 boxes in a day. That's better than the average, however, which is about 80 boxes. The minimum is 50 boxes. If you can't fill 50 during your eight hours, then you can't work for Jerry Fry. The men work rapidly, cutting the bunches from the vines with hook-bladed knives that resemble linoleum cutters. But before they lay a bunch into the box, they inspect it and remove any bad grapes. Fry insists on that.

These Tokays are being harvested as table grapes, about the last of the season, and they will be taken in their boxes to a warehouse in the community of Victor, next door to Lodi, where they will be loaded onto refrigerated trucks that will take them to supermarkets 3,000 miles away.

The juice grapes, those intended for wineries, will be picked last, and less caution is taken with them, the rest of the Tokays and the Zinfandel, Palomino, Alicante, Petite-Sirah and Sauvignon Blanc. Juice grapes are put not in boxes but in fifty-pound buckets, each of which is worth fifty cents to the picker.

Fry approaches the picking crew's foreman, who wears a white cowboy hat, and asks, "Johnny, are we gonna make it today? Are we going to finish up here?"

The face is Mexican, but the language is pure English: "Yeah." Then he wrinkles his brow and says, "Some of the men want to leave for Mexico today if they get paid. Can they get paid today?"

"It's going to be hard to get it done today. I hadn't planned to pay today. I didn't think they were leaving until Saturday."

"No, they would like their money now, the bonus and everything."

"It's not that easy. Each of them is one person, but last week I had eighty-five to pay. You understand?"

"What should I tell them?"

Fry smiles. "Tell them I'll do the best I can."

The bonus that pickers get at the end of the season is a nickel for each box—on top of the eighty-five cents that already has been paid. That's to encourage them to stay for the full season, and most of them do. After they finish with the grapes, some of them return 500 miles to Mexico for the winter. Others find different

jobs and remain in Lodi, which has a substantial Mexican population and where they have friends or can find friends quickly.

A few of the Mexicans work around the year for Fry, pruning
vines, irrigating, fertilizing the cherry and almond trees. The full-
time workers are paid a minimum of $3.10 an hour, and, when I
whistle my surprise, Fry says, "If you want good help, that's what
you pay. Labor has gone up around here. When we started, in
1965, I was paying $1.35 for general labor."

Running a farm that totals more than 1,000 acres is big business, and Fry is a businessman. He dresses like a farmer—boots,
jeans, cotton shirt and nylon jacket—but the years when he actually went to the fields to labor are long gone. He directs the operation through his foremen these days, and he spends much of his
time looking over computer print-outs that reveal where his
money is coming from—and where it goes.

He has a computer terminal in his office back at the house. It's
hooked up to a computer in Gridley, north of Sacramento, and on
a shared-time basis for which he pays $260 a month he keeps his
books and handles his payroll—a far cry, he says, from the days
when farmers scribbled their finances on the backs of envelopes or
whatever they could find.

Fry seems comfortable in his businessman role although, he
says, he wishes he'd taken more business courses in college. He began as an agricultural engineer at the University of California at
Berkeley but transferred to the university's branch at Davis, where
he switched his major to soil science and where he subsequently
got a master's degree in soil physics. "It's not common around
here for a farmer to have a graduate degree, but we'll see more as
time goes on. Things are changing on the farm. It's a different
game now, more sophisticated. You can farm without it, but lots
of things in education are valuable to a farmer."

It was while he was at Berkeley that he met the woman who
would become his wife. She was in a sorority down the street from
his fraternity and after a friend introduced them, he and Peggy
were constant companions. They have three sons, Jay, twelve; Oscar, nine; and Bruce, seven, and Fry seems torn between the time
he feels necessary to run his farm and the time he would like to
spend with them.

As with many fathers, he often finds there isn't time enough to
go around. On this very evening he has an Indian Guides date with

Bruce, while Jay is playing soccer and Oscar has a meeting at school. He and Peggy match their schedules, and she will hit the soccer match before going to the school meeting. He says he feels guilty that he can't be at all three.

At thirty-seven, Jerry Fry is beginning "to realize how time flies. I hope I can spend more time with the boys. I keep telling myself that I'm going to, but then something seems to come up. The days just aren't long enough. I feel I'm always going to have more time a little later, but I know that I won't have more time unless I make it. I've got to do that."

He remembers the days when his father farmed in the San Francisco Bay area. "I'd wait with my ball glove for him to play catch after he came in from the fields. He always played with me—no matter how tired he was. I guess I haven't done that, but then the boys don't ask me the way I asked Dad."

Some of the closest moments with his father came when they were in the fields together, working side by side, riding the tractor that tilled their vegetables. That was a big factor in his decision to become a farmer, but his children won't have that memory with him—because he's not out there on a tractor; he's in the Jeep from one vineyard to the next or he's in the office wrestling with the computer. Will his sons follow him on the farm?

"I don't know. One is a good bet. I'm not sure about the other two. But what bothers me is that they aren't able to do the things that I did with my father, not because they wouldn't want to, but because times have changed."

Jerry Fry has a flattop crew cut, right out of the 1940s, and he looks so much like Mickey Mantle, the baseball player, that it's spooky. He is muscular in the shoulders and legs, and it's difficult to believe that he was a 100-pound runt until his senior year in high school. He never got to play football, because of his size, but he did play some basketball, and he was good enough to make the varsity when he transferred to Davis. Peggy transferred with him, because they were like two peas in a pod, and in many ways they still are. She helps with the bookwork and does some compensation/labor reports, and she is active in 4-H work. She is, Fry says, a full-time partner in the business.

Both enjoy going back to the Bay area for cultural events, but they say nothing in the world equals living out in the country "where you can stretch and yell." Their social life consists mainly of dining with friends, water skiing in the delta created by the

Peggy Fry is a full-time partner in the business.

merging of the Sacramento and San Joaquin rivers, fifteen miles to the west, and snow skiing near the cabin they own in the Sierra Nevada, three hours away.

"Even if you took all of that away," Fry says, "living here is just plain nice. There are no urban pressures, no traffic jams. Some people live here in the valley and drive to the Bay area every day to work. I understand why."

Jerry and Peggy Fry started out in a frame house on the ranch that now is occupied by a foreman and his family. A few years ago they built their once-in-a-lifetime home, back from the highway and nestled behind an orchard of cherry trees. It's a low, flat house, 3,200 square feet, made of adobe bricks with a roof of cedar shakes. The living room is spectacular, eighteen by twenty-four feet with a fourteen-foot vaulted ceiling. They designed the house and, although it stretched them financially, they wanted to build it while their children were living with them. It is, Fry says, "the only house we'll ever build." He could double his money if he sold it, but he wouldn't be interested in four times the price. He says simply: "This always is going to be our home."

Fry's office is off the end of the front porch, and it connects to the kitchen through a laundry room where three cats crunch food from dishes atop the washing machine. It's said that you can tell the quality of a man by the office he keeps. If that's true, then you get your own feeling about Jerry Fry.

A sign on the office door reads: "Beware of cat." A poster on the wall shows a picture of George Washington with a Fry-type crew cut and the caption: "Keep America beautiful—get a haircut." A sign on his cluttered desk declares: "A clean desk is a sign of a sick mind." On another wall is a picture of Jerry and his father, who is now dead. There are framed resolutions from the California Senate and State Assembly honoring Fry for his "outstanding rendering of service on behalf of the Lodi community."

Jerry and his father had grown some grapes along with vegetables, but they'd never farmed grapes on a massive scale and they never intended to, until the state condemned much of their land to build a junior college. They looked for land around Lodi, liked what they saw and were intrigued by the prospect of becoming big-time grape growers.

"If you know how to farm, you can grow grapes," Fry says. "It's not that much different from anything else. What you don't know, you can ask people about."

Some of the land they bought contained established vineyards. They also put in some new ones. What is the life span of a vineyard? "They don't die of old age," Fry tells me. "There's always a reason if a vineyard dies. Most don't die. But at some point they become uneconomical to operate because of decreased production." In other words old vineyards, like old soldiers, tend to fade away. When that happens, the vines are dug up and new vines are started. This is called a "second-generation" vineyard—if it is on ground that held an earlier vineyard. Second-generation vineyards tend not to do as well as first-generation vineyards because of the diseases that linger in the soil. "Thirty years of stuff builds up and you're not able to clear it all up—no matter how hard you try."

With a vineyard planted on fresh land, some production can be anticipated by the third year, with a fair return by the fifth year. A second-generation vineyard takes longer.

Fry's 500 acres make him the largest grape grower around Lodi. Some around the state are bigger, but 500 acres is above the statewide average.

One of Fry's concerns is the increasing number of corporations that are buying thousands of acres of vineyards. An insurance company now owns 10,000 acres of wine grapes, he says, and an oil company also has made substantial purchases.

This has tended to push up the price of grape land across the state, he says, because the corporations, buying with tax purposes in mind, paid more than top dollar and more than could be justified by the income that can be produced by the land. Bare ground around Lodi now is selling for up to $4,000, Fry says, and by the time you start a vineyard you have invested from $8,000 to $10,000 an acre. It's difficult to justify that on the basis of return on investment, he says, but "maybe that's how farming will be done in the future, by corporations that are in it not for profit but for tax purposes. I don't know if this would be bad for consumers, but it wouldn't be good for the people who wanted to make a profit from their own farms."

For now, Jerry Fry doesn't seem too concerned about his profits. If you're serious about farming and if you do what you're supposed to do, he says, things work out in the long run. A good crop one year may not bring as much money as a light crop another year, depending on supply and demand, but that's what makes the business challenging and interesting.

The delicate art of pruning vines.

"The thing I like about farming," Fry says, "is that it's always changing; it's not a static situation. You go to the office and everything looks the same. Farming always is full of surprises. There are not drastic changes daily, but there never is a dull moment, at least for me."

Fry's table grapes are sold across the country, and it's likely that one of these days you'll see his boxes in your supermarket's produce department. The boxes bear the label "Young-Fry, Inc.," which is a corporation he and four other growers founded as a means of "cutting a few costs, like making our own boxes and loading our own grapes." Fry is president of the corporation, and his insistence that the grapes be better than good is rooted in his belief that "you have to be concerned with what goes out under your name."

The grapes are trucked to the Northern California Fruit Growers warehouse in Victor, where they can be held in cold storage from harvest until December. But the grapes usually are cleaned out by orders that pour in from food wholesalers before the middle of November. "We don't hang onto grapes and hope that the price will go up. When you do that, the price generally goes down. No, we sell at the prevailing price."

At the warehouse Fry has 18,000 boxes of grapes waiting to be loaded into the giant trucks that pull up to the loading docks almost hourly. The warehouse manager, Rich Mettler, greets Fry and hands him a clipboard that contains invoices showing who bought how many of his grapes: 780 boxes to A&P in Baltimore; 240 boxes to Kroger in Woodlawn, Ohio; 240 boxes to A&P in Indianapolis; 1,440 boxes to Millgram in Kansas City. And on and on it goes. There are 1,266 boxes to Miami, 1,500 to Pittsburgh.

In many cases, Mettler says, the trucks drive the grapes right to the stores. "They can be picked Tuesday, leave here Wednesday, and be to New York by Sunday night." Each truck has two drivers and travels twenty-four hours a day until reaching its destination. The over-the-road truckers are not unlike people who do other things to earn a living, Mettler says. "Some of them are hippies with their shirttails out, but most of them are clean-cut guys who are concerned about their families."

The cost of shipping a load of grapes to the East Coast is $5,000, and this, Mettler says, is what runs up the price to the consumer. In a supermarket Fry's grapes sell anywhere from forty-nine cents a pound, "if they're an advertised loss leader," to ninety cents a pound. For a twenty-three-pound box that retails for $18.40—at eighty cents a pound—Fry receives $3, the warehouse $7 for holding it until shipment.

While this sounds like big business to me, it really is peanuts when you consider that table grapes represent 15 percent or less of Fry's total crop. Most of the grapes go to the wineries, and Fry recently has signed what he calls a long-term contract with Almadén Vineyards. How long is long-term? "Most long-term contracts are for five years. Ours is for thirty years." That must be a secure feeling, I say. Fry answers with a smile. He's sold to a number of other wine makers in California, but he likes the way Almadén does business. Does he serve Almadén wine at his house? "Yes, I support the people who buy my grapes."

We drive back from the warehouse through Fry's vineyards, which are built on the sandy loam for which this area is known. On the right is a second-generation vineyard, and I'm told it's not doing as well as the first-generation vineyard on the other side of the road. Fry describes the difference as "greater vigor" in the first generation.

Don't birds give heartburn to a grape grower? What protection does he have against birds that could swoop down and gobble up an entire vineyard?

Farmers around Lodi have been lucky, Fry says. The vineyards that birds tend to hit hardest are those near feedlots, and there are no feedlots around here. "But I know some farms that have been picked clean. They come in flocks and there's nothing left."

There are three defenses that farmers have used. One is a battery of propane-fueled guns, which are set to go off every five minutes. The explosions sound like shotgun blasts and tend to be reasonably effective in scaring away birds. A second defense is a machine that emits a tone that, when amplified, is interpreted as a danger signal by birds. Fry says he never heard a bird "make a noise like that, but it seems to work." A third defense is netting that covers the entire vineyard and makes penetration by birds unlikely.

But birds are not the grape grower's primary concern. Right now the raging question is whether farmers will be permitted to use a chemical that they say they must have if they are to remain in business.

The chemical is a pesticide called DBCP that acts against soil parasites that live on the roots of the vine. DBCP has been used since the 1950s to control the parasite, but now it has been banned in California because sterility has been reported among some of those who handle it.

The employee who has handled DBCP at Fry's ranch "has four kids, and so obviously it has been no problem for him," Fry says. "If we don't get the chemical back, we're in real trouble. If there's nothing to replace it—and I don't hear of anything—we'll have to pull our vineyards." That would mean the death of the Tokay grape, since 97 percent of the world's Tokays are grown around Lodi, about 18,000 acres. "This *is* the Tokay industry," he says.

Do grape growers drink their share of wine? Yes, they do, Fry says. California is the nation's biggest state for wine consumption, averaging 3½ gallons per person each year. That sounds high, but consider Italy, where the annual consumption is 30 gallons a person. Californians also drink their quota of brandy, especially around here, where brandy, which is distilled from grape juice, is known as "Lodi Scotch."

As a confirmed bourbon whiskey drinker, I've known brandy only as an after-dinner drink; but in Lodi they mix brandy with club soda, with Seven-Up, even with water, and they use it as their liquor in manhattans, old-fashioneds and sours. I tried it, just to be sociable, and in most drinks it's about as good as bourbon and in some, especially an old-fashioned, I believe it's better than bourbon.

To show how inventive the wine-making business can be, one of Lodi's six wineries is test marketing vodka made from grapes instead of the traditional grain. This winery, like the others, had grapes and alcohol-distilling equipment going to waste after the demand for dessert wines dropped in recent years. Dessert wines are about 19 percent alcohol, compared to 11 or 12 percent for most other wines. It's impossible to achieve 19 percent alcohol through fermentation because yeast dies at about 14 percent, and fermentation stops. So dessert wines must be fortified by adding alcohol, which often is distilled at the winery. Without a heavy demand for dessert wines, the distilling equipment went silent, and there was a surplus of grapes that had been contracted for to be distilled into alcohol. What would the wineries do?

For the one winery, vodka, an increasingly popular drink that is nothing but alcohol diluted with water, indeed may be the answer.

Bearing a silver and blue label, the new product—Silverado, it's called—has appeared in some markets and it seems to be doing well, especially in Japan, Fry says.

Both the vodka and brandy seem a source of pride around Lodi. I went into a liquor store and asked what local brandy they recommended, and a young man handed me the bottle of his choice and said, "I know it's good because my daddy works there." Then he also tried to hustle me into buying a bottle of vodka and, soft heart that I am, I permitted him to succeed.

Does the enormous appeal of foreign wines bother Fry? Are they better than California wines? Such questions cause Fry to bristle and to rage against the restaurants, even in California, that place imported wines at the front of the wine list and California wines on the back page. Fry avoids restaurants that don't promote California wines, and he says that almost all restaurants overprice their wines and discourage consumption. "The restaurant markup on wine is from 100 to 400 percent. Why not cut the price and sell more? To charge $14 for $3 wine is ridiculous."

The problem with foreign wines, aside from their outrageous snob appeal, is that they don't have to meet the same standards as American wines, Fry says. Foreign grape growers can use chemicals that are banned for American growers. And they aren't bound by the same rules on varietal wines. American varietal wines must be made predominantly from the varietal grapes whose names they bear. When you buy a California-made Cabernet Sauvignon, you can be certain that more than half of the grapes that went into it were Cabernet Sauvignon grapes. This is not necessarily true of imported varietal wines, yet the government permits these wines to carry varietal names, and, Fry says, it amounts to playing with a stacked deck.

Today is Thursday, Fry reminds himself, and that means it's Rotary Club luncheon day. Would I like to go with him? Here I am in soiled jeans and a faded orange golf shirt. Does anybody go to a Rotary meeting dressed like this? I'll fit right in, Fry assures me. Many of the people come right out of the vineyards and, without changing clothes, they sit elbow to elbow with those who, in their suits, come straight from their offices. Nobody will think anything about my being there dressed like a tramp.

Fry changes from jeans into blue corduroy slacks, and we're

off, bouncing along the dusty road to West Lane, a four-lane divided highway in front of his cherry trees. In five minutes we're at a combined bowling alley-restaurant, where the Lodi Rotary Club meeting is about to begin. Fry picks up his name badge, which, like all the others, is startlingly different from any I have seen. Most Rotary badges, you remember, have the Rotary symbol, a wheel, in the center. In Lodi the center of the badge is a cluster of grapes, a reminder that this is deep in the heart of wine country.

Before we can sit down, a man in a straw hat nudges Fry and says, "Hey, Jerry, my daughter bought some of your grapes last week in New York and paid ninety cents a pound. She said your name was right on the box. At ninety cents a pound, you must be getting rich. You wanna pay for my lunch today?"

Fry shakes his head and laughs, but doesn't respond. We sit at one of five twenty-foot-long tables that have been positioned so they point at the speaker's table. Many of the 120 people, just as Fry promised, look as if they came straight from their fields. They wear jeans, boots and work shirts, and some have pale foreheads above their suntanned noses and cheeks, identifying them as hat wearers.

A physician they call Doc is the piano player, and the man next to me whispers that Doc is just learning to play the piano. "He's making great improvement," the man says. "When he plays 'The Star-Spangled Banner,' you almost can recognize it now." We stand, Doc plays and we sing. But it's hard to sing as fast as he plays, like a 33-rpm record on a 45-rpm turntable. There is applause at the end and, from the back of the room, a voice cheers: "Way to go, Doc!" This is not your everyday Rotary meeting.

Steven Furry, the man across the table, shows me a page from the local newspaper, the *Lodi News-Sentinel*. On the page is a picture of him and Fry, both of whom have been elected to the Board of Directors of the California Association of Wine Grape Growers. He offers the page to Fry, saying: "I have plenty more at home."

The speaker is traditional Rotary Club fare, a brown-suited, somber-faced representative of the California Chamber of Commerce, whose topic is, "Is There Still a Place for Business in California?"

It's strange, I think, being in California, which so many of us regard as a place to go to escape our problems, and hearing about California's problems. The primary worry, the speaker says, is that government is overregulating big business right out of the state and threatening to "overturn our advantages of climate, water and timber resources and ports from which to export." What kinds of overregulation is he talking about? He gives some examples:

There was the miner who was a one-man operation, but he was forced to have a two-way radio to comply with federal laws. The absurdity was that he had nobody to talk to on his radio.

There was the meat processing plant that was forced by one agency to have a hole cut in a wall to allow samples to be taken. The absurdity was that another agency said it would close down the plant if it didn't seal the hole.

Then there was the cattle rancher, back in World War II, who wanted government permission to slaughter 300 steers. The agency would allow only 150 to be killed, saying that the other 150 should be retained for breeding purposes.

That story breaks up the audience, and the meeting ends shortly after that. Then Fry and I are back in the Jeep, driving through vineyards, and he's talking about the efforts to organize farm labor in California.

"There's no question that we've had severe labor problems. But the newspaper stories have made the problems worse. Our people around here read that the lettuce pickers over there are getting $5 an hour, and they say they won't pick unless we raise their pay. That's reported in the newspapers, but our side is never told. That's why I'm wary of the media. I've not had bad experiences personally, but I think the media should try to be fair. Look at the efforts of [Cesar] Chavez. He's had a lot of publicity. But the growers have to ask to get their side covered. It's not fair."

Some grape growers to the south of Lodi have signed contracts with labor unions, Fry says, often because they have been intimidated by organizers who sent men into the fields with chain saws to cut down grapevines and cherry trees. Some non-union laborers were frightened away, he says, because organizers wrote down their license plate numbers and told them: "We'd better never see these cars around here again."

In some cases law enforcement officers stood at a distance and watched, without interfering. The problems around Lodi have not been so severe, and Fry is hopeful peace will continue. "After all, the people who work for me are happy with their conditions. They don't want a union, and I don't want a union." One of Fry's concerns is that unionization around here might bring the same situation that occurred in the south. After the unions came in, they were unable to produce enough workers at harvesttime, and grapes decayed on the vines.

We're driving toward Micke Grove Park now, down a road lined with almond trees (around here people call them "ammen" trees). Owned and operated by San Joaquin County, the park features a drive-through vineyard, a "sunshine trail" with Braille signs that identify the flowers and trees, and a historical museum to which local people have donated ancient wagons, harvesters, hand tools, even a 1930 air-cooled Franklin automobile. There's also a forty-eight-inch section of a 930-year-old redwood that toppled during a 1970 storm in Santa Cruz County, along the coast.

It is a fascinating park, worthy of a metropolitan area. What makes it so successful, Fry says, is that Lodi people not only contribute gifts and money but also their time, as volunteer guides in the museum or as workers in building the sunshine trail and other projects. "This is what is nice about a small community," Fry says, his voice rising with pride. "You can see the result of what you do. In the big cities, maybe people think, 'What good is it to do anything? We never see the results anyway.' But that's not true here. In a small community, you do see the results."

It's Saturday night almost before I know it. Time really flies when I'm on the road, especially since Marilyn has joined me. It's her first trip to California, and she is excited to see the wine country that I've been talking about. We drive back to Lodi, where the night before Jerry Fry dug the grave-size hole in his front yard and started a fire, getting up every two hours until dawn to fuel it with more logs. At sunrise he wrapped the beef and put it on top of the coals. Then he placed a sheet of tin on top of the meat and filled the hole with dirt.

Before the meat comes out this evening, guests will take turns shoveling away the dirt. The tin will be too hot to handle with bare hands. With gloves they will pull it away and the meat will come out from the smoking ashes.

But it's not yet time for that ritual. Right now we're inside the house, changing our clothes. We climb up the ladder beside the vat, Marilyn and I and six others, as the band blares out with "The Stripper."

Our feet are in the mushy grapes, and we're laughing.

7 ❧ A farmer calls, a doctor answers

This is a warm, sunshine-filled day, a driver's joy, and I remove the sunroof before I ease through the tollgate to enter the Pennsylvania Turnpike.

Two hours and $1.90 later, I exit near Harrisburg, the state capital, and swing west across the Susquehanna River and past byways to Linglestown, Fisherman's Creek and Duncannon. The placid-looking Juniata River is off to the left, well below the highway, which in some places is as broad and straight as an expressway, in others as narrow and tortuous as it was fifty years ago. To my right, a thirty-foot-high screen protects the highway against the rocks that sometimes rumble down from a red-faced mountain, sheared off to make way for the road.

A green exit sign tells me I'm almost there now, State Highway 17. I pass a dozen cars parked beside a cemetery; they belong to car-pooling commuters who work in Harrisburg, thirty-three miles away. I pop over the crest of a hill and I've arrived: The Borough of Millerstown, population 700, tucked away on the northern edge of Perry County, a county in which there is not a single traffic light.

What residents call "The Square" is the town's hub, a diamond-shaped patch of grass in the middle of Highway 17, sur-

---

Dr. James E. Witt, who says a rural physician must pattern himself after the old-time country doctor.

rounded by Bill's Gulf service station, a self-service laundry, the Moose Lodge and the volunteer fire department building. I pull into the Gulf station and before I can shut off my engine, a man appears, rag in hand, and begins wiping my windshield. The name stitched in orange on his blue shirt tells me that this is Bill—yes, Bill, the boss. He stands on tiptoe, leans over the top of my car and peers down at me through the sunroof. "Hey," he laughs, "do you know that you got a hole in your roof?"

This is my introduction to Bill Rouse, who is, as everybody will tell me later, the key man in Millerstown—fire chief, head of the borough council and president of the Greenwood Medical Association, which he helped form in 1975 to attract a physician to Millerstown after the lone doctor retired because of ill health.

This is why I've come to Millerstown. I want to visit the Greenwood Medical Center, the dream that came true for Bill Rouse and other residents who contributed $30,000 in seed money to secure a federal Rural Health Incentive Grant that totaled $130,000 for three years.

They say Bill Rouse personally raised almost all of the seed money, and they say he did it in a direct, blunt way. As Nancy Bratton, a dairy farmer's wife, would tell me later in the day: "He knocked on your door and told you how much he wanted you to donate—and that's what it was, a donation, because nobody ever expected to get the money back. He did the same thing when the town decided to build a municipal swimming pool. He knocked on doors and told people how many shares of stock in the pool they should buy. The guy's incredible."

Bill Rouse wastes no time proving to me just how incredible he is. As soon as I tell him that I'm from Philadelphia, he knows who I am and why I've come to Millerstown. He even knows what they're going to serve me for dinner at the house that the association rents for the doctors who staff the medical center. "I sure hope you like chicken," he says. "You won't find better chicken anywhere."

I ask Bill Rouse why he's so involved in Millerstown affairs, why he spends so much of his time on activities that provide no financial payback. He gives me the best answer I've ever heard: "Because I live here. I've always lived here, and I love this town. I just love it."

I tell Bill Rouse I'll talk with him again tomorrow. Then I drive off toward the Greenwood Medical Center, which is half a mile north of Bill's station, up a hill and past the First Presbyterian Church, just beyond the high school. It is housed in a flat, green building that is also home to two insurance offices, a dentist's office and a pharmacy.

The center is directed by Dr. James E. Witt. He is associate professor of general practice at Philadelphia College of Osteopathic Medicine, which pays his salary and which provides, on a rotating basis, five third- and fourth-year students who work without pay for up to two months. The arrangement is part of the school's "extern" training in rural medicine. These are the physicians—Witt addresses each as "doctor"—who provide the bulk of medical care for the 1,100 persons who each month have come to the center since it opened in the fall of 1976. It is one of seven centers in Pennsylvania affiliated with the osteopathic college.

Witt, forty, practiced rural medicine privately for six years before becoming a medical center director, first at LaPorte in north-central Pennsylvania for three years, at Millerstown since 1976. He introduces me to the student-doctors he is supervising, all of whom are from Pennsylvania: third-year students Mike Lurakis of Philadelphia, Bill Longenecker of Lancaster, Vic Farrah of Meadville; fourth-year students Bonnie Hubicz of Sharon, Rick Hale of Frackville.

All are neatly dressed—the men wear neckties—but nobody, including Witt, has on the physician's traditional white coat. Farrah, who has been with Witt for five weeks and is the veteran of this group, explains why:

"We want to be casual, not intimidating. You see pediatricians in white coats, and I really think that's why little kids become afraid of doctors. I wore a white coat my first two years in school, just like I wore a stethoscope around my neck, and for the same reason: It was a cover for me. But not now. It's just not appropriate here."

Witt, who grew up in rural Bedford County in central Pennsylvania—he still calls himself a "a poor farm boy"—at age sixteen operated a thirty-acre farm for a florist and one summer presided over 100,000 gladiolus. Today he owns a 600-acre farm in Burnt Cabins, forty miles away from the medical center, where he grows grain, has 100 sheep and sixty cows, sixteen of which are being milked. He spends a few nights each week at the farm, supervising his two hired hands. The other nights he stays in an apart-

Bill Rouse, who made the dream of a medical center come true.

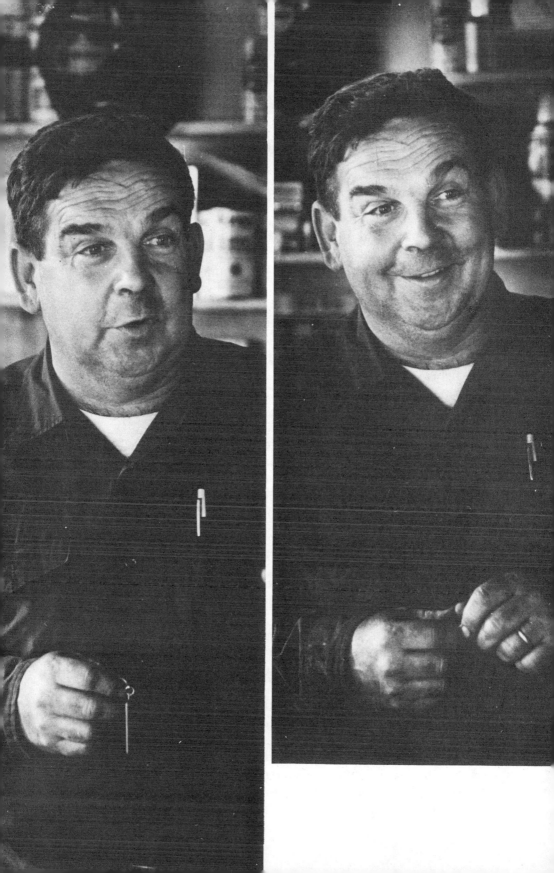

ment in Millerstown, two blocks up the street from the eleven-room house where the student-doctors sleep, eat, study and discuss their cases. Mrs. Witt, Judy, travels with him, does the driving—much of it in their mud-spattered pickup—and Witt refers to her as "my chauffeur."

Witt and Judy met when both were students at Indiana University of Pennsylvania, where he was working on his master's degree in education and she was studying for her bachelor's degree in home economics. He always wanted to be a physician, he says, but he considered the dream impossible until after they married, when Judy began to encourage him and tell him that the dream was possible. "Her father was a school principal in Pittsburgh and he had a lot of friends who were doctors and they encouraged me, too, and helped me apply to medical schools," Witt says.

When he was a student at Philadelphia College of Osteopathic Medicine, Judy Witt worked first as a dietician and later taught home economics at West Philadelphia High School. After he went into private practice—in an area where the nearest pharmacy was thirty miles away—Judy Witt helped him in the office and, in Witt's words, "always was pretty much with me."

Witt's sandy-colored hair hangs down over his shirt collar and into his eyes. As he talks, he leans back in his chair, puts his scuffed, unpolished ankle-high boots on a corner of his desk, folds his hands behind his head. Seated, he appears taller than he actually is—five feet, seven inches, in his boots. His upper body is muscled and he looks a little like a one-time weight lifter, a bit thick at the waist although not overweight at 150 pounds.

He is wearing checked trousers that are short enough to reveal his brown socks when he walks. His flowered knit shirt, snug around his waist, argues with his patterned necktie, the knot of which is left of center of his collar. His speech—"There isn't no better place in the whole world to live than right around here."—is the speech of the patients who sit in the clinic and wait for the treatment, the prescription or the reassuring words that will make them or the children they clutch feel better.

A lot of physicians don't want to practice in a place the size of Millerstown, Witt says, often because they are nagged by city-bred wives who feel isolated from the theater, concerts and country club dances. But the students assigned to him, he feels, are "the cream of the crop, the best people you ever could hope to find." In turn, the student-doctors appear to regard Witt with a kind of awe that approaches worship. "I can't imagine anybody who's more understanding, patient or a better teacher," says Bill Longenecker. "I've made some mistakes, the mistakes you make when you're young, but he's never jumped all over me. He's just told me what I did wrong. You know, Dr. Witt has done well. He's made a lot of money—from his medical practice and off his farm. But you'd never know it—not from the pickup truck he drives or the way he handles himself. He's just not impressed with himself."

I ask Witt what's it's like to be a rural doctor. He shakes his head and says it takes a "different" kind of person to make it, different from most of those turned out by the medical schools.

"The successful rural doctor is patterned after the old-time country doctor. If a kid falls and breaks an arm, the doctor sets the arm. If a woman is having a baby, the doctor delivers it. People [in rural areas] expect this. But the urban doctor is trained not to set the kid's broken arm but to refer him to an orthopedic surgeon. If a woman is pregnant, he's trained to call in an obstetrician. This may be fine in the city, but what if the nearest specialist is seventy-five miles away?

"A rural doctor must be able to handle all emergencies and all the minor things without a specialist—if he wants to succeed. Some don't succeed and it's because medical schools today don't teach them what to do. They teach them what not to do to avoid malpractice lawsuits.

And that, Witt says, is where the rub comes. "A farmer today walks in and expects you to set his broken wrist so he can go back to work. If you tell him to go seventy-five miles to see an orthopedic surgeon, you're inviting him to get mad at you. He won't ever be back to see you—and neither will anybody else you treat that way."

The Greenwood Medical Center's nurse, Mrs. Thelma Patton, interrupts Witt to show him a patient's chart. He scans it, scribbles his name, invites me to talk with some of the patients who sit in the waiting room beneath a handwritten sign that says: "With the number of emergencies we are having daily, we find we are often behind our appointments. If it is impossible for you to wait, please notify the desk so we can try to see you sooner."

What kinds of emergencies? It's incredible, Witt says, how many farmers—and farmers' children—get their hands and feet caught in machinery and come to the center to be stitched up and given shots to guard against infection. "It's more dangerous work than people think," Witt says.

I talk with some of the patients in the waiting room and they tell me that the center has been "about the best thing" that ever happened to Millerstown. It offers them around-the-clock medical coverage for a fraction of what they might pay elsewhere: $8 for an office visit, $4 for each subsequent visit for the same illness.

When the telephone rings at the center, another telephone also rings at the house where the student-doctors live, and one of them is always available—regardless of the hour—to handle any emergency case. They even make house calls, if patients are too ill to come to the center.

Some of the patients like the student-doctors, Witt and their brand of medicine so much that they drive to the center through towns that have "regular" doctors—Newport, eleven miles south, and Liverpool, eleven miles east.

What is the brand of medicine they practice at the center? Here's how Witt describes it and it represents what he calls a major departure from medicine as taught today in almost all medical schools:

"A farmer today is a businessman. He has to milk the cows twice a day, seven days a week, whether he feels like it or not. If he gets a cold, he goes to the doctor to get medication and prevent complications. You can't tell him to take two aspirin, drink juice and go to bed for two or three days. He can't go to bed. He's got to be out in the bitter cold, rain or whatever caring for his cattle. There's nobody else to do it. You tell him to go to bed and he looks for another doctor—or else he goes to the barn and injects himself with some antibiotic he's bought for his cattle. And that really can cause trouble, if he's allergic to it."

What this all means, Witt tells me, is that country doctors must treat with antibiotics more freely than city doctors who put their patients to bed. "Medical schools don't seem to understand this difference, and neither do a lot of young doctors fresh out of medical school."

Witt says he often sees the results of this lack of understanding "of the facts of rural medicine" when "one of those city doctors" from the osteopathic college fills in for him on alternate weekends, when he's off duty, or when he's away on vacation. "I'll come back and there'll be ten or fifteen people in the waiting room, people who aren't better but who would have been better if they'd been put on antibiotics. They come back and their fever is higher than it was before the city doctor saw them, and they don't understand why."

While Witt is quick to treat with antibiotics, he is slow to subject patients to tests that he does not consider essential—tests with the primary purpose of guarding against the possibility of a malpractice lawsuit. This is another difference between him and city doctors, he says.

Is there a chance that frequent use of antibiotics for less-than-severe illnesses can build up a patient's immunity to antibiotics so that they are of limited benefit in an emergency?

That's a good question, Witt says, but it's based on a worry "about remote things. The danger of pneumonia or upper respiratory infection is infinitely greater than the danger of building up an immunity."

What about malpractice lawsuits? Is their potential of no concern to rural doctors? There never has been a malpractice suit in all his years of practicing rural medicine, Witt says. "People here don't treat a physician like God, but they still look up to him."

And, Witt tells me, they also appreciate the economics of coming to Greenwood Medical Center. "A woman was in here the other day. She'd gone to the city with her four kids, who had bad colds. Well, the doctor there ran all those tests and charged her $92. But the kids didn't get any better. She comes here and her bill is $16. After the first two kids in a family we don't charge extra. You could have twenty kids and the bill still would be $16."

The center's cost per patient—Witt calculates that by dividing the number of patients into the cost of operating the center—is $12, less than half the national average of $26 for such centers. How is this possible? Witt smiles and says it's because "my doctors" don't get paid. "I'm probably the only guy in the world who has working for him five doctors who are paying $5,000 a year [tuition] for the privilege."

Now it's getting on toward five o'clock on this Wednesday, when the center continues office hours until nine for the convenience of farm families that can't come during the day. The center shuts down between five and six so Witt and the student-doctors can eat dinner back at the house.

Witt walks out to my car with me and starts laughing as I unlock the door. "Boy, folks can tell you haven't been here long. Nobody locks anything around here. It ain't necessary." He shows me the other cars in the parking lot and he's right—not a single one of them is locked. "The students who come up from Philadelphia lock their cars the first few days, but then they realize there's no reason to. We don't lock our houses around here either."

We start to drive away from the graveled parking lot, but Witt asks me to stop as he recognizes a small, stooped man who is being assisted by another man into the center. "That looks like Caney," he says. And, indeed, it is the man everybody in Millerstown knows as Caney, who, accompanied by a friend, is alternately perspiring and chilling and complaining of chest pains.

Caney is "like the town mascot," says Thelma Patton. He's about seventy-five, semi-retarded, without any family, loved, the target of good-humored barbs at the Moose Lodge, to which he rides his lawn mower-size tractor to drink beer.

"If we needed somebody to drive him to the hospital in Harrisburg," says Mrs. Patton, "everybody in town would volunteer. He's more popular than the mayor."

Caney is wearing a baseball-type cap, plaid shirt, jeans, hightop work shoes. His speech is slurred and difficult to understand, as it has been ever since anybody can remember. Caney tells Witt where it hurts—"right here"—and he points at his breastbone.

Is it a heart attack? No, Witt says, he doesn't think so. "I'm 75 percent sure it's indigestion. But with his symptoms we'll check him thoroughly. I'll have a doctor look at him and run an EKG."

Witt telephones the house and asks that a student-doctor leave the dinner table and return to the center. In three minutes not one but two student-doctors, Mike Lurakis and Bill Longenecker, screech into the parking lot in the Jeep provided by the Greenwood Medical Association. Caney disappears into an examining room with them, and Witt and I leave for dinner. "They'll call me if they need me, if it's a real emergency."

At the house, a mile from the center, Witt and I sit down to baked chicken, mashed potatoes, gravy, carrots, green beans, tossed salad, biscuits and a gelatin dessert. Dinner has been prepared by Sharon Beaver, the housekeeper-cook who owns this house and who rents it to the association. The chicken, just as Bill Rouse said, is about the best I ever ate.

Witt barely has finished his first piece when the telephone rings. "I hope that doesn't mean I was wrong, that the 25 percent has

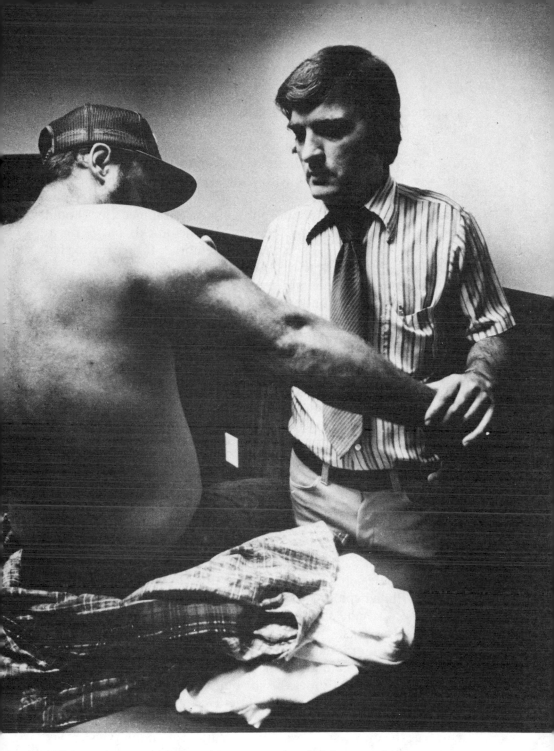

When a farmer gets a cold, you can't tell him to take two aspirin and go to bed. The livestock won't wait till he's feeling better.

happened." But the tone of his telephone conversation quickly reveals that he is not alarmed.

What has happened is something that would not happen in a hospital: They have sent home a patient they think has indigestion—without establishing with clinical certainty that his heart is not the problem. But this is not a hospital, and what is happening is consistent with Witt's philosophy of how rural medicine should be practiced—a philosophy, he says, that he quickly passes on to his student-doctors as gospel they must embrace if they are to succeed in rural medical practice.

Distilled to basics, the philosophy is this: You don't hospitalize people when there's only a slim chance that they might have a serious problem. You treat them for what you think the problem is and you save them money and a fifty-mile hospital trip that is probably unnecessary.

In Caney's case the student-doctors, Lurakis and Longenecker, have found nothing on the EKG to indicate heart disturbance. Their diagnosis is acute indigestion, probably brought on by Caney's consumption of large amounts of beer during the day. They give him some stomach medicine, return him to the friend to take back home. He is to come back at nine o'clock even if everything is all right, sooner if the pain doesn't diminish.

Most of the farm people who come to the center, Lurakis says, pay the bills themselves. They aren't covered by insurance and "they can't afford the $200 work-up a doctor in the city would do to cover his butt" against a possible malpractice lawsuit.

I like Lurakis's candor and the confidence he seems to have in his ability to size up the situation correctly. He is twenty-five, married to a Philadelphia schoolteacher, dark-haired, quick to smile. Sometimes after he says something and watches me write in my notebook, he asks: "Gee, you're not going to print that, are you?" He is a graduate of the Ivy League University of Pennsylvania, looks even in this clinic setting more like a student than a doctor in his pigskin shoes, bright blue corduroy jeans, pale blue shirt and blue-and-red striped necktie. He applied to every medical school in the state, and Philadelphia College of Osteopathic Medicine was the only school even to invite him for an interview. "My grades weren't that good. You look at people who are applying at schools today and they're 4.0, 3.9. I wasn't that good—although I really brought up my grades in the last two years. I think I'm lucky to be here."

Lurakis says he hopes one day to practice medicine in Maryland's Chesapeake Bay area, where he once lived and which, he says, is "country but not as country" as Millerstown.

By seven o'clock all of the student-doctors—and Witt—are busy, funneling patients from the waiting room into examining rooms for consultations that range from a few minutes to half an hour. On each case Witt confers with the student-doctors, reviews prescriptions they submit to him for approval and signature, sometimes seeks out patients for additional information.

The kinds of problems the patients bring to the center are not unlike those doctors find in the city, Witt tells me. But there are a few differences. "We get snakebites and wild animal bites sometimes, some poison ivy, too—you don't see these things in urban medical centers—and the farm machinery accidents. I'd say our people here have fewer colds and upper respiratory infections than the general public. People constantly exposed to the elements seem to build up a kind of resistance. But when they do get a cold, it's usually a good one."

A "good" one? Witt shakes his head. "A bad one, I mean."

Witt says it's rare that he finds a farmer with an ulcer or any stress-related illness. Alchoholism is virtually nonexistent within farm families, he says, because "you can't be an alcoholic and survive as a farmer." He sees some patients with hypertension, but "those who are actively engaged in farming, who keep down their weight and who are in pretty good health, those people don't have much hypertension."

The telephone at the desk rings almost constantly. The appointment secretary answers each call politely: "Yes, I believe a doctor can see you now. Why don't you come on in? How long will it take you to get here?" Sometimes Witt, himself, answers the telephone—as if to emphasize a point:

"In solo practice, the crazy telephone kills you. My last year in solo practice I don't think there was a single evening meal at home that wasn't interrupted by at least one telephone call. That's one of the reasons I quit and went into clinics. You can't continue like that forever—but it's hard to turn down people, when you're the only doctor in town. I couldn't do it, turn them down. And a lot of other docs can't either. That's why so many country docs have high blood pressure and heart attacks—those in solo practice, I mean. Clinics, like this one, are the answer, the wave of the fu-

Farmer-doctor Witt and wife, Judy, visit with a neighbor on the

gingerbread porch of the Witt farm home in Burnt Cabins, Pa.

ture. I think one day it will be rare to find a doc in solo practice.''

One reason it's hard to turn down patients, Witt says, is that rural people tend to be ''less tolerant'' than city people about a physician's need to have time for himself. ''I'd finish at the office about 1:00 A.M. and come home and somebody would call at 2:00 and ask me to see them. And I usually did—because if you tell them to go to a hospital emergency room, they won't talk to you for two months. Their attitude is that if you're needed, then you should go—regardless of what time it is or how tired you are.''

Lots of rural people, Witt says, also aren't reluctant to approach a doctor in a nonmedical setting and ask for medical advice or a prescription refill. This happened so often during his last year in private practice, Witt says, that ''I got to where I wouldn't go shopping anymore with my wife. I'd wait for her outside, in the car, because I didn't want people to ask me to get their prescriptions refilled. You know, you hear a lot these days about how unfeeling and cold some doctors are. I can't help thinking that maybe a lot of that is a defense mechanism—a way to put some distance between themselves and patients who otherwise might be after them all the time.''

The parade of patients continues—a social worker with an ailing back, fifteen-month-old twins with diaper rash, a five-year-old with a ''croupy-sounding'' cough, a young woman in skintight jeans whose neck aches and who says she's generally tense all over. Tonight, Witt says, it's mostly family night, no farmers, mostly children and adults who live around Millerstown but work in Harrisburg or Lewistown, twenty-eight miles to the west. Lewistown is where most of Millerstown goes shopping, Thelma Patton says. ''You can park in back of the stores and walk to your car after dark and know you'll be safe. It's not like that in Harrisburg anymore. It's getting more and more like Philadelphia. I don't know how you people can live in Philadelphia.''

With permission of the patients I enter some of the examining rooms and watch and listen as the student-doctors work. I am amazed by the time they take with each patient to explain the problem and the proposed medication or treatment.

They talk in the language of those they serve and they keep it simple, free of medical jargon. Lurakis tells a man who is suffering from hypertension: ''We're going to give you something that will make you pee up a storm. This will help lower your blood pressure, just like we'd lower the oil pressure on a tractor if we took out some of the oil. If we can get some of the fluids out of your body, we probably can bring down the blood pressure." When Lurakis gives the man a prescription for a diuretic, there is no question about the man's knowing the reason why.

Rick Hale looks at the infant twins, Randy and Rodney, who, because their parents are working the night shift, are accompanied by their grandmother and their baby-sitter, a teen-ager in jeans, sweat shirt and high-heel shoes. Hale takes one of the twins in his hands and interrupts his bottle feeding. "OK, Champ, time to take a break," he says. Grandmother beams.

The baby-sitter tells Hale that the rash on the babies' bottoms has been there for three or four days. She's tried to treat it herself, she says, by putting the babies in a tub of warm water and coating their bottoms with Vaseline.

Hale shakes his head. No, that's not right. "You've got to keep them dry. Use powder, but don't put anything wet on them. They're very sore. I'll bet they cry when they get wet, don't they?" Yes, the baby-sitter says, looking at the floor, they do cry when she puts them in warm water, and she never understood why.

The grandmother calls Hale's attention to a rash on the heads of the twins. It's prickly heat rash, Hale says, common among crib-age babies. "Cut the heat back three or four degrees in the bedroom and cover them with blankets. That'll get rid of it. It's not serious. It'll go away."

At 8:52 Caney returns, in his friend's tow, and reports that "it don't hurt so much no more. I feel better. That medicine is good."

Witt smiles. So do Lurakis and Longenecker. What would have happened, I ask Witt, if Caney had gone home and died of a heart attack?

"People know we do what we think is best. You could have a myocardial infarction and still have a normal EKG. Sometimes an EKG change may not show up for six to twelve hours. We do all we can, and we try to save people a fifty-mile trip to the hospital if it's not necessary."

Fortunately, says Witt, "it's rare that we miss" in a diagnosis.

Lurakis and Longenecker again examine Caney, talk with him almost the way sons would talk to their father:

"Gee, you've changed your shirt; you must be feeling better. Don't eat anything until tomorrow and be sure and take your medicine. How much medicine are you going to take tonight? That's right—two small pills and then one spoonful when you get home. Take a spoonful every four hours and you'll feel a lot better. Tomorrow eat applesauce, bananas, things that are soft and bland and won't upset your stomach. And no more beer. That's what messed up your stomach.''

After Caney shuffles out the door to rejoin his friend, Lurakis turns to me and asks: ''You know what would happen to him if he lived in the city? People would abuse him, make fun of him. Thugs would rob him because he can't defend himself. But here, people take care of him. If he died, everybody in town would come to his funeral. That's the difference.''

It's that difference, Lurakis says, that has helped convince him that rural medicine is where he wants his future to be.

It is almost 10:30 when the last patient leaves the clinic. ''We never get finished by nine o'clock,'' Witt says.

During the evening I have stood for awhile beside the desk and watched the patients pay in cash for their visits—usually $4 or $8. Is that unusual? Does everybody always have the cash? Doesn't anybody ever ask to be sent a bill?

Well, Witt says, the welfare patients don't pay at all. The Greenwood Medical Center handles 20 percent welfare patients, he says, higher than average for rural clinics because ''some private doctors around here refer their welfare patients to us. They don't want to treat them.''

How many welfare patients would a big-city clinic customarily handle? In Philadelphia's inner city, Witt says, about 97 percent.

Do the other patients always pay their bills? Witt gives me the expression I last saw on his face when I was unlocking my car in the parking lot. ''That's one thing you learn about rural people: They pay their bills. I'd say about 75 percent pay on the spot. We bill the other 25 percent. Our collection rate for the last two years was 98.5 percent. We don't use a collection agency. We don't need a collection agency.''

What's the collection rate in a big-city clinic, in Philadelphia, for example? For the few paying patients, Witt says, it's about 20 percent.

''We're a community nonprofit association. If a patient runs up a bill that's too high, we'd offer only emergency service if he made no attempt to pay. But nobody so far ever has been restricted. I have talked only to two people about paying, and both paid promptly after that.''

We walk out to the parking lot and Witt—it's getting to be a habit—laughs again as I unlock my car. He suggests we pick up Mrs. Witt at their apartment and then visit some of their farm friends. At this time of night? Yes, he says, they're expecting us. With Judy Witt we drive through what they call Raccoon Valley, south of Millerstown, along a narrow road between the 1,700-foot-high Tuscarora Mountains to the west, a nameless ridge to the east that seems almost as high.

"It's beautiful country," Witt says. "You ought to drive through here in daylight. I bet you never saw nothing—anything—like it."

We stop at the dairy farm of Don and Nancy Bratton, three miles from town, where conversation is held over ice cream and Coca-Cola. Their home would be fashionable by suburban standards—with its curved driveway, closed-in back porch, basement garage and patio where they and their three school-age children sometimes enjoy a meal barbecued on their outdoor grill.

In front of the house is a sign that identifies Nancy Bratton as an agent for a company that specializes in insuring farms and farmers. "It's something I really enjoy doing," she says. "Did you know that dairy farmers have about the highest premiums of anybody? It's because of all the machinery they're around all day. It's dangerous. Don knows how dangerous."

Don Bratton is missing part of a finger on his left hand—the result of a farm accident a few years ago when "I wasn't as careful as I am now." He has seventy cows and 510 acres of land on which he grows the grain to feed them. His monthly checks from the cooperative to which he sells his milk average $10,000, which, he says, "sounds like more money than it is when you figure the cost of doing business."

He likes dairy farming—his father was a dairyman, too, and owned the farm on which the Brattons now live. The worries about herd disease, too much rain, not enough rain are diminished, he says, by being his own boss. "There's a difference between worrying when you work for somebody else and worrying when you're in business for yourself. I don't believe I could work for anybody else. I'm accustomed to giving orders—not taking orders."

Nancy Bratton giggles into her ice cream and says, yes, that's right, her husband is accustomed to giving orders—to her, their children and the two hired hands who help them with the farm. "I can't imagine that he'd ever get up every morning to go to work for somebody else.''

But Don Bratton gets up to work for himself—at five o'clock every morning. His voice carries a sound of pride when he says he hasn't missed milking his cows one time in the last seven years.

Witt stares at me across the table and I know what he's thinking: "You can't tell a sick farmer to go home and go to bed. You have to treat him so he'll be able to go home and milk the cows.''

The talk switches from dairy farming to the difficulty of attracting doctors permanently to rural areas. Nancy Bratton, who is a member of the board of the Greenwood Medical Association, says she thinks the medical center, with its revolving corps of student-doctors, is the answer.

It's a topic that ignites a spark in Judy Witt, who until now has been more of a listener than a talker. She is from suburban Pittsburgh—"a city girl"—but she's lived her entire married life in the country, except for the time Jim Witt was in medical school in Philadelphia. She is slender, about three inches shorter than Witt, customarily dresses in blue jeans, sweater and sneakers. She has, she says, almost nothing in common with most wives of doctors.

And then she offers her perception of why a doctor's wife might be unhappy in a rural area:

"There's not a lot of socializing, not much to do. She has to drive to Harrisburg or Hershey if she wants to eat out, and that frustrates her. She's got to be independent and she's got to change her whole living style and her attitudes.

"There is no fashion show at lunch to entertain her. She has to learn to entertain herself. Some doctors' wives think a lot of local women are beneath them, not sophisticated enough for them, backwoods mamas who don't know anything. But some of us [country women] are better educated than they are. We can go into their environment and blend in; nobody can pick us out of the crowd. But they come here and don't blend in. Now, who's better rounded?''

It's nearly midnight when we leave, just five hours before Don Bratton's regular getting-up time.

"I bet he'll hate us in the morning,'' I say.

"No, he won't,'' Witt answers. "He'll be glad we came.''

When I drop them off at their apartment, Witt and his wife ask me to stop in for coffee, but I decline—I'm so sleepy I barely can see to drive.

Back at the house where the students live, I walk through the blackness, up the steps and through the unlocked door and into the second-story bedroom I am sharing with Bill Longenecker. I sleep well and, as I reflect on it the next morning, I am somewhat amazed because it's the first time in my life—I'm sure of that—that I've slept behind unlocked doors, or, as in this house, behind doors that don't even have locks.

When I come down for breakfast at 7:15, housekeeper-cook Sharon Beaver, who starts working at 6:30, hands me a cup of brewed coffee. She has the best job in the world, she says, because she enjoys what she does and she likes the medical students who work at the center. She and her husband, who commutes daily to Harrisburg for construction work, live not in Millerstown but in the crossroads community of Seven Stars, ten miles away. Millerstown, says Mrs. Beaver, who is expecting her first child, is too big. "It makes me feel cramped."

She serves me orange juice, two eggs over easy, bacon, biscuits, sweet rolls and a cup of strawberries. I go outside to walk off the effects—normally I don't eat breakfast, except on weekends—and I head up the street, toward Bill's Gulf station, where, I'm told, the cream of the town sits each morning, drinks coffee, eats doughnuts and swaps stories.

I get to Bill's at 8:15, and there they are, mostly middle-aged men, some of whom wear maroon nylon jackets that bear the emblem of Millerstown's volunteer fire department, which is next door to the Gulf station. They talk about how the "new" U.S. Highway 322, relocated ten years ago, has affected the borough. The good is that it has made Millerstown less inaccessible and Harrisburg easier to reach, putting outside jobs within commuting distance. The bad is that, with easier access to other communities, the borough is no longer so self-contained; it has lost, they say, its small-town flavor, the town band, the Fourth of July parade and the unity that comes when everybody works where he lives.

Today, one man says, Millerstown is just a spoke in the wheel of which Harrisburg is the hub. The man says he has the feeling that life "is less better" because of the road and what it has brought, an influx of people who "basically moved here because they wanted to get away from something somewhere else."

It's at the station that I meet two of Millerstown's three preachers, the Rev. Donald Bailor of the First United Methodist

Church and the Rev. Douglas DeCelle of the First Presbyterian Church.

They perhaps reflect the old and the new in Millerstown, where 100-year-old homes of natives contrast with modern homes of commuters, those who have moved out from the cities and built their castles on a hill that the natives, depending on their frame of mind, call either "Debtors' Hill" or "Snob Hill."

Bailor is fifty-one, a native of the area who "knocked from job to job and never was satisfied" until he enrolled at a Washington, D.C., seminary at age thirty-nine to become a minister. "I kind of got booted by the good Lord, who said to me: 'This is what I want you to do.' And I've been happy since the day I made my decision." He's been back in Millerstown for four years.

DeCelle, the son of a General Motors executive, is from California. He was a psychology major as an undergraduate and he prepared for the ministry at Princeton Theological Seminary in New Jersey. He's been in Millerstown a year and a half—it's his first pastorate—and he describes himself as "a twenty-seven-year-old in a sixty-year-old's job. You know you're young when the people you're marrying are older than you are."

Bailor's wife is an ordained minister and is active in the church. She preaches from the pulpit once a year—on Father's Day. DeCelle's wife is a fourth-grade teacher, not especially active in the church. "My wife, on the exterior, is a good-appearing pastor's wife," DeCelle says. "She satisfies the image. She doesn't wear jeans or T-shirts without a bra—but that doesn't mean that below the surface there's no friction with the role."

Bailor says he preaches in a "more oratorical" style than DeCelle and is prone to "call a spade a spade" when he perceives something in town that's at odds with what he thinks the Lord would want. It's said that Bailor was instrumental in getting a house of ill repute shut down a few years ago after it became a town attraction and folks gathered across the street to ask: "Gee, who's going in next?"

DeCelle says his preaching is more conservative and tends to deal with man's struggle to discover who he is and who God is and how the two can become one. He directs his sermons to adults, he says, and never preaches to children "because they get enough preaching from everybody else."

We walk up the street toward the First Presbyterian Church, the three of us, Bailor in the maroon Millerstown fire department

When he's not doctoring, Witt works on his 600-acre farm.

jacket, DeCelle in a black nylon jacket with a single word printed in orange on the back: "Princeton." We stop at the church office a few doors before we get to the church. The sign on the door says, "Please enter without knocking."

It is late morning by the time I get to the medical center. Witt is waiting to take me on rounds at two nursing homes where he is medical director. He drives the pickup and his wife sits in the middle, between us, as we bounce along country roads, zip through Seven Stars, where Sharon Beaver lives, almost before I'm aware we've been there.

The first home we visit is Nipple's Convalescent Home in Thompsontown, fifteen miles away. It's a place, Marilyn Nipple tells me, where people don't come to convalesce. They come to die. It's a home for those with advanced senility and terminal illness—those who require skilled care—and Medicaid pays the home $24.71 per day to take care of each of them while they wait to die.

Ms. Nipple, who is blond and wears blue jeans, is a licensed practical nurse and administrator of the home, which has twenty-three "guests," as she calls them. Witt, she says, comes at least once a month to check on each guest, more often if he is needed.

The guests seem happy, she says, being "with people their own age. It helps them come out of their shell." Only one of the twenty-three is able to walk by himself outside of the home. Two are able to walk with assistance. The rest stay inside. Many never leave their rooms. Many are "so out of it"—that's how Ms. Nipple describes it—that they are only vaguely aware of what is happening to them, that they are taken out of bed, dressed, fed, placed in chairs, fed again, undressed and put back to bed.

To me it's depressing. To Ms. Nipple it's not, she says. Her mother founded the home and she's worked here almost all of her life, she says. "It's made me mature a lot quicker, made me think what life might be like for me someday. But it's not depressing to me. I see people die at sixteen in car wrecks, from leukemia. To me that's depressing."

The second home is a $31-a-day home, twenty miles away near Mifflintown. It's called Brookline Manor and, while it has a wing for the terminally ill, its population basically is made up of reasonably healthy people who have been placed here because they have nowhere else to go. The atmosphere is livelier here.

Witt stops at the room of Robert Hanley, who is eighty-seven, stooped and fragile-looking. He is wrapped in a sweater because, he says, "I feel cold." Witt tells Hanley that he looks in better shape than many of the people in Millerstown. Hanley laughs and in a croaking voice tells Witt about a red-letter day in his life the previous week: "They came up and took me for a ride in the fire truck. I really liked that."

That's right, Witt tells me later, some of the Millerstown volunteer firemen drove a fire engine to the home and took Robert Hanley for a spin through the country. "Wouldn't that thrill you, too?" he asks me.

Hanley complains that his new hearing aid, just two weeks old, is "driving me crazy. It whistles. Is it supposed to do this?"

I look at his right ear and, since I've just finished collaborating with an otolaryngologist on a book about hearing aids, it's immediately obvious to me what the problem is. The ear mold isn't snug in his ear canal and the sound is leaking out of his ear and coming back through the amplifier, producing feedback—that whistling noise about which he is complaining.

I give my diagnosis to Witt, who adjusts the ear mold into Hanley's ear and asks if he still hears whistling. "No, it's stopped. That's lots better." He grins and thanks Witt. "I always knew you were a good doctor," he says.

We climb into the pickup and head back toward Millerstown, through towns named Port Royal, Mexico and East Salem, alongside the Juniata River. It's late afternoon when we arrive at the clinic. I thank Witt, get into my car and start for home, three hours away, hungry and wondering what's for dinner.

As I come down Highway 17, I pass Bill's Gulf station and Bill Rouse is still there, pumping gasoline and talking. I wave and he waves back. I think about a question I asked him earlier in the day: What happens when there is a fire and he has to leave the station? Does he close down the gas pumps? "Well, I'll tell you," he had answered, "I just leave and anybody who's around takes over until I get back, pumps the gas and handles the money. That's the way we do it here."

I zoom over the hill, out of sight of Millerstown, and I'm thinking: "That's not the way we do it in Philadelphia, but, oh, how I wish it were."

8 ⊰ In Idaho, years of discontent

Around the country most people may remember 1974 as the year that Richard Nixon resigned as President and Patricia Hearst was kidnapped. But in Idaho they remember 1974 as the year of $9 potatoes. In the short run it was the greatest thing that ever happened to some potato farmers. In the long run it was a disaster for many.

Consider the case of Glenn Matsuura, a real-life potato farmer since he was old enough to walk the fields and help his father. He rocks along with a stable market, making a little when prices reach $4.00 for a hundred pounds, breaking even at $3.50. Then without warning, across much of the nation, there is too much rain here, an early freeze there. Potato crops fizzle and fail, creating a general shortage. The ten-pound bag of potatoes that normally costs $1.29 at the supermarket rockets to $2.39. The price to farmers who have potatoes is an incredible $9.00 a hundredweight, unheard-of in the history of the market.

In Idaho some farmers do have potatoes because they have been spared the natural disasters. Overnight fortunes are made. Borderline farmers become successful. Successful farmers become wealthy.

Some farmers who contracted in advance to sell their potatoes to processors for $3.25 can't resist the lure of big money. They

---

Glenn Matsuura, an Idaho potato farmer who says he is "married" to his occupation.

renege, and sell their potatoes on the open market at the going price. One of Matsuura's neighbors does this; then, because he feels guilty and he realizes that he may be on the processors' blacklist forever, he asks Matsuura to let him have some of his potatoes. Matsuura, who does little advance contracting because "that takes the fun out of the business," refuses, even though the neighbor offers him a 240-acre farm in return for 35,000 bags of potatoes. "Maybe we needed the money worse than he did," Matsuura says.

Across the land potato growers go wild. They think that the pot at the end of the rainbow is filled not with gold but with potatoes. The $9 price is burned forever into their minds and into the minds of those who now are eager to get into this get-rich-quick business. More acreage is devoted to more potatoes by more farmers. Nonfarmers become farmers. The potato farm is heaven on earth.

But not for long. The next year prices fall to $4.00 as supply comes more in line with demand. In the years that follow, prices continue to decline, and now they've hit $1.50. That means that a farmer is losing $2.00 for each hundred pounds he trucks to market. If you're farming in Michigan, Washington, Maine or somewhere else, you can switch from potatoes to other vegetables. But if you're in Idaho, the potato capital of America, you come up short when you look at options. Because of climatic favors and soil make-up, your land is excellent for potatoes, but not for too many other things. You can't get out of the business because you have a fortune invested in land and potato equipment. If you sold, taxes would wipe you out. On paper things look good because your land is valued at more than $1,200 an acre. But you can't eat your land, and you can't continue to lose $2.00 on each bag of potatoes.

What do you do?

I'm meeting Glenn Matsuura at 7:30 this morning to ask that question. He is forty-seven, and he has lived his entire life in Idaho. His father, a Japanese farmer, came to America early in the century and settled in Rexburg, Idaho, near the Wyoming border. Matsuura's Japanese mother came a few years later, and she and her husband had five sons, all of whom were given American names: Jack, Gene, Brent, Glenn and Tom.

That was because the Matsuura family wanted everybody to know that they were in America to stay. But then the war came and the Matsuuras weren't at all certain that America wanted them to stay. All people of Japanese descent living on the West Coast were forced by the United States government to move inland. Because the Matsuuras already were inland, they weren't affected by that. But they were affected in other ways. People who had been their friends suddenly weren't so friendly anymore. Neighbors weren't so neighborly. Merchants who sold necessities to other families now seemed to run out when the Matsuuras wanted to buy.

At the time, Glenn, the fourth-born son, was nine, and it was difficult for him to understand why his classmates no longer seemed to like him. One day, while he was ice-skating, another youngster crashed into him, "probably because I was the only black head on the ice." He suffered a concussion and was hospitalized, unconscious for seventy-two hours. His parents tried to explain what was happening, why people had changed because of the war, but still it made no sense to Glenn. Then one day he heard the Matsuura family physician, a native-born American, tell a crowd outside the Matsuura home: "My God, these people didn't start the war!"

Suddenly, it began to make some sense. Glenn Matsuura's father had come from Hiroshima, and Glenn often had heard him talk about what it was like, back home in Japan. Yet when the atomic bomb was dropped, Matsuura felt no sense of loss. Rather, he reacted as other thirteen-year-old American boys reacted: "I was glad the war finally was over."

In Rexburg the family rented land but was unable to assemble any substantial acreage at one place. "We had forty acres here, fifty acres there, and we spent too much time on the road, driving from one farm to another," Matsuura said. So they came south, found land they could buy and settled in Blackfoot, in the southeast corner of the state near Pocatello, about a thirty-minute airplane ride from Salt Lake City, Utah.

The father died of cancer but the five sons continued to work in the fields, then hired others to work with them and for them. They invested in modern equipment and bought more land. By 1966 they had put together 3,500 acres, and they were becoming well known in the area and reasonably prosperous. All five sons, Glenn Matsuura said, were perfectionists. "If something wasn't right, we made it right." All devoted long hours, literally dawn to dusk, to the farm. Three, including Glenn, never married, and that probably was because, as Glenn said, "When you're serious about a farm, you sort of become married to it. I think that's what happened to me."

I'm driving north toward Blackfoot on Interstate 15 from Pocatello, where I've spent the night. It's a thirty-mile trip, and I'm looking more at the scenery than at the highway. Off to the east the sun is inching up behind 500-foot-high hills and streaking the clouds with pink, purple and orange. The hills are brown, almost evil looking, like the hills out of which the bad guys gallop in the cowboy movies. It's not only the hills that are brown; it's everything else, too. This is semi-desert country, where the average annual rainfall is ten inches but where nobody is surprised by a year that yields just two. Farming is done by irrigation, either by diverting water from the Snake River or by driving wells 400 feet into the lava rock and tapping into the never-ending underground stream that is fed by the melting snow from the north.

To the east an irrigation system sprays drops of water that fall gently to the ground. Through its mist a rainbow forms, while up ahead, a green sign announces that I'm approaching the Fort Hall Indian Reservation, which is home for 2,000 members of the Shoshone and Bannock tribes. Then I'm in Blackfoot, population 8,700, and there on my left is where I'm to meet Glenn Matsuura for breakfast, the Riverside Inn, on the banks of the Snake River.

I've heard a lot about the Snake River, and I'm expecting to see something that looks like the Mississippi River, or maybe the Missouri or the Delaware. Instead, the Snake River looks more like a drainage ditch. Is this what daredevil Evel Knievel tried to rocket across? Well, no. That happened 150 miles to the west, beyond Twin Falls, where the Snake River looks like a river and runs at the bottom of a deep canyon.

Inside the inn I go directly to the coffee shop, walking past a painting of Indians who are doing a rain dance. No, that's not right. I look again and the plaque under the painting says the Indians are sun dancing.

I order coffee and wait. Fifteen minutes later a Japanese-looking fellow walks in, and I'm betting my life that this is Glenn Matsuura. It's a safe bet. Matsuura is grinning broadly beneath jet black hair that sticks out from under a black cap with a yellow emblem that proclaims, "Cat diesel power." He is short—five feet, four inches—trim, and wears a tan work shirt and blue jeans. His

Dry weather in Idaho potato country provides natural protection against rain at the wrong time. Irrigation systems like this one make it possible to apply water just when it's needed.

face is what Americans think is classic Japanese: round, with deep, dark eyes and a flat nose that might pose a problem if called on to hold up eyeglasses. But when he speaks, the illusion is broken. Matsuura's voice is deep, like a radio announcer's, and his English is as flawless and accent-free as a college professor's. I will spend fourteen hours with him today and not once will I recognize a mistake in grammar.

As a youngster, he learned Japanese from his parents, and he and his brothers often spoke Japanese around the house. But they learned their English lessons well in the public schools and, as they got older, seldom used their Japanese.

"I used to be a little bashful," Matsuura says. "You speak Japanese around Caucasians and they think you're a foreigner. But that doesn't bother me now. My feeling now is that if you're bilingual, you have something extra." But he is finding that with language, as with some other things, you have to use it or lose it. Not long ago some Japanese youngsters came to Idaho on a 4-H tour and "it was hard for me to communicate with them. I'm losing command of the language because I don't speak it regularly."

A dozen or so people are in the coffee shop, and most of them seem to know Matsuura. On their way out, some of them stop by the table to talk:

"How's your crop?"

"How much are you storing?"

"What are you charging for storage?"

Others don't stop but they call out: "Hey, Glenn, how's it going? Good to see you."

The questions about storage are the result of an advertisement that Matsuura has placed in the *Blackfoot News*: "Don't give away your potatoes; store them." He is telling potato farmers that he has storage room to spare and that he is willing to rent it to them so they can withhold their potatoes from the market, hopefully until prices are more realistic than $1.50.

Why is it that he has storage space available?

In the answer to that question is to be found the answer to the question that brought me to Idaho: What does a potato farmer do when prices fall and he can't afford to stay in the business but, because of taxes, can't afford to sell out?

Matsuura has rented 1,500 acres to tenants who, in the bloom of youth, still want to gamble with potatoes. He has stepped up a cattle-breeding operation that until a few years ago was strictly a sideline to his potatoes. He has planted 900 acres in grain and seed peas. But, more importantly, he has taken some of the money that traditionally would have been plowed back into farming and put it in the city.

In the city?

"When our accountant told us we needed to diversify, I thought he meant to get into some other kind of farming. But he said, no, the problem was that we had too many eggs in one basket and that the basket was Idaho. He wanted us to get out of Idaho with some of our money."

And Matsuura and his brothers have done just that, investing in real estate in Sacramento, California. All of this means that Glenn Matsuura, who calls himself a potato farmer, is growing absolutely no potatoes—for the first time ever.

"That's exactly right. Until things change, I believe I'll sit on the sidelines and let the substitutes play the game."

Besides the year of $9 potatoes, what are the other problems? Matsuura talks about the state of the crop:

"It used to be an art, growing potatoes. You had to know what you were doing. Now, with the new herbicides, anybody can grow potatoes. A boy with a high school education easily can take over his father's farming operation. Too many people are coming in, and not enough people are getting out. Both ways, it's the government's fault."

The government encourages new people to begin farming, Matsuura says, by making low-interest money available, and it entices others who are faltering to stay in by propping them up with loans that are well below bank rates.

"You take the FHA, the Farmers Home Administration," he says. "That was meant to help young guys get a start and to help in disaster situations. It's fine to help young guys, but now they're helping the big corporations, too. The big corporations are into farming. There was one here in Idaho and Oregon that bought out some farm people. They had 10,000 or 15,000 acres of potatoes. But they got in trouble, because of the prices. I hear they owed $32 million to one bank. The bank wouldn't bail them out, but they were going broke and so they went to the FHA. I can't knock it. Look at what Chrysler did. Well, the FHA bailed them out with 3 percent money, and they're still going."

The problem with that, Matsuura says, is that it amounts to un-

Until prices are better, Matsuura isn't growing any potatoes of his own. Instead, he's storing potatoes for others and has stepped up his cattle breeding operation.

fair competition. "We can compete and produce as well as any-body if we have an equal chance. But we can't if others are sub-sidized. I'm paying 2 percent above the prime rate for my money and some of the other people are getting money from the govern-ment for 3 percent or 5 or 8 or whatever. You need to go broke to qualify for government money. Then these farms that should be out of it because they can't make it on their own are still in there, contributing to the surplus that causes the low prices. No, I believe we're going to wait and see what happens."

That means the hundreds of thousands of dollars' worth of po-tato-farming machinery owned by the Matsuura brothers is idle. "There's a reason for not getting rid of it. If the tenants get too tough, we always can tell them to find another place to farm, that we're going to do it ourselves here. This is our only leverage.

"But we may get back in at some point. I don't know when, but we're still young enough. We need about $3.50 to break even. If Mother Nature is on our side, if we have no hailstorms, if we have a 100-day frost-free growing season, we can get 280 to 300 bags of salable potatoes an acre. And we can hold our own with that. But how many years does everything go right?"

In the future Matsuura predicts that potatoes will be grown as peas now tend to be grown. It's a system called "vertical integra-tion" in which the processor furnishes the seed, tells the farmer how much to grow and buys the crop from him at a predetermined price. The problem with that, from Matsuura's standpoint, is that it takes the fun out of farming and "if it's not fun, why stay in it?" The fun, he says, is "trying to get the highest market, to see what you can do. Take away that, and you just go through the motions, as far as I'm concerned."

In a 1975 story in *Forbes* magazine, Matsuura was described as a "millionaire gambler." Half of that was accurate, he says, downing his second cup of coffee. "I do like to gamble on prices. But a millionaire?" That would crack up the accountant. "The only thing that would make me prosperous is to sell the land. Be-cause of inflation, land values really have gone up."

But there is another problem in selling the land besides taxes. That is the price of the land. The going rate around here is $1,250 an acre but "at these (potato) prices, you couldn't even service the debt with what you'd get off an acre." What that means is that it might be difficult to find a buyer at the right price—unless it was somebody armed with cheap government money.

The thought of that, of selling out to somebody who is the embodiment of what he perceives to be the problem, is enough to make Matsuura wince, which he does, spilling some coffee.

There are other problems, too, that are peculiar to Idaho. Idaho potatoes are a long way from their major market, the population centers of the East Coast. Transportation costs, $3.75 for each hundred pounds, mean that the Idaho potato can't compete with Maine potatoes for price. What's more, as a means of protecting the image of the Idaho potato as the world's finest, Idaho ships out only its premium potatoes. This further puts the Idaho potato at a price disadvantage, since it often is competing against potatoes that aren't premium grade.

The Idaho potato is a good potato and it probably is better than anybody else's potato, Matsuura says, but Idaho potatoes "cost more, and families buy less when money is tight." Maybe an answer is to be found in changing the way the potatoes are promoted. "Maybe we need some leadership. Farmers aren't the smartest people on earth, and maybe we need to get some smart people to lead us along."

Maybe more farmers need more accountants, he says. "Maybe farmers need to go to business school. This whole business is changing. You got words like 'cash flow,' 'prime rate,' 'debt servicing.' You think these are for accountants to talk about at cocktail parties. But they're all coming into play in farming and, by God, you have to know what they mean or you're left out."

Despite his newspaper advertisement about storage space, Matsuura doubts that potato growers ever are going to get together in any kind of significant attempt to influence prices. "In a bad year the growers get together and ask what they're going to do. Then they go home and do their own thing. They all say they'll cut their acreage, but they're afraid the others won't. What happens is that we go home and continue to grow the same amount of potatoes we always did."

Farmers can store their potatoes and ship them throughout the year, but "it takes a lot of guts to hold onto your potatoes and wait for a better price. Some larger farmers are going to storage, but there isn't going to be any general hold-off. You could say that we are a homogeneous group with heterogeneous ideas. Let's just call it that. You get ten potato farmers together to solve a problem and they have eleven solutions."

It's a shame, Matsuura says, that our problem is that American farmers can raise so much, while people in parts of the world are going hungry. "Why we can't get the distribution worked out, I don't know."

We leave the Riverside Inn after scrambled eggs and six cups of coffee. The question, I tell him, is this: If the problem is too many potatoes, why does the government continue to prop up farmers who can't make it without help? Matsuura thought I'd never ask. "It's the cheap food policy of the government. Without it, there'd still be enough food for everybody, but you'd be paying three times more. And there are more consumer votes than farmer votes. Isn't that what everything comes down to—votes?"

We drive through Blackfoot, which is named after the Blackfoot Indians. Nobody would ever confuse it with Times Square on New Year's Eve. It looks neat and pleasant, but there is almost nobody on the streets. It's as if Matsuura is reading my mind. "When farmers have money, they spend it. Now Blackfoot is almost a ghost town. There's an agriculture-based economy here, and when the farmer is in trouble, the businessman is in trouble, too." And right now the potato farmer is in big trouble.

We stop at the building that houses the offices of the Potato Growers of Idaho. The name sounds bigger than the organization really is. It's not statewide. Rather it is a collection of southeastern Idaho growers who banded together to promote their potatoes and to bargain with the processing plants on the price that will be paid for advance contracting. The growers hired an executive director, but now in these hard times they have come to a friendly parting. Some say the growers couldn't afford to pay him any longer. Others say he found a better job. But for whatever reason, Gerald Murphy, whose background is public relations, is on the way out.

Today Murphy is in the office, finishing up some business and talking, he says, not as somebody on the payroll but as somebody who has learned a lot about potatoes and who has some feel for what's going on.

The picture he draws is less grim than Matsuura's: Things are bleak now because of the big surplus of potatoes and low prices. But, historically, prices have run in cycles and, if you believe that the future is a reflection of the past, then you can believe that good times are headed this way. The way it works is this: When prices rise, as in 1974, production rises, too, and before long supply outruns demand. Then prices drop and production drops, too. Before long prices are back up.

It takes about four years for the cycle to switch from down to up, so the farmers who make it through this low spot can look ahead to something good not too far down the road, although it probably won't be a bag of $9 potatoes. Something like that comes along once in a lifetime. And thank goodness for that.

Murphy, I find, is a genuine gold mine of information about potatoes. He really does know his stuff:

• Four processing companies produce more than 60 percent of the frozen French fries that are used by McDonald's, Burger King and other fast-food markets.

• Idaho's summer temperature range was designed with potatoes in mind. It doesn't get too hot. When temperatures exceed eighty-five, potatoes are susceptible to heat damage, which results in a black spot in the center of the potato. At night it gets just cool enough: sixty degrees or just below when the transfer of starch from the vines to the potatoes is accelerated for maximum growth. Even the brutal winters—sometimes it gets to forty below zero— are a plus, because they inhibit bacteria development in the soil. What about lack of rain? Murphy has the answer to that, too. This insures natural protection against rain at the wrong time, such as harvesttime. With irrigation farmers apply the water as the crops need it—not as Mother Nature releases it.

• The prime potatoes are those that weigh from seven to twelve ounces and are well shaped and without defects. These are the potatoes that are bought by first-class restaurants to serve to first-class customers. We can buy identical potatoes at the supermarket, but we'll have to pick them out of the bins and pay more for them. The prime potatoes aren't in the ten-pound plastic bags that often seem to be bargain priced.

• Potatoes that sell for 35 cents a pound in the supermarket are bought by the processors from the growers for 3½ cents and sold to wholesalers for 10 cents.

Does Murphy know everything? All right, how did the name "spud" originate as a synonym for potato? There's even a Spud candy bar, made of marshmallow and chocolate, that is produced and marketed in Idaho. Well, I thought Murphy was against the wall, but, by golly, he answered that one, too. Long ago in Europe, the elite scorned the potato because they thought it was an unspeakable fungus, and they organized anti-potato societies all over the place. Among these was the Society for Prevention of Unwholesome Disease—SPUD. But a political prisoner in France survived by eating potatoes, and when he eventually returned to power, one of his first unofficial acts was, in Murphy's words, "to make the potato fashionable." The anti-potato societies are gone but the "spud" is still with us.

Is that a true story? Who knows?

We leave Murphy, and I'm glad—because who likes to hang around a know-it-all? But Matsuura, who has chuckled through the spud story, tells me that there is some basis for regarding the potato as "one big disease. It is susceptible to a lot of diseases. We rotate crops, potatoes for one year, grain for two years. If we planted potatoes a second year, we'd get a lot more diseases."

Matsuura heads toward the "ranch," which is five miles outside Blackfoot. "I always called it a farm, but then somebody asked me where my ranch was, and I liked the way that sounded."

Although he is as American as apple pie, Matsuura says the Japanese culture has some things going for it that he would like to see more of in America. Like respect for elders. "In a Japanese house when the parent says to the child, 'OK, this is what you should do,' the child does it. He doesn't say, 'Oh, Mom!' But we're losing that. I notice that second-generation Japanese families are getting westernized. As much as I remember, if my dad said no, he meant it. He didn't hit us, but no was no. That's not the way it is in my older brother's family. They're just like American kids, and there's nothing wrong with that. But I do hate to see loss of respect for elders. These young kids have minds of their own, but maybe the wisdom of elders could help straighten out a lot of their problems."

If Japanese tradition had been followed, all five of the older brother's sons would be farmers, like their father. But not one is farming, and this is typical of what is happening today. Kids who grew up on farms are abandoning farms. It's mostly those who didn't come from farms who are taking the government money and growing potatoes, Matsuura says.

Why are farm kids abandoning the farm? "Maybe we were too tough on them. They don't like to work on Sundays when they're growing up. It's tough not to see a paycheck, like other kids get. But this is changing today. Now you pay them, even if they're working on their father's farm."

Matsuura, who has a bachelor's degree in agricultural economics from Utah State University, is Buddhist. The predominant re-

If farming is not fun, Matsuura asks, why stay in it?

ligion in this part of the country is Mormon, but there are enough Buddhists around Blackfoot so that a Buddhist "reverend" visits once a month to lecture. Matsuura doesn't attend, and he says he now practices no formal expression of religion. "If I want formal religion, I take it out of books." The core of his religion, he says, is simple enough: You should know right from wrong. "We all have our beliefs. You've got to believe in something, even if only that hard times will get better. But, pricewise, it's been a long time." Even when he talks about religion, it's difficult for Glenn Matsuura to act like anything except what he is: a potato farmer.

That's why it's difficult to imagine that he's no longer growing potatoes. But even so, he leaves the house he shares in town with his eighty-four-year-old mother bright and early every morning and heads out to the ranch to supervise, unofficially, the work of those who are growing potatoes on land they rent from him. They're out there now, the renters, harvesting potatoes from soil so soft and sandy that you sink in past your shoe tops. In one pass a harvester digs the potatoes out of the ground and scoops them onto a conveyor belt and then deposits them in a truck that moves alongside the harvester. These are russet Burbanks, Idaho's prime baking potatoes, big and firm and delicious.

Matsuura walks the plowed rows and doesn't like what he sees. "They're digging at eight inches, and that's not deep enough." On the next pass of the harvester he yells at the crew: "Go deeper! You're missing some!"

The potatoes vary in size, from five or six ounces to twelve ounces or more. Why aren't they more uniform? Matsuura doesn't know, and nobody else knows. "That's what the agronomists ask: 'If you want all big potatoes, why don't you grow all big potatoes?' But it's not that simple."

One reason it's hard to make money on potatoes is that they're expensive to grow—from $800 to $1,000 an acre. Because potatoes require tremendous amounts of nitrogen to develop, from 250 to 300 units of nitrogen must be applied to each acre each growing season—at a cost of about $75 per acre. Other chemicals must be added, too. And then there is the cost of irrigating. Potato fields must be watered at least once every five days. Ten years ago the cost of operating a watering system was $6 an acre. Now it's almost $25 an acre.

Watering is done in a variety of ways. The most spectacular—and the newest—is a system in which a giant wheel attached to the end of a water line pivots around an anchor in the center of the field. It's possible to water a circle of 140 acres, and from the air you can see these circles dotting the landscape, spots of green in an ocean of brown. Another system has a water line that is 400 yards long with motor-driven wheels on each end. Each line costs $5,000, and one line is needed for each 20 acres. "We have 3,500 acres, so you can figure out the cost yourself," says Matsuura.

The water for the system is pumped up by 400-horsepower motors that suck so much current that the wires feeding them jump each time they are switched on. You can hear the surge of the current—a steady hum—without getting close to the pumps.

The fields on which all of this is happening are neat as a pin, without rocks or growth other than potato vines. Yet the areas that surround the fields resemble the surface of the moon, lava rock pocked with craters big enough to drive a truck into. Sage brush thrives in these sparse surroundings and cedar trees do well, too, but most of the cedars have been cut for firewood. White rocks, some almost the size of a man, have been dragged from the potato fields and dumped into some of the craters, and they are stark looking against the dirty gray of the lava rock. If you were filming a movie about another planet, this is where you might come, to this gigantic lava flow that extends, in hit-or-miss fashion, all the way to Boise, nearly 300 miles to the west. And yes, you guessed it, astronauts came to this part of the country to get ready for voyages to the moon.

We leave the moon, and go over to one of Matsuura's storage cellars, where he is to meet a reporter from the *Blackfoot News.* It's big news around here when somebody like Glenn Matsuura advertises storage space and suggests withholding potatoes from the market. A storage cellar is enormous, 400 feet long, 45 feet wide, 20 feet high. The floor of the cellar is cut six feet into the ground. The roof is the ultimate in insulation: slabs of lumber topped by bales of straw that are covered with four inches of dirt. Potatoes are stacked 16 feet high in the cellar, the equivalent of 70,000 hundred-pound bags. They can be kept there for months in temperatures that, because of the insulation, remain a constant 50 degrees. But they'll spoil before a year is up—and that's why any holding action by potato farmers must be short-term.

Potatoes are not like grain that can be stored indefinitely. Because potatoes are living, breathing organisms that give off carbon dioxide, they have a life span that is limited. When a potato "dies," it shrivels as the 80 percent of it that is water begins to run out. This is what happens when you keep potatoes too long with refrigeration in your home. You say they've spoiled, but actually they have died.

Potatoes come out of the soil, during harvesting, at about fifty-five degrees and in the sophisticated storage cellars of the potato processors, the temperature is reduced half a degree a day until it reaches forty-five. At that temperature the potato's breathing rate slows down, and it can be bumped around without much fear of injury. But even under these conditions, about ten months is the longest that potatoes can be stored.

All of this is explained to me by Jeff Lynn, field department manager of Sun Spiced, Inc., the fresh potato division of the American Potato Company, which is headquartered in Blackfoot. This is one of the processors that contracts to buy potatoes from people like Glenn Matsuura. The best are earmarked for the fresh market—restaurants and grocery stores—and the rest are processed, to appear later as various forms of instant potatoes. The scientists at American Potato Company developed and patented the process of hooking potato granules together to make "buds" that hydrate into fluffier potatoes than granules.

The plant operates ten months out of the year, from mid-September to mid-July, and as many as 450 truckloads a day roll in, mostly potatoes that farmers have removed from their own storage cellars.

The $30,000 potato trucks are lined up on this wind-swept afternoon, waiting for their turns to be weighed and then to empty their cargoes, which average $900 each to the grower. Many of the trucks are driven by young women, and the men in the storage cellars seem not to notice—because there's nothing unusual about women who drive potato trucks. In fact, Matsuura says, he's heard that in some parts of the country women are paid more than men because they are considered more desirable drivers. Why? Because their safety record is superior.

It's getting on toward the cocktail hour now, Matsuura reminds me. How about something to drink? How about dinner? Off we head for the Colonial Inn, a remodeled residence that has a reputation for good food and even better drinks.

Well, Glenn, you've talked a lot about potatoes. But you haven't talked much about yourself. What do you like to do? Do you ski? After all, Blackfoot is just 160 miles east of Sun Valley.

"I tried it once, but I had an accident. I don't ski now."

This is close to elk hunting country, which is only two hours to the west. Do you hunt?

"No, I never liked that much."

What about traveling?

"I travel sometimes, but when I go on a fun trip, I still feel guilty. I think: 'Gee, I should be back on the farm.' At times that bothers me. I don't know why I feel that way. I know I don't have to account for my time. I know that some people can take off and never be bothered. But I can't help how I feel. I guess that's what happens when you're more or less married to your occupation."

Inside the bar of the inn we find what Matsuura identifies as the usual Tuesday evening crowd. In fact, he says, "they're also the Wednesday, Thursday, Friday and Saturday evening crowd. The bar's closed on Sunday and Monday, and they can't wait to get back Tuesday to tell each other what's happened."

The crowd is not really a crowd at all. It's five men, and they are joined together by a bond that maybe can be found only in a town of 8,700 called Blackfoot. The bond: They all grew up in Blackfoot. They've all known each other since they were kids.

And so here they are: Blackfoot's prosecuting attorney, a patent attorney for American Potato Company, a state court judge, a sheep grower and a lawyer who's rumored to be the next town magistrate. The judge, who wears a yellow golf sweater, orders a round of drinks for everybody, including Glenn and me. Next the sheep grower, who wears a cowboy hat and sheepskin jacket, orders drinks for everybody, including Glenn and me.

Then Glenn buys a round. We have won, he beams. He and I have outlasted the Tuesday night regulars. They totter out the door, one after the other, reminding us that it was not a fair fight, since they arrived earlier.

The two of us adjourn to the dining room, where we both order rib eye steaks. The steaks arrive, accompanied by their customary baked potatoes. I'm eager to see if he thinks his is a first-rate potato. After all, who could evaluate a potato better than a potato farmer?

Mine tastes delicious, I tell Matsuura. How's yours?

He nibbles at it, then purses his lips, almost like a wine taster in his ritual. "I don't like the texture," he says. "On a scale of ten, I'd give it about a six. I'm not even sure this is an Idaho potato."

9 ⇜ Dairy cows and suburban sprawl

The date is September 20, 1978, another morning like so many before it in the life of Henry Retzlaff Sr., a retired dairy farmer who refuses to admit that he is retired. The land and the herds that were his for more than forty years have been passed on to his son, Henry Jr., but every morning father still gets up first, goes to the barn and waits for the milking ritual to begin.

He can't do the milking anymore. With arthritis it's painful for him to bend down and attach the suction cups of the milking machine to the cows as they contentedly munch hay from troughs before them. But he can help his son herd the cows into their milking stalls. And, for the ones that balk, he still has in reserve a hard slap with his right hand that tells them he means business, while at the same time he's soothing them with: "Come on now, baby, it's time to eat."

He's glad that his son has followed him into the dairy business, but he's a little surprised by it, too. Henry Jr. always made good grades in school and there was hope in the father's heart that he would become a physician. But that never was part of the son's plan. He wanted the farm, the cows, the freedom to do what he wanted when he wanted to do it—and the responsibility of facing up to the consequences of what he did and did not do.

Henry Retzlaff Jr. operates a farm just across the street from a suburban development that was once dairy land.

The dairy business, they both agreed, had changed over the years, even since son bought out father in 1965. On a broad scale there was the scare about the cholesterol from the milk. Was it a massive contributor to heart attacks? If so, then what exactly was the future of the dairy business? On a narrow scale there was the pressure from land developers to sell out. Nowhere was this greater than around this part of Wisconsin, in Cedarburg, twenty miles north of Milwaukee. On land where cattle grazed and corn grew just a few years ago, there now were houses, $100,000 castles of wood and brick, from which executives left with their briefcases every morning and to which they retreated every evening from their Milwaukee offices. The prices offered for farmland were becoming so tempting that maybe one day . . . .

Henry Retzlaff Sr. pushes that thought out of his mind. Now as he waits outside the barn, he looks down the hill from his 100-year-old house, where his son was born, to the new house, 300 yards away, where his son now lives with his wife and three daughters. A light blinks on in the kitchen. That means Joan is up, probably with the new baby. After all, new babies do have strange hours. Henry Jr. will be up and around in a few minutes and by six o'clock they'll be milking and talking. And then they'll have breakfast and son will head for the fields and father will tend his produce stand, to which people from as far away as Milwaukee have been coming for years to buy fresh vegetables.

Henry Retzlaff Sr. squints into the heavy black clouds that curl in from the east off Lake Michigan. On a clear day, standing here by the barn, he can see the lake, shimmering like silver in the sunshine, just off to the left of the Milwaukee skyline. It's an illusion, he knows, but it never fails to amaze him that the lake looks higher than the land. From the top of this hill, 200 feet above sea level, he feels as if he is looking up at the water and in danger of being flooded.

But he can't see the lake this morning. Even when the sun comes up, the sky will remain dark with the clouds that carry the smell of a rainstorm. Lightning crackles off to the east, and then thunder rumbles through the valley and seems to climb up the hill. It won't be long before the rain comes. Henry Sr. moves into the barn and waits as the first raindrops spatter into the dirt. Now the rain is harder and the lightning seems closer. It's not a big storm, though, and it's almost pleasant to hear the water beating against the sides of the barn.

At ten minutes before six, Henry Sr. is jolted by a burst of thunder that sounds as if a cannon has exploded right above him. "That hit something pretty close," he tells himself. The barn is dark because the lights are out. That's something he always preached to his son: Don't waste electricity. There is plenty of time to turn on the lights when the cows are brought inside for milking. But what's that?

Through the ceiling, up in the loft, there is a light. Did Henry Jr. leave it on when he was up there yesterday, checking the bales of hay? No, Henry Jr. wouldn't do that. Oh, my God, that's no electric light! There's smoke drifting through a corner of the ceiling. It's a fire! The barn has been hit by lightning!

There are five calves in the barn, tied to stalls by baling twine. He'd better get them out. No, he'd better call the fire department and then his son. In the house down the hill Joan Retzlaff answers the telephone. Then she screams: "Henry, the barn's on fire!" Her cry jolts him out of bed and he tears open the curtains to see a reddish glow on top of the hill. He frantically pulls on his trousers and runs for his truck. As he turns into the driveway that leads to the barn, the fire sirens atop the poles that line the street screech their message of urgency.

Where's Dad? Now son is inside the barn and it's not dark anymore. The flames that lick through the ceiling have coated the barn with a sheet of orange light, like a million candles in the night. There's Dad, over in the corner, with a knife, cutting loose the calves. Three are dancing around, bellowing, confused. Even though they no longer are tied to the barn, they don't scramble for the door. This is their safety, the barn, and they don't want to leave it.

"Get 'em out of here, Dad! Get 'em out! You get out with them!" The smoke is beginning to thicken, and the sulfur bites at his lungs. One of the calves is down on the floor, kicking crazily. God, that one's gone. She's choking to death.

He slices through the last piece of twine and frees the fifth calf. Then he stumbles for the door, rubbing his burning eyes and calling, "Dad? Dad?" There he is! He's all right.

The fire trucks are arriving, manned by volunteers who, like Henry Retzlaff Jr., have been torn from their beds. They seem unexcited as they go about their business, almost as if they are training for the time they have to fight a real fire. But this is real, and the dreams of a lifetime are being swallowed up by the dust and the smoke and the flames. The water hose is attached to a hydrant across the street, right behind the suburban castles, where windows come alive with light and pajama-clad bodies lean forward for a clearer look. Along the street, a jogger, in white shorts and wearing a white sweatband around his forehead, watches motionlessly. A bicyclist joins him. One man from across the street, as if by instinct, begins to direct traffic.

The barn burns to its foundation, fueled by the hay from the loft. Father and son watch it collapse and then they walk away, because there is nothing they can do. There is nothing anybody can do. For a week the ruins smolder, and then a man on a tractor digs a giant hole, sweeps the ruins into the hole and covers it. Only then is the crisp fall air free of smoke and the smell of broken dreams.

● ● ●

There's a new barn on the hill now, grander than before, and a new dairy herd, too. After the barn burned, Henry Retzlaff Jr. sold his other cows, keeping only some calves, because he had no place to milk. He and his wife took the winter off, flew to the West Coast, toured the movie studios and then invested a few of their dollars at the Las Vegas gambling casinos. It was the trip of a lifetime, just what they needed. Then in the spring they bought a new herd, for $100 a head more than the price at which they sold. They were back in the dairy business. The land was green in celebration; the eighty acres they own and the 150 acres they rent were heavy with oats and hay for the cattle. And there were cucumbers, green beans, potatoes, pumpkins, tomatoes and corn for the produce stand, which had been moved up from the road and into a new building adjacent to the barn.

Henry Retzlaff Jr. is expecting me at fifteen minutes before six o'clock on this morning and I am there right on time, driving Interstate 43 from my Milwaukee motel in less than half an hour. I pull into the driveway and this, I think, is not your typical dairy farmer's house. Instead, it looks as if it's been stolen from the subdivision across the street, a four-bedroom house with the brown wooden second story cantilevered out over the red brick first story. The porch light is turned on. When I ring the doorbell, I am greeted not from the door but from the garage, which is attached to the left of the house.

The old Retzlaff barn goes up in flame and smoke, along with the dreams of father and son.

"Hey, is that you?" The voice is friendly, unmistakably Wisconsin in accent. The face that goes with the voice is smiling from under a green cap, a tan face with even, white teeth and eyes that size me up from my white sneakers to my navy blue sweater.

"I didn't know that people from the city got up this early or dressed like that." It's Retzlaff's way of welcoming me to the farm. He is thirty-five years old, but he looks younger as he stands there in his heavy, brown work shoes, jeans and rainbow-like shirt of red, white, blue and yellow stripes. We can have coffee later, he says, but right now we need to get up to the barn, where Dad will be waiting, and start the milking. If there's one thing as certain as death and taxes, it's that the cows are going to be milked at six in the morning and six in the evening. These are times that are inviolate, times around which everything else must be scheduled, including meals, play with his daughters and attendance at meetings of the county Farm Bureau, of which he is a board member.

We ride the short distance to the barn in Henry's green 1974 GMC pickup and when we climb out, there is Henry's father, just as he is every morning. Henry Retzlaff Sr. is seventy-eight years old and while his pace has been slowed by arthritis, his love for the land and the cattle burns as strong as it did that day back in 1935 when he bought the farm from his father. He is wearing a yellow golf cap, green pants, blue shirt and suspenders of red, orange, yellow, green and blue. With those suspenders and his son's shirt, I think, all of us need sunglasses. But I keep my thoughts to myself as father and son automatically go about the business of preparing to milk.

While Henry Sr. waits in the barn, Henry Jr. goes outside for the twenty-seven cows that will be milked—twenty-six Holstein and one Brown Swiss, each worth about $1,100 during the prime of their milk-giving lives, which average seven years. After that they are shipped to market, and Henry Jr., while he is reluctant to admit it, sometimes is saddened. "It's not like it was when I was in 4-H, as a kid, and showed cows. I really got attached to them, and it broke my heart when they were gone. I don't feel quite that way now, but you have to like them because you make your living off them. You worry if they're sick. You hate to see them go. They're like, well, some of them are almost like friends. Maybe they look the same to you, but when you're around them every day, you can tell them apart. You don't have to look at their ear tags. They all look different, just like people."

The five calves in the barn fire all escaped and survived, even the one that was on the floor and choking. Henry Jr. remembers that firemen dragged her out fifteen minutes after they arrived and "I thought for sure she was dead. But firemen gave her oxygen and artificial respiration, and pretty soon she came to and took off for the pasture. For a couple of days she had a raspy cough. But now she's OK, just like all the rest."

The calves are among thirty-two on the farm, thirteen from two weeks to six months in age, nineteen from six months to two years. At about two years they are ready for milking and they are eased into the dairy herd as replacements for cows that are weeded out.

Retzlaff wants to hold the herd steady at twenty-seven because he's able to milk that many in the barn on one shift. When he had more, he had to have two shifts and that gets to be more than one son and one father can handle—or want to handle. If he could get good help, young men who knew the business or who wanted to learn it, maybe he'd change his mind. But good help is hard to find. There aren't many farm boys left in this part of the county. Most of them moved out when their parents, unable to refuse offers for as much as $7,000 an acre for their land, closed their dairies. The neighborhood boys now mostly come from the subdivisions, city-bred kids whose expectation of farming is jolted by the reality of the hard work and the long hours.

"We had some to come out and do some hoeing for us," Retzlaff says. "They did good for about an hour. Then they wanted to lean on their hoes and talk. They don't know what hard work is—not like farm boys know."

Now the cows are shuffling into the barn, in single file, complacent looking, like people who know there is no sense in rushing to the table because there's plenty of food for everybody. And like people who sit in the same pew every Sunday at church, some of the cows have their same stalls for milking, and they walk straight to them, past empty stalls that they don't even pause to investigate. They head into their stalls, extend their necks so that they can eat from the troughs in front of them and wait to be locked into place with clamps that are controlled by a single lever at the end of the barn.

The milking begins. There are enough lines from the milking machine to milk three cows at one time. The father washes the udder, which stimulates the milk glands, and then the son attaches four suction cups, which pulsate rhythmically and draw out the milk as human hands once did. From the cups the milk is sucked by a vacuum up through a clear tube and into a line that runs the length of the barn and into a tank.

Each cow gives about 13,000 pounds of milk a year, Retzlaff says. At about 8½ pounds to a gallon, that adds up to a lot of milk. How much milk a cow gives at each milking depends on where it is in its cycle of motherhood. The "fresh" cows, those that recently have delivered calves, may yield up to 60 or 70 pounds twice a day. This is maximum production and it continues for two to three months. Then it tapers off, Retzlaff continues, as the cow is impregnated again; as the pregnancy reaches its final two months, the cow drops to five to ten pounds a milking and then it goes completely dry.

After the next birth—Retzlaff tries to get a calf from each cow a year—the cycle begins again. The calf is weaned after the third day because milk is worth money and Retzlaff doesn't "want to waste the milk on a calf."

Baby bulls are castrated at three months, fattened and sent to market. The female calves mature and some are sold to other dairy farms, some are kept to become part of Retzlaff's herd.

Retzlaff moves quickly from cow to cow, removing the cups when each milking is finished and starting a new milking. It's a sense, more than anything else, that tells him when it's time to go to a new cow. If the sense fails, however, the cows reminds him that time is up by bellowing softly. The danger of keeping a cow on a milking machine too long is that the cow will develop mastitis, an inflammation of the udder, the dairy farmer's major health concern. Mastitis usually can be cleared up with one shot of a special antibiotic, but the cow's milk can't be used for about 10 milkings after that—and that's like throwing away money since milk is bringing about $12 for each 100 pounds, up $8 since Henry Retzlaff bought out his father in 1965.

"That sounds like we're making a lot of money," he says, "and I guess we are. But everything else costs more, too. And I don't have any more money than before. It's all relative, what you make and what you spend, and that's what a lot of people off the farm don't seem to understand."

In an hour the milking is finished. The cows are ushered out of the barn, and the cleanup begins. It's amazingly rapid, the cleanup, because a gutter behind the cows catches most of the waste material and a conveyor belt at the bottom of the gutter pulls it out of the barn and deposits it in a pile that later is worth its weight as fertilizer. The milk is in a 230-gallon holding tank, which is emptied every other day into a transport truck from the Golden Guernsey Cooperative in Milwaukee, to which the Retzlaffs have been selling milk for more than forty years. "They started out with just Guernsey milk, but they had to expand. They had a lot of customers and not enough milk," Retzlaff explains. "Dad started with them and we've been at it ever since."

The size of the check they receive from the cooperative once a month is pegged to the butterfat content of their milk and also, more recently, to the protein content. All of the hubbub about cholesterol "has people concerned" about butterfat, and there is talk that one day protein will be the basis for payment rather than butterfat. This would encourage dairy farmers to increase the protein content of their cows' milk, but this is where the rub comes in, Retzlaff says.

"You can feed your cows better and increase the butterfat in their milk. But protein seems more like it comes from heredity rather than from food. There'll have to be some research into ways to increase protein. I just don't know what's going to happen with that."

Another thing that Retzlaff doesn't know is what is going to happen to his land. "The real estate people knock on your door and ask if you want to sell your land. I'll probably sell someday. Three years ago land around here was selling for an average of $5,000 an acre, right across the road. Seven years ago a man died and they settled his estate for $3,000 an acre. So you can see how much it's growing in value. Now it's $6,000 to $7,000 an acre, and you can't afford to farm at those prices. Lots of people can't, anyway. Those near retirement have sold and moved to town. Maybe I will, too. That's a lot of money."

The houses that are built on the rolling dairy lands are snapped up as quickly as they are completed, some for as much as $175,000. They are occupied for two or three years by people Retzlaff calls "corporate gypsies" and then they are sold and resold as the gypsies are transferred out and transferred in. It seems like a crazy way to live, Retzlaff remarks, having no control over where you are and how long you remain there. "But they seem to like it, I guess."

Many of those who live in the subdivision directly across the street from Retzlaff's farm have moved from the city, and some of the small children never have seen live cows or corn on the stalk. "They're welcome to bring the kids over," Retzlaff says. "They know that. We don't make a big deal of it, and we don't know any of them very well. But they know they're welcome."

The kids and their parents seem fascinated by farm life, by the animals and by the tractors that pull the giant machines that fertilize the corn, pick it and then grind up the stalks into green feed for the cattle. They learn quickly, and they're almost like farmers compared to the dyed-in-the-wool city folks who come out in response to ads in the newspapers to pick up their own potatoes for $2.50 a bushel. They come in their station wagons, dressed as if they're headed for a football game, and they get their potatoes and then bring out the wine and food baskets for tailgate picnics.

The mess they leave behind sometimes takes half a day to clean up, and it irritates Henry Retzlaff "because they don't know how to behave." Yet he doesn't discontinue the practice of opening his farm to city people, less for the money than for fulfillment of his philosophical dream that one day city people will understand what farmers and farms are really like. When that happens, he says, there will be less grumbling about food and milk prices, and more appreciation for what he calls "still the best bargains in the world."

We're back at the house at the bottom of the hill now, just the two of us, since Henry's father has decided to have a quick snack at home and open up the produce stand a little early. We enter the house through the back of the garage, take off our shoes in the mud room and walk into the shag-carpeted living room, where Joan Retzlaff and two daughters, Lori, five, and Julie, three, are seated in front of a twenty-four-inch color television set.

The baby, just two months old, is sleeping, so would we please not make too much noise?

Joan Retzlaff is thirty-three, and she was Joan Pagenkopf—"so German that kraut was hanging out my ears"—until she married Henry eight years ago, despite her feelings, as a child, that she never would marry a farmer. "But Henry changed my mind. Boy, did he change my mind."

She is blond and to me she looks not unlike the maiden pictured on the box of Swiss Miss chocolate drink mix—blue-eyed, buxom, her lips curled into a smile that seems certain never to leave. But unlike Swiss Miss, she wears no frilly frock. To the contrary she

Henry Jr. finds out what daughters Lori and Julie did today.

has on jeans that fit the way a designer dreams and a purple T-shirt with white lettering on the front that reads: "Try it, you'll like it." When I look puzzled, she turns around and reveals the back of the shirt: "I tried it, I liked it."

She says she's glad I've come and asks if I'm ready for breakfast. I am ready—boy, am I ready—and we move into the kitchen.

Joan Retzlaff was a hairdresser for ten years and she worked right up until her first child was born, putting all of her earnings into the house mortgage and enabling them to pay it off in just seven years. She doesn't miss working, she says, despite frequent jibing from friends who ask: "Don't you want to get out of the house? What on earth do you do all day?" What she does, she says, is savor every moment of what she is doing. "I love my family and I love my home. I enjoy being here. Children are little only once. They grow up so fast. There is plenty of time to work later, if I want to, and I probably will."

Her parents farm not too far up the road, mostly cauliflower and red beets, and it's thought that the beets eventually will be their big-money crop since the coloring now is used for dyes and "it's about the only thing the government hasn't found to cause cancer." Her mother comes over once a week, and Joan does her hair. Mother and father go dancing two or three times a week, and "they usually ask us to go with them, but Henry's not much for that. He likes his sleep."

She's smiling again when she says that, and Retzlaff recognizes a ribbing when he hears one. He smiles back and pours himself and me a cup of coffee. He has a day's stubble on his face and a tired look that wasn't apparent when I first arrived. "I need eight hours of sleep if I'm going to feel good. Last night we had a Farm Bureau meeting and I didn't get home until eleven. I was up at five, and I'm tired. But I'll make up for it tonight."

The baby cries, ever so softly, and Joan leaves the room, returning in an instant with Kathy, who is wearing yellow pajamas and whose head is crowned with more black hair than I ever have seen on a baby. "She was born with it, the most of anybody in the nursery," Joan says proudly.

We dig into a breakfast of pancakes and eggs, and Retzlaff says that he never for a minute doubted that he'd return to the dairy business after the barn burned and he sold his cattle. "I like this. I like the way we live. I never worked in a factory. I never did anything but work on a farm. It's all I know. I don't think I could

Some comfort for Julie from her mother, Joan Retzlaff.

make it in a factory, with regular hours, with somebody telling me what to do. I don't think I could be bossed. Here on the farm if I don't want to do something, I don't do it. Of course, then it don't get done, and I have to do it later. But it's my choice. And I really like that.''

He asks me about newspaper work and if I'm happy. Do newspapers always tell the truth? Do writers have to pass a test—like doctors—before they can write on a newspaper? He unfolds a copy of the *Milwaukee Sentinel,* "the paper that Dad always subscribed to.'' And then he repeats an earlier question: "Do you think newspapers ever exaggerate the facts? Are things as bad as they sound sometimes?''

I tell him that, yes, some newspapers do exaggerate sometimes and, no, things aren't always as bad as they sound. I make a lot of speeches to newspaper groups, I tell him, and they don't always like what they hear from me. Newspaper people, like everybody else, enjoy listening to a recitation of what they do properly. Like everybody else, they are less entertained by being told what they mess up. But, Henry, I didn't come here to talk about newspapers. Let's talk about you and cows and dairy farming.

Retzlaff seems almost embarrassed that he will remain the focus of attention. "I'll tell you one thing I learned from the fire: Keep your insurance up-to-date. We'd just roofed and painted the barn, in June before the fire in September. And I didn't have enough insurance. I hadn't changed it since I bought the farm. It still was insured at 1965 values, and it cost us a lot of money to build a new barn, a lot more than the insurance paid.''

Joan Retzlaff asks if the newspaper has anything about the phantom who has been terrorizing the countryside about 20 miles to the north, burning five barns and one wagon. No, there is no story, but Retzlaff provides me with the background, just as a good editor would in briefing a reporter before he sent him out on a story. "They saw a guy in camouflage clothing running from one of the barns. You know, a camouflage suit, like soldiers wear. But they never caught him. We've been upset, everybody has, because the fire department around here got an anonymous call from somebody who said: 'If you think what happened up north was bad, just wait.' But nothing has happened. Maybe it was just a crank.''

Retzlaff shudders. "The guy has to be crazy. Don't you think? They say maybe it's somebody who worked on a farm and was fired. But I don't think that's a reason to burn down barns, do you? Well, maybe they'll get him. I hope so. A barn is such a big thing to a farmer. I know. . . ."

Joan brings out a collection of pictures taken the day of the fire. One shows her husband with his head down, staring into the smoking ruins. "That was a sad moment, really sad. It makes you realize how quickly you can lose what you have," he says.

Joan hands me some of the letters written by students at the school of First Immanuel Lutheran Church in Cedarburg, where the Retzlaffs worship. From the third grade: "Dear Retzlaff Family: We are very sorry that you had a fire in your barn. We collected some money for you. It isn't enough to buy a new barn, but we know you need extra money."

From the first grade: "We love you. We pray the Lord will take care of you." From the second grade: "We are very sad about the fire. God loves you . . . and He will take care of you."

There is a personal letter from a fifth grader whose father is president of one of Cedarburg's three banks: "I hope you rebuild your barn and that you don't sell the farm and leave, because you are very good, hardworking friends."

With those letters came $135, which represented a $1 gift from each student in the school. They were touched by that, Joan and Henry, as they were by the friends and neighbors who descended on them with food immediately after the fire. "It was almost like a funeral. But that's when you find out who your friends are," Joan says. "We had so many apples. Everybody brought apples. We had more apples than I knew what to do with. I laughed about it, but I appreciated it."

The Retzlaffs have some other pictures on the table, pictures of Lori and Julie from last winter, standing on snow piled up by a road grader, their heads almost even with the power lines strung from poles. "You can see how much snow we had," Retzlaff says. "I think it was our worst winter. I've heard Dad talk about the winter of 1936, when all of the roads were closed. But at least there were some bare spots. Last winter everything was covered, a foot or two feet deep, and the drifts—not where they plowed, just the drifts—were ten feet high. It can be really tough here in the winter. The winds come in from the east, off the lake, and there are a lot of sleet and ice storms that tear down the trees and power lines. I've had to buy a portable generator so we can do the milking, even if the lines are down."

The baby begins to cry—it must be snack time—and Joan Retzlaff kisses her on the forehead, then turns to Retzlaff and tells him: "This is the last baby. If you have any more, they'll be with your second wife."

"You know there'll never be a second wife."

"That's good to hear. Just be sure you understand that there'll be no more babies."

They exchange smiles that say it all, and then Retzlaff gets up and says it's time to grind up some cornstalks for cattle feed. Would I like to go along? Yes, I would, and in a few minutes I'm aboard a $25,000 International Harvester tractor that is pulling a corn chopper, a red-colored machine that snatches up cornstalks, funnels them into a series of revolving blades that reduce them to bite-size morsels and then sprays them through a tube into a wagon that is behind.

Retzlaff drives the tractor in a giant square, following the boundaries of the cornfield and almost filling the wagon in three trips around the field. Then he stops and remarks that the corn chopper probably is the most dangerous of all farm equipment. "I've heard all the horror stories about people who were pulled in it. Their arms were cut off or they were decapitated. I don't know if the stories are true. But I do know that you have to be careful. Around all machinery, not just this."

We unhook the chopper and tie the wagon to the tractor, and then we're off for the barnyard. The cattle have not been turned out to pasture. Instead they wait for their wagon of fresh food, almost as if they expect it as payment for being denied their run of the land. They eat as if it is their last meal, ever, and Retzlaff talks about how he enjoys going into Milwaukee to watch the Brewers play baseball but how he's never seen the Packers play football, even when they leave Green Bay, 104 miles to the north, and come to Milwaukee two or three times a season. "It's just too cold to watch a football game. I couldn't enjoy it."

But he did enjoy the trip to California and then to Las Vegas, where he and Joan saw Elvis Presley's last appearance there and where they also attended shows featuring Dean Martin and Bobbie Gentry. "Yeah, sure, I'd like to travel more, and maybe we will someday, if we sell the farm. We're tied down now, but I don't think it always will be this way. I know the girls will want to go some places when they're older, and that's part of growing up, don't you think?"

Hard work for Henry Jr. on a cold winter morning.

Henry Sr. is retired now,

but he still helps his son with the daily chores.

Back in the pickup, we drive through the subdivision across the road from the dairy farm and into Cedarburg, population 10,000, a town so clean and tidy that you suspect that somebody gives it a bath every morning. The main street is Washington Avenue, lined with neat shops that look not unlike some of those in colonial Williamsburg. "That's what they're trying to do, look like Williamsburg. They even want to get rid of all the signs that hang out over the sidewalks."

There is a mill built of native limestone in 1855. It still grinds 120 barrels of flour a day under the sign of Cedarburg Supply Company. Henry's father once was president of the firm and now Henry is vice-president. How much longer the mill will grind depends on what the preservation society that bought it decides to do with it. Presumably, the society will turn the mill into a museum someday. We leave the mill and drive along a street lined with mountain ash trees that hold fiery red berries and then we're into the subdivisions and then into the country. Retzlaff will take the long way home and will show me Joan's parents' farm with the beets that look red even as they grow in the field.

We pass a truck loaded with sweet corn and bound for the cannery in Belgium, fifteen miles to the north. Then, up ahead, there is a farm that Retzlaff makes a point of my noticing. "There's a twenty-five-year-old man with that farm. Either his daddy gave it to him or sold it to him, after giving him enough of it so he'd have equity to borrow money to buy the rest. I'd say he's $200,000 in the hole right now. I wouldn't want to be in that position. The only thing we ever owed a lot of money on was the house, and we paid that off in a hurry. I don't like to owe money. But it's getting harder to pay cash. Dad taught us to save money and then to buy something when we had enough. I could do that until the fire. But now I'm borrowing like everybody else, although not any more than I have to have."

Now we're driving beside Woody's Vegetable Farm, where a sign invites us to come in and pick what we want. This is a coming thing in this part of the country, Retzlaff says, because you don't have to hire any help to pick your crops. People come right in and do it themselves and pay you for doing it. Lots of apple orchards work this way, the orchards with dwarf trees that permit pickers to reach even the highest apples without climbing a stepladder. That's to avoid the possibility of a fall that could be the basis of a lawsuit. Even at Retzlaff's place, in the fields that he opens to the

Cows are almost like friends, Henry Jr. admits. And when their milking life is over and they are shipped to market, it's sad to see them go.

big-city potato pickers, he carries a $1 million liability policy, not because anybody is going to fall but because somebody possibly could get hurt by the machinery that plows up the potatoes. That's not likely, Retzlaff says, but these days a man can't be too careful.

Retzlaff has been careful with planning his future, whether or not the land eventually is sold to real estate developers. He has incorporated his farm for tax purposes, and he is the corporation's lone stockholder and only employee. A good-sized hunk of the corporation's profits is plowed into the stock market, and this is both the retirement fund for him and his wife and the college fund for his three daughters. He pays into Social Security but "I don't think we'll still have Social Security when I'm ready to retire. It'll be busted before then."

His father, who has joined us near the barn, agrees. He thinks the country is in bad trouble and fading rapidly.

"When I started in 1935, during the depression, I was lucky if I made $2,500 a year. But we raised our own food and we could make it. But in a lot of ways I think the country was more solid then. At least people worked. There was no welfare. Now we have all the giveaways. People can get more by not working than by working. This is why the country is going broke. The government gets in the red and it prints more money. Farmers can't do that." He glances at his son and adds: "But I wish we could, don't you, Henry?"

A teen-ager in an orange-colored Dodge that sounds souped-up rumbles up the hill. He is the son of a local optometrist, the exception to the rule that city boys don't work hard on the farm. He has been hired by Retzlaff, who is pleased both by his eagerness and by his knowing what to do and how to do it without being told. "A nice kid what we got here" is the way the senior Retzlaff describes the boy.

I decide to go down to the produce stand and see not what's cooking but what's selling. Henry Sr. seems to enjoy minding the stand, which is a series of vegetable-laden tables in a row inside a steel utility building. Signs advertise cucumbers four for twenty-five cents, green beans at thirty cents a pound, a dozen ears of corn for ninety cents. He sits in a straight-back chair, strokes a yellow cat that alternately climbs in and out of his lap and listens to a thirty-year-old radio that still pulls in distant stations, even in the daytime.

His wife, Viola, is seventy-nine now, just home from the hospi-

tal and housebound. That's the nice thing about having the produce stand so close to the house, back away from the road: He can
be right with his wife if she needs him. All she has to do is call,
from the window that he keeps within sight.

For twenty years he has sold vegetables from the farm and he
has his steady customers, people who come because they want the
best food for the best price. There are two young women with
small children who get out of an Oldsmobile station wagon and
say they'd like to go into the garden and pick their own bushel of
tomatoes. A man asks if it's possible to get twelve dozen ears of
corn by the end of the week.

"You don't look that hungry," Henry Sr. says.

"No, it's not for me," the man says. "It's for our company picnic. Can I get a special deal?"

"Sir, you are getting a special deal. Where you going to find
corn like this for ninety cents?" The man smiles, climbs back into
his car and says he'll be back Saturday morning for his corn.

A woman asks if he has red peppers. No. "Oh, darn, I just
knew you'd have them. You always have everything." That is
music to the elder Retzlaff's ears. "Well, we try. Maybe we'll have
some next year."

A woman brings in a child, perhaps her grandson, to look over
the pumpkins. The boy, about five, is wide-eyed, and he selects
the biggest pumpkin of them all, twenty-five pounds. "How
much?" the woman asks. "About a dollar and a half," she is told.

They pay and they leave with the pumpkin, which, while large,
isn't the granddaddy of them all. There was a time, Henry Sr.
says, when they had pumpkins as large as seventy pounds, but
they couldn't sell them because nobody could handle them. Ah,
those were the days.

We walk outside the building into hazy sunlight, and Henry Sr.
tells me about the time a woman brought back a cauliflower and
asked for a refund because it had a brown spot on it. "She said she
had paid seventy-nine cents for it. I said she couldn't have bought
it here at that price because we charge seventy-five, eighty or
eighty-five cents, never seventy-nine cents. That made her mad. I
think she did buy it here, but not for seventy-nine cents."

Did he give her a refund anyway?

"Of course I did. Isn't that the way to keep happy customers?"

Yes, it is, Mr. Retzlaff, but when you live in the city, sometimes
you forget.

10 ❧ Where gobble, gobble means money, money

My wristwatch shows five o'clock on a dark and cool morning, and here I am, in jeans and golf shirt, with a dust mask over my mouth and nose and with a push broom in my hands.

That's right, a push broom, the kind that janitors use. But, unlike a janitor, I'm not pushing dirt. Like a turkey farmer, I'm pushing turkeys—broad-breasted, twenty-five-pound toms that before today's sun has set will be trucked 100 miles, shackled upside down on chains, electrically stunned into semi-consciousness and funneled into throat-slitting "kill machines."

This is big business, the turkey business, and nowhere is it bigger than in Minnesota, the turkey capital of America, where dreams can be made or broken in a single year, where good luck and a boom market can promise eternal prosperity, where misfortune and tumbling prices can challenge not only a family's pocketbook but also its soul.

I'm with Glen Harder on his turkey farm near Mountain Lake, in the southwest corner of Minnesota. Harder, his wife and their three children live in a futuristic-looking house that has orange carpet instead of shingles for a roof. The house is on a hill that overlooks the barns in which the turkeys spend their entire lives, about nineteen weeks, without ever being exposed to the sun that

Turkey grower Glen Harder in a sea of 20,000 baby turkeys.

bakes this part of the country in the summer or the snowstorms that paralyze it in the winter.

By nineteen weeks the turkeys have reached their prime—at least from the standpoint of converting into meat the corn and soybean meal that is augered to them two hours out of every six. For every three pounds they eat, they gain one pound, and this is the stuff from which money is made, lots of money—sometimes.

In a year's time Glen Harder buys from a hatchery on the first day of their lives about 400,000 turkeys. If he sells them for an average of $10.00—and that's not a high average—you don't have to be very good at arithmetic to figure that he's grossing $4 million. What does that sift down to after expenses are paid? Harder aims for $1.00 a bird, but prices can fluctuate rapidly and not too many years ago he realized $3.25, which he regards as an unrealistic, almost absurd price.

Like most things that run in cycles, there are the bad years that inevitably are spliced in with the good and average years.

There was one year when Harder lost $400,000 because "nothing seemed to hit. Those are the times when you struggle to get out of bed before daylight and ask yourself why on earth you're in this business." But in the next breath he says: "It's a fantastic challenge. I can't imagine I'd ever be as happy doing anything else."

Glen Harder is my kind of person. He's direct. He looks you straight in the eye when he speaks. His smile comes easily and often. He talks about his wife and children as if they are the most important components of his life, and they are. He's forty-five, a former president of the National Turkey Federation, and he's been in the turkey business for more than twenty years, every minute of it with his wife, Luetta, as active partner and companion.

It is, both of them say, a good life, and part of what makes it good is the necessity to confront adversity, to try to turn wrong into right or to learn from wrong so that it doesn't plague you in the very same form next year.

Harder doesn't have many sleepless nights—even when he is losing $400,000. "I do the best I can. After that, there's nothing else I can do. Once you get a banker in far enough, he's got to stay with you. If the farm is in such bad shape, he could liquidate, but who would want to buy it? If a banker has somebody else who can run it better, I invite him to send him in. But I know that's not going to happen. Nobody can do it better than I can."

The unique Harder home is a local landmark.

Harder has dark hair that curls around his ears and down his neck to the collar of the blue cotton shirt he is wearing this morning. He is well-muscled in the arms and chest, the result of his working so much of the time alongside the men he pays to do the hard work, like getting the turkeys ready to go to market.

He rarely plays golf these days, although in college he was a par shooter. When he does play, he scores in the nineties because he's lost his touch. With all the lifting and handling of turkeys, it's almost as if he has become musclebound.

This is a day when we're doing some of the hard work, loading turkeys on the slaughterhouse-bound trucks. There are eight of us, Harder and I and six other men, including his two sons, and we're inside a hangar-like barn that is 600 feet by 60 feet. Right now it is a sea of white-feathered turkeys, about 10,500 of them, standing almost wing to wing and showing a marked lack of eagerness to do what we want them to do.

We have divided the barn in half by erecting a waist-high wooden fence. This is to keep half of the turkeys out of our way while we work with the other half. Then we put up boards that form a funnel-shaped chute, perhaps ten feet wide at the mouth and four feet wide at the other end. With our brooms and with sticks to which plastic flags have been nailed, we push and scare the turkeys toward the chute.

Once they're in the chute, the hard work really begins. We use the brooms to drive the turkeys toward the other end to the conveyor belt that takes them out of the barn through a canvas-covered passageway. The passageway is about twenty feet long and ends where two men stand and alternately seize turkeys off the belt and stuff them into cages that are stacked on a truck that is called the "Iowa Turkey Express."

After this truck is loaded with 1,000 turkeys, it will leave on a two-hour journey to Storm Lake, Iowa, where the slaughterhouse waits for its frightened cargo. Then another truck pulls up outside Glen Harder's barn. Then another. And another. On and on it goes—until all of the turkeys have been loaded. With good luck we'll be finished by midafternoon. Good luck is when the turkeys walk onto the conveyor belt. With bad luck it may be after dark. Bad luck is when the turkeys run away or have to be carried.

While the work seems difficult to me, Harder says it will be tougher later. The "good" birds go first. They require less effort to get into the chute. The "bad" birds want no part of what's hap-

pening. They get as far away from us as possible, like soldiers trying to hide when the sergeant is looking for volunteers.

The masks we wear are to protect us from the dust of the barn's
dirt floor and from the down of the turkeys, many of which flap
their wings, scream their "gobble, gobble" and insanely fly into
the side of the chute. It is a scene that could belong in a horror
movie, the eight of us in the barn's dim light wading among the
turkeys, whose cries almost drown out the hum of the conveyor
belt that is the beginning of their death ride.

For the turkeys this must be an experience in undiluted fear. It's
not unusual, during loading, for six or eight out of the 10,500 to
die from heart attacks. On this day three will die, at the end of the
chute, seconds before they would have been on the conveyor belt.
Harder takes one of the dead turkeys outside the barn, slits its
throat with a pocketknife and hangs it upside down so the blood
will drain. Later in the day we will have part of this turkey at the
dinner table.

The men who herd the turkeys inside the barn seem resigned to
what they are doing, almost bored, although they are efficient and
waste no time or motion. This is called "chasing" turkeys, and it
is by anybody's yardstick not much fun. What it is, is hard work
from which there is no relief except for a fifteen-minute break
after the loading of every other truck, each of which takes about
an hour.

One of the workers is George Hiebert, who is Glen Harder's
brother-in-law and a partner in the turkey farm. Hiebert has been
in what he calls "this business" for ten years and he likes it,
despite the long hours spent chasing turkeys.

Turkeys are not very smart, he says, and in fact they are downright dumb. All turkeys are frightened easily, especially by strange
noises from above them. This is a problem for turkeys that are
raised outdoors, on the range, as they still are on many farms.
When an airplane flies over or when thunder booms, they get very
jittery and they are prone to dash toward any shelter they can find.
Sometimes they pile up and smother the turkeys on the bottom of
the pile. It's not unusual, Hiebert says, for farmers to lose thousands of turkeys this way in a single year.

This is less a problem when turkeys are kept inside barns,
which, while a relatively new concept in growing turkeys, seems to
be the wave of the future. But it's still possible for turkeys to panic

Harder and his partner, George Hiebert, chase turkeys onto a

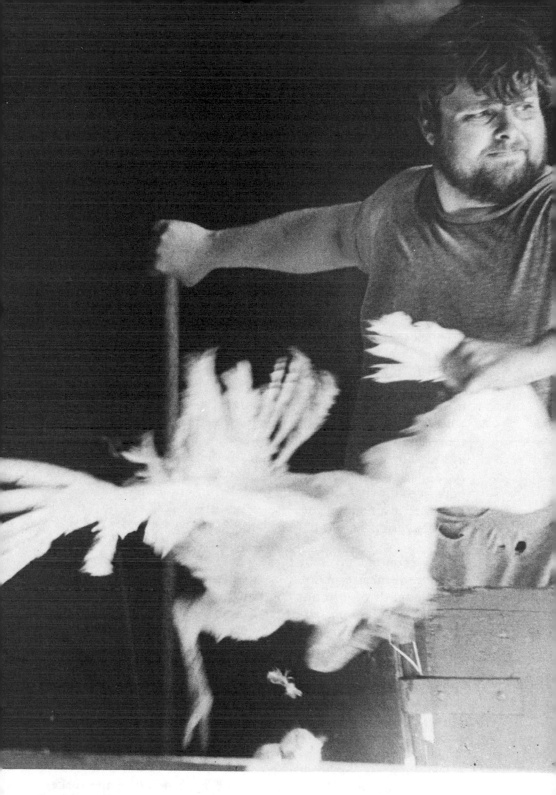

loader that moves the birds into a truck destined for market.

and smother if a coon or dog gets into the barn and scares them.

While turkeys are dumb, they are smart enough, Hiebert says, to know when it's time to eat and time to sleep. When the lights in the barns are turned on and the feeding machinery is revved up, the turkeys seem automatically to be hungry. They eat for two hours, almost without stopping, and then the lights go out and the turkeys sleep for four hours. When the lights come back on, the turkeys are up and eating again. Is it any wonder they become so plump so quickly, that in less than five months they go from chicks you could hold in the palm of your hand to big birds that, with the flap of a wing, can damage a man if they hit him in the right—or wrong—place? Pound for pound, Hiebert says, a turkey probably is stronger than a man.

Up close, a turkey is about the ugliest animal you can imagine. The red skin on its head and neck is wrinkled, almost like the skin of a person who has lost too much weight too rapidly. The tip of the upper beak has been clipped off and the toenails have been removed to keep the turkeys from pecking and scratching each other when they fight, as they often do. Once skin is broken, turkeys automatically are relegated to a lower class by the federal inspector at the slaughterhouse and this means they are worth less money. As a matter of fact, if skin is broken, a turkey may never even make it to the slaughterhouse, because turkeys seem to have a cannibalistic instinct and they attack and try to kill any bird that is bleeding, crippled or otherwise imperfect.

As we continue to chase turkeys and as the dust and down grow thicker, the men seem not to be tired or uncomfortable. I hear not a single word of profanity although we are in a situation that seems to me to lend itself to some choice language, particularly as birds you think you have in the chute suddenly back away and dash to momentary freedom.

There is never much profanity, George Hiebert says, because "it's something that people around here don't think is necessary. It just doesn't help things to talk that way." But, he says, if I'm interested in hearing some good, old-fashioned cussing, I should go along with the truck to the slaughterhouse, where men called "pullers" take the turkeys out of the cages and hand them to men called "hangers," who shackle the birds to the chains that lead to the kill machines. This is the hardest work of all in the turkey business, and the hangers and pullers constantly are in danger of

Turkey farming is a dusty business that requires face masks and, to keep disease from spreading, frequent changes of clothing.

being injured by the turkeys, which can be downright nasty by the time they've bumped along for 100 miles on country roads.

Hangers and pullers are paid an hourly wage plus so much for each turkey they handle, and it's not unusual for them to earn as much as $290 a week. Even at that salary, however, there is heavy turnover, and it doesn't take long for a man to gain seniority—maybe just a few months.

I'm fascinated by the crew that is loading the turkeys onto the trucks outside Glen Harder's barn. They travel the turkey country, almost like migrant workers, and show up at any turkey barn where loading is scheduled. The two men who stand at the end of the conveyor belt are called "chuckers" and they are paid about $280 a week for seizing turkeys by head and tail and stuffing them into the cages. This is hot, dirty, unpleasant work, too, but the risk of injury is less than at the slaughterhouse because the turkeys, at this point, are so terrified that they are docile.

There are four of these men and they rotate their jobs: Two cage the birds; one operates the conveyor belt; one goes inside the barn and helps chase the turkeys. The chuckers are perspiring heavily, even though the predawn temperature is less than sixty degrees. They wear coveralls with long sleeves, gloves and caps and they talk about how they have loaded for as long as thirty-six hours without stopping, except for their break after every other truck. If the birds are good, they say, they can load a truck in an hour. As the hours—and the trucks—pass, they reach a point where they work by instinct, without thinking about what they are doing. They chuck ten turkeys into each cage and then they move on to the next cage. The truck bed is ten cages long, five cages high and two cages wide. When one side is loaded, the driver turns his truck around and it is in these few precious minutes that a chucker may run for a drink of water.

One of the chuckers is an aeronautical engineering student from Iowa State University. He has a perfect 4.0 grade average, and this is his summer job before he returns to the classroom for his senior year. He fits right in with the other chuckers, who seem to accept him as one of their very own. His speech appears tailored to his environment: "This sure ain't no place for a lazy man." He laughs, and so do the other chuckers. But, he says, he'll be glad to get back to school. "The money is good, but this is hard work, really hard. The hours are long, and I get tired. But I think I'm in the best shape of my life."

Having said that, he turns to another chucker and says, "Hey, ain't it about time for a break?"

Inside the barn, we continue to push our brooms and wave our sticks at the turkeys. All of these turkeys are supposed to be toms, but it's obvious that some of them are hens because they are less colorful around the head than the toms. These hens, says Glen Harder, have been "missexed" by the Orientals who work at the hatchery and who, somehow, within hours after turkeys are hatched, are able to determine their sex. "They do it by feeling the genitals," Harder says. "It's a real skill, and I don't know how they learn to do it. It's something that only Orientals seem to do. I've never seen a sexer who wasn't Oriental."

The sexers are given a 2 percent error allowance, but it looks as if this group of toms has more than 2 percent hens. Toms tend to bring a slightly better price than hens because they're larger. They also cost more when Harder buys them from the hatchery on Day One. Toms are $1.05 each, hens sixty-five cents.

On that first day the turkeys not only are sexed and their beaks and toenails clipped but they also are injected with a drug that helps them get through their first few days of life without illness. Drugs are used only to prevent illness and not to stimulate growth, Harder says, and this is why a move to do away with all drugs makes no sense to him.

"Without drugs, prices would go sky-high because we'd lose so many turkeys. But some people are obsessed with the idea of perfection. They don't want anything to interfere with what they think is a natural turkey."

Back in the 1940s the biggest killer of turkeys was a liver disease called "blackhead." This has been wiped out virtually by antibiotics, but viruses now are the main problem. The Minnesota turkey industry gives $150,000 a year to the University of Minnesota for disease research. This represents two cents from each turkey that is marketed, two cents that the grower never receives, since it goes directly from the slaughterhouse to the university.

When Harder was raising his turkeys outdoors, he anticipated—and usually got—a death rate of 12 to 14 percent in the first ten days after he bought them from the hatchery. Usually the birds that died were "starve-outs," birds that, for whatever reason, didn't get in and push and shove enough to get their share of the food. Since he brought the turkeys into barns and put them on their schedule of two hours of eating and four hours of sleeping, the death rate is under 2 percent.

Does that make Glen Harder happy? Does a wheel roll? "A lot of people don't think this is the way to do it, but I'm convinced it is." Confined within the barn, the turkeys get all they want to eat—and more—and they don't exercise off the weight, since each turkey is allowed only about 3½ square feet within the barn.

Glen Harder is one of about 350 turkey growers in Minnesota, which annually produces more turkeys than either California or North Carolina, which rank second and third in production. All told, there are about 1,500 turkey growers in the country and because the business "is so small, we all kind of know each other. The pipeline [of information] is terrific. Something happens and everybody knows it."

Harder's annual crop of 400,000 turkeys makes him a medium-size operator, he says. Three million a year would be considered big, but, he says, he's in no hurry to get that big. More time with his wife and children is what he is aiming for—not more time with turkeys.

Harder and I leave the barn to check on the loading. Off to our right the compressor that drives the conveyor belt chugs contentedly. A sign proclaims the machinery as the property of "Bil-Mar Foods of Iowa, Inc. Storm Lake. Premium Quality—No Matter How You Slice It."

Harder climbs onto the side of the truck and asks the sleepy-eyed driver if he's about ready to go. "Yuh, I think so," the driver responds. The truck is loaded and gone before the sun has climbed over the horizon. The next truck, which has been parked 100 yards away, roars to life. The headlights come on, and it inches into position to be loaded.

I notice that my golf shirt, which was blue and white striped when I first entered the barn, now is mostly white and fluffy looking. That's white and fluffy, as in turkey feathers. I rub my hand through my hair and all of a sudden it appears to be snowing. No, it's not dandruff. It's that white and fluffy stuff.

It's chilly, even in midsummer, but it won't be chilly for long, I'm told. Temperature swings of thirty or forty degrees are not uncommon between early morning and late afternoon. The aeronautical engineer from Iowa State suggests that it'll be ninety-five degrees in a while. That means it will be another good day for swimming, Harder says, and he invites the loaders to take a dip in the swimming pool when they've loaded their last truck.

The Harders' swimming pool, like their house, always is open to visitors, especially those who end the day bone-weary after chasing and loading turkeys. Glen Harder and I walk a quarter of a mile up the hill from the barns toward the house, and he looks out over part of the 1,800 acres on which he grows corn and soybeans and says: "Isn't it beautiful?" He asks the question rhetorically, without expecting an answer. But I give him one anyway, because it is beautiful, with the dark green of the corn seeming to melt into a sky that has become bright blue as the sun has climbed and already begun to shoot up the temperature.

Corn and soybeans grow to within a few yards of the house, which is the realization of a dream for Glen Harder and his wife of twenty-four years. It is spectacular, with six fireplaces connected to three rock chimneys capped by orange-colored rain hoods that curve toward the sky and give the house a decided Oriental appearance. It's not Oriental, I will be told later; it's starkly original. But people call it Oriental because they don't know what else to call it. The siding is cedar shingles, stained pale tan, and they, combined with the rock chimneys, unite the house with the ground, while the soft, carpeted roof and the rain hoods seem to knit right into the sky.

We enter the front door, which actually is on the side of the house, and Luetta Harder is there, reminding us to take off our shoes and put on slippers that are waiting for us. She has no hired help to clean the house and this is her way of making her work load a little lighter, by keeping out dirty shoes from the fields and turkey barns. She has forty pairs of slippers inside a closet in the slate entrance hall and nobody, not even guests at their Christmas parties, wears shoes beyond this point. Only a handful of people object to taking off their shoes, she says, and their objections fade quickly when she explains her reasons.

Luetta Harder is forty-four, a year younger than her husband. She, too, is from this immediate area, the daughter of a part-time farmer whose main business was the hardware store he owned. She and Glen, whose father was a turkey farmer before him, knew each other in high school, but they didn't date until they both went away to Bethel College, a Mennonite-funded school in Kansas. She was attracted to Glen because "he was fun to be with, and we just hit it off.'' They were married after her sophomore year and Glen's junior year. His major was social science with a minor in business and economics. Her major was home economics and education and "if I couldn't get a job, I figured I'd get married and be a housewife. I thought that was my future. Women are awfully dumb, you know. At least women from my time.''

She never considered that she was marrying a farmer because, at that time, Glen seemed to have no notion of returning to his father's farm. And that was fine with her because she viewed farming as "hard work without satisfaction, and it was nothing I wanted any part of.''

As Glen's graduation approached, he began to look at alternatives to entering military service through the draft since he, as a Mennonite, was a believer in the pacifism taught by the church.

His choice was to work as a volunteer in an underdeveloped area. It wasn't something that his draft board looked at with a great deal of pleasure, but he was given permission. The summer after his graduation, he and Luetta went to Canada and worked in a home for disturbed boys. That fall they packed up and went to the backwoods of Newfoundland, to a village, population 100, that had no access roads within 30 miles. They had to get in and out by boat.

Luetta taught grades one through four and Glen taught grades five through eleven. There were forty-five children in the school, which was sponsored by the United Church of Canada. The school tax the families paid daily was four pieces of firewood, brought in by the children. "We had to have the firewood,'' Harder says, "because there was no other heat. The stove would get red-hot and the walls would be ice-cold. We had to keep moving the kids around to keep warm and to keep from getting too hot. We didn't get much learning done.''

At the time they arrived the school had no report cards, which the Harders promptly introduced. "The parents treated us harshly,'' he remembers. "They thought we were judging their children, and they told us that the Bible said we were not supposed to judge. We pulled back off the report cards, although at the time I was upset by the parents. But in retrospect I think we tried to do too much too quickly—as outsiders.''

Glen and Luetta taught at the school for two years and lived in a little house without electricity or running water. It was a spartan life, but they liked it. Still, when the opportunity arose to come

Keith gets some help with a fund-raising project from Luetta.

back home to Minnesota, they didn't hesitate. That opportunity was in the form of land that Harder's father had acquired with Glen in mind. He bought 160 acres from his father and moved into a frame house that still stands on the property near where the turkey barns now are located.

That was in 1958 and, as the years passed and the turkey barns were erected, Harder kept promising his wife that one of these days they would have a new home, a home that would be grand and permanent and worth the wait. But Luetta began to wonder and at one point threatened to move into the next building that was put up, whether it was a barn or a house. But they waited, and by 1970 they had a "whole folder" of plans that represented what they wanted in their dream home.

But who would design it? And who would build it? In a magazine they read a story about architect Bruce Goff, who was described as somebody who liked to build with natural materials and who was not only willing but eager to listen to his clients and give them exactly what they wanted.

Goff, they agreed, sounded like their man; they both felt that the heart of building a suitable house was starting with somebody to whom they could relate. Goff was living in Kansas City and Glen, as president of the Minnesota Turkey Growers Association, went there to attend a meeting of the National Turkey Federation.

Right from the start, Glen hit it off with Goff, who was near eighty but still active. "I asked him: 'Would you consider designing a farm home in Minnesota?' And his answer was: 'I'd be honored.' "

Two months later Goff showed up at their house, notebook in hand, and spent two days interviewing them not about what they wanted in their house but about their life style and their family. "He hardly took any notes," Luetta remembers, "but four months later he came back with the working drawings, twelve color sketches. Essentially it was this house."

Who could build such an unusual house? Where, in the countryside, could you find someone with the necessary skill, which reached beyond the ability to build an ordinary house? The Harders thought of a carpenter they knew who had done many barn buildings. "Nobody ever had asked him to build a house," Glen said. "I asked him, and he seemed delighted to do it."

They broke ground in September of 1970 and moved into the house in March of 1972. Glen was his own contractor because "I wouldn't have it any other way.'' He gathered the chimney rocks from the fields himself and washed them in what he called a labor of love. Some of the rocks weighed more than 3,000 pounds and he brought in a crane to move them since they were more than his tractors could handle.

They wanted a house that would be timeless, a house that, twenty years from now, somebody wouldn't look at and say it was built in the early 1970s. They got just what they asked for—a house that in some ways is like a classic sports car: so unique in design that it always will seem to be new.

As the house went up and as a carpet layer—not a roofer—put the orange carpet on the roof, it became a landmark. Goff wanted a carpeted roof to lend softness to the appearance of the house. He chose orange as the color—with the Harders' blessing—because he wanted to tell the world that vibrant people lived in the house. It really was an experiment for the architect, because he never before had carpeted a roof. Now, with the passing years, the carpet has been bleached and weakened somewhat by the sun and is frayed in places. The Harders have been in contact with Goff to find out what he thinks they should do.

During construction of the house, there were rumors around Mountain Lake that the Harders were conducting guided tours and charging $5 admission. People screeched their cars to a stop on the dirt road 300 yards below the house, got out and rubbed their eyes in disbelief. Some called it a "bunch of rocks up on the hill.'' Others said it looked like something from outer space. Some wondered why anybody would build a Japanese-looking house in a remote corner of Minnesota. Others asked the Harders point blank: "How on earth can you live in that?''

Some people thought there was no way to get in to look at the house and so they never tried. Others were scared off by the rumored $5 admission.

Luetta Harder recalls those days: "For our friends the house always was open. We had no qualms about letting in strangers who were interested in the architecture. But if people just wanted to look at the color of our bathtubs and the brand of our appliances, they were not so welcome. If their first question was, 'How much money did you spend?'—then we didn't spend much time with them.''

It is a house designed with what the Harders call casual elegance and truth. There are no false beams, no vinyl floors made to look like stone, no plastic plants. Instead there are real beams, stone floors and plants that flourish in the sunlight that floods through the glass paneling that connects the cedar shingles and the carpeted roof. Architect Goff was so impressed by what he had created that he showed pictures of it at conventions all over the world and even brought members of his family to look at it.

From the rear deck, which overlooks a swimming pool that is bigger than any I've seen at a Holiday Inn, you can watch the sun set and turn the sky a brilliant mixture of orange and purple. From the screened-in porch in front, you can see the turkey barns and endless acres of corn and soybeans, and you can lie in the hammock and enjoy the warm winds that roll in from the south.

If there is one thing the Harders won't talk about, it is the price of their castle up on the hill. "We like to think of the house as a work of art that is priceless," Luetta Harder says.

Not long ago a reporter and photographer came to Mountain Lake from a Minneapolis newspaper and, in Luetta's words, "harangued Glen for half an hour about how much the house cost. They kept telling him the most important thing was the price of the house. But we never discussed it with them. We don't discuss it with anybody. What the house is worth to me and what it is worth to somebody else, well, there's no correlation."

And that was the end of what discussion there was about the cost of the house.

By now it's getting beyond sunset time. We've had our swim, and we've had gin and tonics on the patio around the pool and then turkey steaks charbroiled on a grill. The Harders' daughter, Brenda, who is eighteen and almost ready to leave for her freshman year at Iowa State University, has invited three friends—two boys and a girl—over for a swimming party. Brenda is a strikingly attractive girl who takes her turn in the fields picking up rocks and pulling up stray plants in a ritual known as "walking the fields."

The sons, Anthony, twenty, a sophomore at the University of Minnesota, and Keith, sixteen, a junior at Mountain Lake High School, are still in the barns, chasing turkeys. The loading has taken longer than expected because some of the trucks didn't arrive on time and because some of the turkeys were balkier than usual.

Finally the boys are home, tired, down-covered, hungry as tigers. Anthony is thick-necked—like a football lineman, which he

After a hard day's work, Luetta and Glen enjoy the pool.

was in high school and during his freshman year at Bethel College. He quit that school and football because he didn't get to play enough. "The coach kept bringing in kids from the South. They'd play for one season, then flunk out and he'd bring in another group." He says it matter-of-factly, without bitterness, although he quickly adds: "I know I should have played. I was good enough to play."

Keith is taller than Anthony, about six-two, rawboned, with a skeleton that one day will be fleshed out and will make him a 240-pound athletic terror. Right now he plays nose guard on the football team and center on the basketball team. He is less talkative than his brother. He hurries inside, eats, showers and roars off on his motorcycle to be with "friends." A girl friend perhaps? Glen Harder shakes his head, grins and asks: "What do you think?"

In the meantime Anthony has wolfed down enough food for a man and a half and he asks his father: "Is there anything else you want me to do before I go to bed?"

Just think about that. Here's a young man who has worked from before dawn until after dark, tough, debilitating work, and he's asking if there's anything else that needs to be done. When his father tells him it's all finished, Anthony says good night and goes up to his bedroom. (I'm so impressed by what has just happened that I will seek Anthony out the next morning and ask about his philosophy of life, what he thinks about farming. He will speak slowly and seem to choose his words with caution: "I feel sorry for anybody who hasn't had the opportunity to grow up on a farm. I've been lucky, because I'm part of a family that allows me great opportunity to do things at an early age. You can live in town and get a job as bag boy at a grocery store. But that's not responsibility. The responsibility is out here, and it's more than driving tractors and chasing turkeys. It's making decisions, not always having somebody tell you what to do. I don't think it's likely that you could have this away from a farm. I've always had a good relationship with Dad. We've had our problems but it's been good most of the time. I like living out here. It's my home, this house of ours. I can't explain to anybody what that means. Living here is more than our home; it's our life style. I guess this is not normal by farm standards, but I've grown up with it and it's not unusual to me. I really can't say. 'Normal' and 'unusual' are words that can't be defined."

(I will ask if he feels that he's missed anything by not living in the city. "It's all in how you set your mind. Wherever I am is the most important place to me. Everything else doesn't matter. Once you believe that, then you can be happy anyplace. That's the way to stay happy and never become discontent.")

After Anthony heads for bed, Luetta, Glen and I leave the patio and walk upstairs to the living room, seat ourselves in orange- colored foam chairs around a fountain spewing water that is turned blue-green by the lights beneath it. Glass panels above the fireplace give us a clear view of a black sky that is specked with stars. Behind us, on the landing that leads to the screened-in porch, decorative glass tubes sway on cords suspended from the ceiling. They are artificial insemination tubes—can you believe that?—but they fit right in with the natural tone of the house. The beams in the open ceiling are two-by-twelve boards that have been bolted together. The bolts have been left exposed and they have been painted orange, every one of them, by Luetta Harder. "Most people would try to cover them up," she says. "We want to accent them." We talk into the wee hours of the morning about the kind of people Glen and Luetta Harder have become: people who live life to the brim, drive 50 miles to Mankato to attend a movie, 135 miles to Minneapolis to watch a football game, hear a concert or sometimes just to have dinner. They entertain often and each Christmas they give two parties, one for their friends who drink, one for their friends who don't.

They travel—they're planning a Caribbean cruise with eight other couples in a few months—and they hope to travel more. In the summer they swim, and in the winter they ice-skate on their pool until the snow piles up so high that they can't shovel it away. Then they ride their snowmobiles.

They have dared to be different, and for this they have paid a price. In some ways Luetta and Glen have become cut off from people who once were close friends, people who don't have the money or the desire to keep up with them. They openly discuss their needs to have broader interests than many of those who live around them. Many of their friends are from outside the farm community—business people whose life style matches theirs and who, like the Harders, consider it a challenge to drive to a Minnesota Vikings football game without tickets and try to buy tickets from those who gather at motels near the stadium for fun, drinks and scalping.

They have "strayed," they say, from the simple life preached by the Mennonite church—although not so far as you might think. Their church is related to the conservative, isolationist Mennonite church only by name and by belief in pacifism. The cultural background and religious practices are different, and at their church, the Harders say, services are "pretty much like any other Protestant services."

The Harders spend their money—on the farm, the house and on themselves—because they don't believe in hoarding it. "What good does money do in a bank?" Harder asks. "Money is to be used. It's not an end in itself, but a tool to be used."

They are willing to take chances if, after calculating the risks, the odds seem reasonable. One of their biggest gambles was their decision not to hatch their own turkeys anymore but to buy them from commercial hatcheries. They made that change after their accountant told them they hadn't made any money during a year in which they wanted to buy more land.

"When you operate a farm," Harder says, "it's difficult to see what's happening—if you're making money or losing money—on a month-to-month basis." But the accountant's report prompted them to study the economics of their operation. They concluded that the labor costs of hatching their own turkeys were excessive. "We couldn't be sure" that buying turkeys would be more profitable, Harder says, "but we wanted to try it," even though it was a change so drastic that it almost was like going into a new business. So far they are happy with that decision, and so is their accountant.

Glen and Luetta Harder work as partners, and Luetta feels so strongly about it that she once made a speech in Washington, D.C., to a group of farm women and told them: "I feel the strength of the concept of a partnership is *not* in the combining of two equals. . . . I feel the primary asset of any partnership lies in the combined strong points of two unique individuals. This way everything, even the worries, can be subdivided. Each partner can be knowledgeable in different areas. . . ."

And, she says, they put this kind of partnership to work every day of their lives. Glen is in charge of the farm, and she is in charge of the house. "He could lose everything, and I wouldn't be upset. That's his worry. The problems with workers are his worry. What happens there is there. He seldom discusses financial business with me. Why should I worry about our business? If it doesn't go, it doesn't go. My worrying won't help.''

But what goes on in the house is her business—and that's her responsibility, her worry, if something goes wrong and has to be fixed. Her husband has little knowledge of or interest in the day-to-day operation of the house. As a result, when Luetta leaves the house for any length of time, she sticks a note to the refrigerator door telling him what food she has prepared and where she has put it. "Otherwise he can't find it."

The decision to buy rather than hatch their turkeys was her husband's, and in making that decision, Luetta says, Glen taught her "not to be indecisive. He worried over that decision. He'd wake up in the middle of the night and think about it. But after he makes a decision he never looks back. His philosophy is: If we're wrong, we can go back and figure out how to change it so we can try again. This has helped me not to be wishy-washy, and do nothing."

So it wasn't a difficult decision for her when she felt it was time to do something outside the home. "I felt depressed for about six months. We'd moved into our new house and I needed another challenge, another goal." Glen encouraged her, and she enrolled in a vocational school and took a course in retail fashion merchandising. She now works three days a week in Windom, twenty miles away, buying, designing window displays, and merchandising at Lady Bug, a women's clothing store advertised as "the shop that's different."

It is one of five dress shops in Windom, a town of 4,000, and it attracts women from all over southern Minnesota. Half the checks are from people who live outside of Windom. Luetta seems to enjoy the challenge of her work, especially the window displays, and welcomes it as a change from her life at home.

Yet it is her life at home around which everything else revolves. On a bright, sunshine-filled morning she stands in her kitchen, figuring out the day's menus, opening the double doors of a six-foot-tall in-the-wall refrigerator-freezer to check food supplies, talking about her conviction that marriage is for keeps. "I am going to make it work, forever," she says. Then she quickly adds: "We have a marriage as good as anybody I know, but still we've had our hard times. Everybody has them. I wonder if we'd moved away to the city, away from relatives, if we'd have stuck it out during some of the hard times. Nobody knows, and I guess that's just as well."

Brenda comes into the kitchen and asks her mother what the schedule is for today. "You want me to walk the bean fields?" Luetta says that will come later but right now she wants Brenda to do the laundry, which is overflowing out of the storage room—not because they haven't washed for a long time but because Glen and the boys go through clothes like Sherman went through Georgia, often changing two or three times a day. This is not because they're dirty but because they must change each time they go from a barn with mature turkeys to barns with younger turkeys, to prevent carrying germs that might be harmful. This includes shoes too, usually sneakers that are washed right in with the jeans, shirts and socks.

Brenda says something that Luetta interprets as lack of interest in doing the laundry and she responds: "No, I want you to do it now. Right now, please. I don't want to talk about it."

Anthony comes into the kitchen, pours himself a glass of orange juice and drops a slice of bread into the toaster. He's agreed to take me out to the storage building to look at the family's snowmobiles. He can't believe that I've never seen one. "We got some of the first ones in the area," he says, pointing to two green and gold machines that are made by John Deere, the tractor people. They have skis on the front, tractor treads on the back and, on hard frozen snow, they can reach speeds of sixty-five miles an hour. But that can be dangerous, Anthony says. One neighborhood boy rammed his snowmobile into a barbed wire fence and was cut extensively. Another boy was killed when his snowmobile hit a culvert.

They are expensive toys, Anthony says, from $2,000 to $3,000 each, but they become the main form of transportation when roads become plugged by snowdrifts that can reach ten or twelve feet in height. "You have a choice when it snows," Anthony says. "You can stay inside and kind of hibernate from the world, or you can go on about your business. It depends on your mind-set. You can get out if you want to."

The winters are severe here. Nobody denies that. Glen Harder last night talked about the year when sixty-three days passed without temperatures even climbing to zero. "We'll stay here—and I think people our age will stay—because of what we have here. But I'm not sure the younger people will stay. I think in time most of them will get out and go somewhere that's not so severe."

But Anthony says he has no intention of leaving and he doubts that others his age will. "People have been here for 100 years. There have been some good winters and some bad winters. But they've not moved out. Winters are bad, but not as bad as people who don't live here think."

Back in the house, Luetta Harder tells me that the family eats thirty or forty turkeys a year and that a week never passes in which turkey isn't eaten in some form. What forms are there? Well, there is turkey salami, turkey pastrami, sausage, bologna, hot dogs, turkey ham, ground turkey—the list seems endless. Ground turkey is used like ground beef and because it is quite bland, it can be highly seasoned and is excellent for tacos, pizza, meatballs and meat loaf.

And turkey salami? I had a sandwich and, so help me, I thought I was eating my same old salami. The advantage of eating turkey, I'm told, is that it contains much less fat than beef or pork.

It's getting on toward afternoon and I'm riding into Windom with Glen Harder. Like a turkey farmer, I've changed clothes before visiting the baby turkeys in their barn and since I've run out of my own clothes, I get some from the closet: size 34 jeans that almost fall down over my hips, black sneakers, light blue terry cloth socks and a gold and maroon T-shirt with a picture of a football player on the front and the caption: "Saturday Afternoon Fever—Catch It."

I look like a clown compared to Glen, who is wearing jeans that fit and a white golf shirt with red, navy, green and yellow stripes and with a Neiman-Marcus label inside the collar. In Windom we visit with his parents, Jacob and Anna Harder, who live in a green shingled, round house that was designed by the same Bruce Goff who designed Glen and Luetta's house. "They saw our house and they knew he was the man they wanted," Glen says. We drive through Windom, and the results of a tornado from two weeks ago still are much in evidence. Seven homes have been destroyed and, although rebuilding is going on, the street still looks as if it had been . . . well, hit by a tornado. "It came through about 5:15 in the afternoon," Glen says. "They say it sounded like a freight train."

We pass a farm implement dealership that has gone out of business. Glen offers some words of advice: "Never prepay for a piece of farm equipment. Never pay for a machine until they have it in the yard. Your chances of getting the machine are better if you don't pay for it until they have it. But some people put $10,000 down on a tractor the dealer doesn't have just because they think they're getting a good deal. And then the dealer goes out of business, like this one, and they don't get their tractor or all of their money.''

Glen parks his pickup and goes into an optometrist's office to get the screws tightened on the frames of his glasses. On the way back to the truck we walk past the weekly newspaper office and he becomes philosophical:

''Since 1973, farm grain prices have been higher and farmers have made some money—and spent some money. That's the thing about farmers: They spend their money within the county. Businessmen in town are trying to bring in industry, and farming, the largest industry, already is here but nobody does anything about it. There's a Toro plant here, but the profits are sent somewhere else. Farmers export grain, and the money stays here. A store spends $50,000 to remodel, and it's a page one headline. A farmer spends $100,000 for equipment, and nobody knows it.''

It's said that in a few years almost everybody will be living in metropolitan areas, that farms will be run by a few people, that many of today's farmers will pack up and move to the city in search of their pot of gold. As Glen Harder talks about that, his forehead wrinkles and he shakes his head in dismay. ''I can't understand why they're doing it. The quality of life here has that beat. The city can't equal what we've got here.''

There was the time when Luetta was visiting her brother in Chicago, Glen says, and the family was telling her that she didn't look like a farm wife. ''They were saying: 'You poor thing. What do you do all day? You should move to Chicago.' How could she explain to them that we have a better life style than they do? Who'd ever believe her?''

Then there was the time when Glen Harder, as president of the National Turkey Federation, took a symbolic turkey to the White House for Thanksgiving and then went on to New York with another turkey to appear on a television talk show.

''At first the taxi driver wouldn't let me in his cab. He said, 'Hey, mister, you can't get in here with that thing.' Finally I convinced him to let me in, but then at the hotel I couldn't get the turkey cage through the revolving doors. I said to the bellman, 'I have this big turkey . . . ' and he said, 'Listen, buddy, I got enough nuts without adding more.' But then he saw the turkey and let me in. On television I was on for all of thirty seconds. The guy had some pregnant women as other guests on the show and he tried to use the turkey as a gimmick to scare them. It really was insulting. After the show the host said he needed to talk to me. He wanted to know if I would give him 200 turkeys for an office party. Can you imagine? I didn't want to take this turkey back home with me so I gave it to an employee of the television station. He said he'd drop the cage off at the airport and ship it back to me. He never did.''

Glen Harder says he has less and less desire to get away from home, especially to the big cities for long periods of time. "It's such a hassle. You take a vacation, spend a lot of money, and your standard of living drops."

Now we're back at the grand orange-topped house on the hill, out by the swimming pool, eating smoked turkey and looking into a sky that has both stars and the hint of daylight.

It's 9:30 and, because we're so far north, the glow from the sun still flames on the horizon. It is quiet and the water in the pool is warm. I take my final swim and head for bed.

11 ◆§ The search goes on

If you blink your eyes and miss the signs that point south to San Francisco, west to Woodland and north to Yuba City, you'd swear that you were in Iowa at the peak of a rain-starved summer.

The land is pool-table flat, and the wind, because there is nothing to break it, picks up the loose, dry soil and hurls it in sheets across the highway. Except for an emerald-green cornfield, the land offers no brightness. Everything is the color of corn-flakes, golden brown, and just as crunchy, too. When you walk in the fields, the star thistle, wild oats, timothy and ryegrass crackle under the soles of your shoes. Dormant, they wait for the rain that will come in October to bring them back to life. By Christmas the valley will be a green paradise that will endure for five months, un-til it is so thirsty that its color evaporates into a sky that seems forever cloudless.

This is the Sacramento Valley of northern California, and, as the blowing dirt becomes grit in your mouth, it's hard to believe that some of it once was swampland incapable of growing any-thing except the squiggly little creatures that ran and swam in fright when somebody sloshed too close to them.

For most of the year, the Sacramento River, which turns and twists through the valley, is higher than the land. Sacramento, the

---

In a misty California orchard, Marc Faye climbs the ladder and shows a new hand how the pear trees are to be pruned.

state capital and the heart of the valley, is only twenty-five feet above sea level. Farming began a century ago in the upper foothills, but it didn't reach the valley until World War I, when technology provided the huge equipment to cut canals that drained off the water, which was pumped back into the river. The Sacramento River levees date back to 1915, gentle grass-covered ridges that keep unwanted water away from the rice fields and the orchards.

Because it rarely rains during the growing season in this part of California, the crops exist only by the grace of irrigation. Where they once pumped water off the land, they now pump water back to the land, out of the river and over the levees, into big irrigation ditches that feed little irrigation ditches.

I'm on my way up from Sacramento to Knights Landing, population 846, which is thirty miles to the northwest. I'm going to visit Marc Faye, who grows prunes, rice, pears and walnuts on a 1,600-acre farm about five miles on the other side of Knights Landing.

"How will I know when I get to your farm?" I asked Faye by telephone.

"Keep going until you see a house," he told me. "That'll be ours. It's the only house you'll see."

And he was right. It's lonely, isolated-looking land that surrounds the narrow state road on which I'm bumping along at thirty-five miles an hour out of respect for a sign that warns: "Rough Road." Off to my right, where the shoulder of the road should be, is a steep-banked canal, which looks to be twenty feet across and fifteen feet deep. Where the road bends left, a brown station wagon is nosed into the canal, its tailgate barely visible. The driver, coming from the other direction, didn't make the curve, and he paid the price. I stop and take a look, but nobody is in the car and there is no sign of injury. At least no windows are broken. I resume my journey, only to slow down again when I come upon a green sedan, shiny, with whitewall tires that seem freshly scrubbed. This obviously is a car that somebody cares about, yet it's out here in the middle of nowhere, and all of the windows, every single one, are smashed. What's going on?

Oh well, no matter. Here's a house up ahead, the first house I've seen, and this must be where Marc Faye lives. And what an extraordinary house it is, nestled back in a grove of oak trees, a blend of precast concrete slabs and steel beams, the color of a gray flannel suit.

The screened-in porch is big enough for a game of six-man football, but before I can walk across its polished concrete floor, I hear a voice behind me. It's Marc Faye, who more resembles a college professor than my idea of a prune farmer.

He is forty-seven, graying at the temples, quietly handsome. He even talks like a professor—precisely, without wasting any words: "I'm happy that you found us."

Faye is holding an empty coffee cup and wearing a yellow oxford cloth button-down shirt, a blue nylon jacket and jeans that are anchored by a belt with an oval buckle inscribed: "California Pear Growers."

Faye has a funny name. Actually he has two funny names. Officially, he is Eyvind Marcus Faye Jr., and his father, E.M. Faye Sr., lives right across the road in a house that is totally obscured by oak trees. That's Eyvind as in "Ivan," a Norwegian name that he put on the shelf as a boy and never used. His last name is not Faye as in Alice Faye but as in "fie" that rhymes with "pie" and "yuh" that rhymes with nothing. It's "fie-yuh," with the accent on the last syllable, a French name with which folks around here are so familiar that they never stumble over it. If you drive to the corner gasoline station in Knights Landing and ask directions to the "Fay" farm, they might snicker at you.

Family ownership of this land goes all the way back to 1917, when Marc Faye's grandfather bought it and formed a corporation, made up of his eight children, to which ownership passed after this death. In 1945, one of those children, Marc's father, bought the land from the corporation after he returned from the war. The father is semiretired now, and Marc and his older brother, Peter, are the active farmers in the family.

Peter Faye, a civil engineer, didn't come back to the farm until 1965, when Marc and his father asked Peter to help them. There was a time, in the decade before that, when Marc wasn't sure he wanted to stay on the farm. He went away to Stanford University, below San Francisco, to major in psychology because "I wanted a broad education. If I decided to farm, I figured I also could learn when I got to it. But I was not at all certain that's what I wanted. Halfway through Stanford, I changed my mind. I can't tell you what happened, but I realized that there was nothing else I wanted to do. I love it out here in our little world. I'm not interested in doing anything else. If I went bankrupt, I don't know what I'd do, because farming now is my whole life."

He completed four years and received his degree in psychology at Stanford, but then decided that he needed an education that related more directly to farming. So he went to the University of California at Davis, thirty miles away, and got a degree in agricultural economics. So is it any wonder that he talks and looks like a professor?

We're inside the house and, golly, it looks sort of like a . . . well, says Marc Faye, that's exactly what it is, a commercial-type building that they decided would give them the most space for their money. So the contractor poured a concrete slab, hauled in the beams and pieces and put it up, paneling off rooms but keeping the ceiling open all the way to the rafters. In full view, suspended from the ceiling, is a round duct, about a foot in diameter, that brings warm air into the house from the furnace. Instead of trying to hide it, the Fayes painted it bright yellow, turning it into a decorating centerpiece about which visitors inevitably ask: "Gee, that's nice. What is it?"

Faye is a musician, and the tools of his hobby are on display in the den, which opens off the kitchen. He plays bass with friends "when I can get them to come out. It's mostly Kingston Trio, Limeliters kind of music." He also plays the guitar ("folk, camp-fire music") and the ukulele ("Polynesian stuff, as part of a dance group").

He's scoutmaster of the troop to which his sons, Eric, sixteen, and Olen, thirteen, belong, and back in the summer he went with them to an International Boy Scout Jamboree in Sweden. Four years before that he was part of an "agricultural leadership program" that took him and twenty-one other farmers to China for two weeks. His impressions of the Chinese: "They know how to farm, but they have their problems in the city just like everybody else—what to do with industrial waste and the black smoke that pours from the factories."

Eric Faye has just realized the dream of a lifetime: a 1967 Mustang that appears to be set up for racing, with the rear higher than the front and exhaust pipes that bellow "Vroooommmm! Vroooommmm!" He's off for the day, Olen is heading in another direction and Marc's wife, Gerda, needs to run errands, although in her plaid skirt and white blouse, she looks ready to attend a Junior League meeting.

Pretty soon there won't be anybody left around here, including us. I've come on an unusual day, Marc Faye says. He has decided

A tender moment: Marc and Gerda.

to go sixty miles north, to Oroville, to look at an organic fertilizer said to be working wonders for some farmers and gardeners.

Why is he looking at fertilizer?

"This isn't the first time. It's kind of become my project. We simply have to develop alternatives to commercial nitrogen fertilizers. I'm talking about 'us,' everybody who grows something. It takes a lot of petroleum-based chemicals to develop nitrogen fertilizers, and you look down the road and what do you see? Well, I see high prices, and maybe scarcity so great that you can't get it at any price. So we have to look for alternatives. For years we thought that trees responded only to nitrogen. Now we know that other things are involved, and that's why we're looking into natural fertilizers."

Faye hasn't yet found any suitable substitute for the nitrogen that is applied heavily to his prune-plum trees and pear trees. But it's not because he has failed to be exposed to those in the fertilizer business.

You simply wouldn't believe, he says, the people who have come around, knocked on his door and tried to sell him fertilizer, each of which is promoted with greater vitality than the one before. There is, Faye says, a certain "snake oil" aspect to the fertilizer business, extravagant claims that precede the purchase, disappearing acts that follow it. "You buy something from them and then they're gone the next day. They're selling fertilizer this week, encyclopedias next week and used cars the week after that."

Just the other day two men who looked to be about college age presented a product that managed to arouse a flicker of interest in Faye. "But the smallest amount they would sell was $500 worth. I said, 'Let me try some and if I like it, I'll buy it.' But they said they weren't allowed to do that. They expected people to buy something they'd never heard of without having a chance to try it out. They kept telling me it was guaranteed, but I know how that is. If you can't find them, the guarantee isn't any good."

So Faye's quest continues, a trip here, a trip there, conversations with traveling salesmen on the porch or over in the yard next-door, where the trucks are, the trucks that take the prunes and pears to market. There's even a fire truck—because when you're this far out in the country, you have to be prepared to put out your own fires.

The Fayes painted the overhead warm-air duct a bright yellow and made it part of the decor.

When do we leave for Oroville? Just as soon as Richard arrives, says Faye. Richard Sachs is a professional gardener, a young man who, after he got his degree in the humanities from Chico State College, decided that there was nothing more human than getting on his knees, digging in the dirt, planting and watching things grow. He's a gardener in a subdivision in the university town of Davis, and originally he was hired by the developer to maintain a fruit and green belt within the subdivision. After the developer pulled out, residents asked Sachs to stay on, and now he is paid by them.

It's a labor of love, and Sachs, who looks like a very young Richard Widmark, never stops looking for ways to do it better. Like Faye, he is keenly tuned to organic fertilizers, but his interest seems almost as much philosophical as practical. He talks about the necessity to "work with nature's system instead of imposing our own system." Chemicals with the greatest short-term results don't always do best in the long run, he says, "not for the farmer or for the quality of the food. The problem is that we've got too many people whose overriding concern is for short-term profits. That's not the answer. In the long run the answer is for us to be like stewards of the land, to take a humble approach instead of trying to dominate."

Sachs talks about land the way some men talk about their wives, lovingly, as if it is a divine mandate to honor and cherish. Then he turns more practical and says he is convinced that the organic way is *the* way, that by controlling naturally the condition of the soil, you also control insects and diseases, to a great extent, without spraying so many chemicals. "There are ways to farm that don't result in deterioration of the environment. I know that."

So here I am, with one farmer who has two college degrees and plays bass in a jazz group and a gardener who is a philosopher. It seems as if this is not going to be your everyday trip to Oroville.

But there's more. We're going to stop on our way to pick up the Pear Doctor. That's right. Faye has insisted that Broc Zoller, a plant pathologist who has a doctoral degree, come with us to offer his opinion on the fertilizer. Zoller, who does business as The Pear Doctor, Inc., near Yuba City, regards it as a command appearance since Faye, with 160 acres of pear trees, is one of his primary clients.

But on top of that, they're friends, and this is apparent as the four of us settle into Sachs's twelve-year-old station wagon and roll to the north.

"You got another one for me?" Zoller asks, feigning despair.

"This one looks different," Faye says. "It's a liquid concentrate that is supposed to take the place of *all* chemicals."

That, says Zoller, "is a blanket claim that's hard for me to swallow."

"Please try to look at it with an open mind."

"I'll try not to be totally close minded about it, but I tend to be close minded."

Sachs has heard about this fertilizer first, and it was he who brought it to Faye's attention. The fertilizer, called Shur-Crop, reputedly is made of kelp and molasses, and Zoller, when he hears that, says: "Even if it doesn't work, maybe it will smell good."

No, be serious, Sachs says. He's tried a lot of so-called alternative fertilizers, peddled by "fast-buck artists who made promises but delivered no results," and he's had a lot of failures. But Shur-Crop may be different. "I tried it as a lawn fertilizer, and the lawn turned green, just like I'd applied nitrogen, and there's no question that the nitrogen in the product is insufficient to do that. The product is supposed to take nitrogen from the air."

Zoller groans. For seven years he has been the Pear Doctor, and while he works with all other plants and trees, he really does specialize in the care of pear trees, not just fertilizing but also pruning and watering. There is a demand for him because pear trees, unlike other fruit trees, "involve so many cause-and-effect relationships that I'm not competent to sort out myself," Faye says.

Before he was a full-time Pear Doctor, Zoller worked with Agricultural Advisors, Inc., near Yuba City, and there's where he, like Faye, got fed up to the gills with fertilizer salesmen. "They'd come around, these strange guys, and want us to tell farmers that they should buy this fertilizer. The salesmen were guys who'd retire from the air force after twenty years as corporals. You know what I mean?"

Zoller has bushy brown hair and a bushy mustache, and he looks like a twin brother of somebody I used to work with, somebody I liked very much. He even talks like my friend, laughs like my friend. I am drawn to him immediately.

Does a plant pathologist have the best-looking lawn in his neighborhood?

"I have Bermuda grass," Zoller admits. "For years it drove me crazy, the way it creeped into the flower beds. I spent all my time pulling up Bermuda grass. But I couldn't pull fast enough. That stuff was impossible to kill. I've seen it grow up through driveways. But then I found this new spray. I spray around the flower beds and the Bermuda grass doesn't invade. You oughta try it."

Zoller likes being the Pear Doctor, says he could retire if he had a nickel for every time somebody asked him: "Hey, Doc, do you make house calls?" Yes, he tells them, unless they figure out a way to bring the trees to him, he will continue to make house calls, working out of a one-story white building on the road to Yuba City. What he does with fruit trees is practice preventive medicine that results in prime yields but also jumbles the balance of nature. He feels bad about that, but what can he do?

The name of the game is to entice trees to produce the best, most marketable fruit possible. This requires irrigation and fertilizer that also make the trees more susceptible to disease. Then he has to combat the disease that wouldn't be present if he hadn't irrigated and fertilized.

When he sprays pesticide in an orchard, he kills the moth or insect that is his target. But what happens to the little bugs that these moths or insects normally feed on? You guessed it. When he wipes out the eaters, those who would have been eaten mushroom in population and then they become another problem that he must go back and deal with.

Wild fruit trees don't have these problems. In some ways wild fruit trees are healthier than trees in orchards. But wild trees yield scrawny fruit for which there is no market. "What's the answer?" Zoller asks. In a way he is like a physician who builds up an Olympic athlete. with pills and injections and then has to treat him for ailments that exist as a direct result of the pills and injections.

We're passing through Yuba City and for an instant it's as if I'm not in glamorous California but on Main Street, U.S.A. Yuba City was born as a gold rush town, Zoller says. It looks like a Midwestern town because it was erected by Midwestern people on their way west to strike it rich. Around here irrigated land sells for up to $4,000 an acre, and people buy it not because their crops can justify that price but because they can sell it later to somebody else at a profit.

We have arrived in Oroville, at the edge of the foothills. The elevation here is 170 feet but just twenty miles to the east, Forbestown is 2,823 feet above sea level. The mountains look brown through a blue haze that hangs above Oroville. Our destination is Hi-Bar, Ltd., the firm that produces not only Shur-Crop, which we have come to sample, but also Shur-Go, a sewage-treatment agent, and Shur-Pak, a soil-compacting agent, something a farmer might put on his roads to keep down dust.

"I don't believe I'm here," Zoller says.

"Don't be mean to him, Broc," says Faye.

"I'll try to keep a straight face."

"Here" is a green metal warehouse-type building that houses the company offices and the giant vats in which the fertilizer is mixed. "Him" is Bill Hibbard, head of Hi-Bar, the man we have come to see.

Hibbard is not in at the moment, a secretary says, so to kill time we walk through the warehouse, sniffing the heavy odor of molasses. "Well, one thing's for sure," Zoller says. "It really does have molasses in it." Unmarked barrels, presumably containing molasses, are stacked on a balcony that is even with the tops of the vats, which are two stories high. White plastic bags are piled against a back wall, and their contents are clearly identified: sea kelp from Iceland.

In ten minutes Hibbard arrives, a slightly paunchy man in his fifties with gray trousers, gray and white striped shirt, cowboy boots and a wristwatch that is held in place by a rhinestone band. He invites us into his office and he sits behind a desk, beneath a sign that says: "To accomplish great things we must not only act but also dream, not only plan but also believe."

Hibbard talks with the rapidity of a machine gun, telling us how years ago his search for a better way led him to discover, quite by accident, the Shur-Crop formula. He produces letters from people who say they are satisfied users. Their tomatoes have no hornworms. Their almonds have reduced insect damage. Their walnut trees are fuller and require less watering. The sugar content of their apples has increased.

And on and on it goes. Zoller says he's impressed by the letters, but isn't there some scientific evidence? No, there is no scientific evidence, Hibbard says, without apology. The only way you can get scientific evidence is to have the university run experiments, and the university won't work with organic products, only chemical products. But Hibbard does have a greenhouse out back, and he'll be glad to show us some rice he's planted and nurtured with Shur-Crop. We walk to the greenhouse and, by golly, there are some green shoots that seem to reach right up to the sky.

He has degrees in psychology and agricultural economics and is

a musician, but Marc Faye says, "Farming is my whole life."

Amazing, isn't it? Hibbard muses. Zoller stares at Faye, who returns the stare. Finally Faye says:

"I hate to tell you this, but that's not rice. That's water grass."

Hibbard seems patient. "No, it's rice. I planted it myself. I got the seeds right out of a drawer in my office."

Zoller shakes his head. "Marc's right. It's not rice. You've been fertilizing water grass. That's the stuff the rest of us are trying to kill. It's my business to know rice from water grass and you can believe me. It's not rice."

How can this be? Hibbard wonders. But back in his office he finds out. He pulls out the drawer with the rice seed, and Zoller fingers through it. "This is rice seed, all right; most of it anyway. But it's got some water grass seed in it. That happens all the time."

There is a pause, and Faye, rushing in to fill the vacuum, says to Hibbard: "But I'm convinced that Shur-Crop works on water grass."

It works on everything, Hibbard tells us. Don't these letters prove that? Faye interrupts to ask what it does for hail damage, but Hibbard keeps right on going: Don't use "the product" in combination with anything else. Why? Because, if the crop doesn't do well, "who the hell are you going to blame? You're going to blame me, and if I'm going to get the blame, I want to make sure I deserve it."

Would it be all right if Faye used "the product" on one corner of his orchards, something else on the rest, just to test it out? "Why don't you do that?" Hibbard asks. "That's a good idea."

We all go next-door to the Feather River Opportunities Center, a place where handicapped young people work, a kind of sheltered workshop. Hibbard, who is on the board of directors, takes us out back and displays a strawberry patch that has been raised exclusively with "the product." Zoller taps me on the arm and whispers, "I'm impressed. The strawberries look good, really good."

The grass on the center's baseball diamond is just twenty-one days old, Hibbard announces with pride. Nothing except "the product" has touched the grass. Zoller whispers to me again: "I'm not so impressed by the grass. It doesn't look so good to me. I believe anybody could grow grass that good in twenty-one days."

We're back at the warehouse. I'm interested in what Faye, Zoller and Sachs are going to do. Before they can do anything, how-

Marc and sons Eric and Olen on a Boy Scout camping trip.

ever, two young men drive up in a truck filled with incredibly good-looking red apples. "Hey, Bill," one of them calls. "We wanted you to see these." The apples are another testimonial for "the product." They give us a half-dozen apples, which we bite into and, without question, they are superb—firm, juicy and sweet.

"Well, boys," Hibbard says, "what can I do for you?"

Faye buys $32 worth of fertilizer—and one carton of Shur-Go, which he is going to put in the drainage ditches to keep down the odor. Zoller buys one carton of fertilizer to try on some trees at his home. Sachs is the big spender. He buys $70 worth of "the product" to use on grass and trees at the subdivision. Hibbard bids us a good afternoon and hopes we'll be back for more. He also gives each of us a green cap with a Shur-Crop emblem on the front.

Only time will tell if "the product" works, but Zoller will give it a fair try. "It all sounds so crazy, and I'd like to think it won't do any good, but I keep thinking about those strawberries."

We drop Zoller at his office outside Yuba City, and he gives me his Pear Doctor business card. Then we head into Knights Landing, where Sachs spends $18 to fill up the gasoline tank and where Marc walks briskly to a drugstore to buy a copy of the *Wall Street Journal*. I don't see a soul on the streets, but not long ago, Marc says, the town was a hotbed of excitement. A movie-making company was here, shooting scenes for a film that is set in a small Louisiana town. Why were they here if the setting is Louisiana? "It was cheaper than going to Louisiana," Faye says.

We're almost to Faye's place now. The brown station wagon has been pulled from the canal, but the green sedan is still there, forlorn-looking and now dusty. The windows probably were smashed by people from around here, Faye says, kids probably. "That's not the first time something like this has happened. Somebody has mechanical trouble and leaves the car, and when he comes back it's all torn up. I don't know why people behave that way. Maybe they don't have anything better to do. Or maybe they're angry."

Off in the distance a crew is harvesting in a section of the 200 acres that Faye devotes to rice. Right now it looks very much like wheat, at least to me, but, as we get closer, there is a big difference: The harvester is moving not on wheels but on tracks, like a tank. This is because it's still muddy in the rice fields and a harvester on wheels soon would be mired down to its axles.

Why is it so muddy in the rice fields when there has been no rain for months and when watering is controlled by irrigation? Faye smiles, lifts his rimmed glasses and rubs his eyes. It's as if he can't grasp how somebody wouldn't know the answer to that question. Rice, you see, is grown in about six inches of water. The fields are flooded because while rice thrives in water, most weeds do not. So the water becomes an economical means of weeding. The growing season is about 120 days, and near the end of it, they drain off the water. As the rice reaches maturity, the heads of the plants begin to tip over from the weight of the seed. When half the plants are tipped, a farmer can bet his harvester that the entire field will be ready in two weeks.

One of the problems that rice farmers face in this area is what to do with the stubble left from the harvest. All of it is infected with stem rot, a fungus that develops at the point of the stem where air and water come together. In the past farmers have burned the stubble, but in this valley there is little wind and the smoke tends to hang. People from Sacramento and Davis have complained that rice farmers are polluting their air.

If a farmer doesn't burn the stubble, what does he do with it? He can spray the field with stubble-leveling chemicals, but that's not very popular these days. He can plow it under, but this is expensive because of the labor and because the ground can't be farmed for a year or two, since massive amounts of nitrogen are pulled from the soil during decomposition of the stubble.

Well then, what? One answer is to develop a shorter strain of rice, so there won't be so much stubble. Another answer—and this is what Faye hopes for—is that some use will be found for the stubble that will make it profitable to harvest. Among the possible uses: A fireplace log that would be made mainly of rice stubble.

Now we're into the prune orchards, 600 acres of trees that bear the prune plums that, when dehydrated, become the prunes that we know and love—or at least that I know and love. One of the problems, Faye says, is that lots of people don't like prunes. Another problem is that lots of people who do like prunes find it easy not to like them if the price goes too high.

"If we have too many good crop years, we're in trouble. A surplus builds, and we can't get rid of it. The reason is that there is an inelastic demand for prunes. When the price comes down, we don't sell any more. We just sell less when the price goes up. The ability of people to refuse to buy prunes is infinite."

The biggest customers are what Faye calls the "geriatric trade," older citizens who recognize the laxative benefits in prunes and who prefer prunes to commercial laxatives.

Prune-plum trees resemble small apple trees, squat with plenty of branches. They produce some fruit in the early years of life but don't become commercially profitable until about their seventh year. The prune harvest begins in late summer when the prunes are taken from the trees and dehydrated for one day in a 160-degree tunnel that is fueled by propane gas. They are bluish-red when they go in, and more red than blue when they come out. But as they age in bins, they turn black, and their shriveled skin bears no resemblance to the smooth-skinned fruit that went into the tunnel.

But ugly or not, prunes are on my list of favorite snacks, dating back to childhood when my mother always kept a bowl of stewed prunes in the refrigerator. When I'd drag in after a hard day of play, I'd ask, "Whatcha got to eat?" And she'd get out the prunes. It wasn't love at first bite, but, like true love, it did grow over the years.

Right now Faye and I are standing behind a wooden bin that holds 3,000 pounds of prunes that are ready to be shipped to the Sunsweet cooperative. The prunes look like the prunes you'd buy at a supermarket, except that they vary in size—they haven't been sorted and graded yet—and they have a little trash in with them. But that doesn't bother a veteran prune eater. I'm chewing away and so is Faye, who's reminding me to be careful. "Some people stand here and talk and eat prunes without realizing how many they're eating. Then they get home and they wonder what happened to them."

When these prunes get to the factory, they'll be inspected and those that are too dry and hard will be hydrated a bit so they'll be nice and plump and edible right out of the package without soaking. Some will be shipped and sold with the pits in them. Others will be pitted, by a quick trip through a Sunsweet-developed machine that uses a series of pins to push out pits without distorting the prunes. One pound of prunes with pits becomes three-quarters of a pound of pitted prunes, something to keep in mind as you compare prices in the supermarket.

Faye worries about prices. Not low prices, as you might expect, but high prices. "This year I'm getting forty-five cents a pound. That's what the co-op is paying me. That means that prunes will be ninety cents to a dollar in the stores. Will people buy them at that price? I don't know. A lot of people didn't buy them a few years ago at fifty-nine cents. Prunes are not that essential."

It's time for me to be on my way. Tonight Faye has a meeting of the State Board of Reclamation, of which he is a member. He dips into the 3,000-pound bin of prunes and fills three plastic bags, which he gives to me.

"You like prunes; you got prunes," he says.

I put them beside me in my car and head back toward Sacramento. Years from now, I'm certain, people who live along that highway will tell their children about that late afternoon when the fellow drove past and left a trail of prune pits thirty miles long.

12 ❧ No more home on the range

It's said that nobody ever conquers the brush country of south Texas. Instead, the brush country bends and shapes the men to fit it, and those who survive become as crusty and tough as the land from which they earn a living.

I'm on my way to visit one of these men today, Jack Dunn, sixty-four, who is raising cattle on rangeland that has been in the family since 1900, half a century after his grandfather came over from Ireland. This is dry, dusty-looking country, for the most part, and rain can seem almost as precious as gold. There's never enough, and the story is that it rained only ten inches around here while Noah was building his ark.

When it is so very dry, ranchers go to bed after watching the weather report on television and they curse silently when the weatherman smiles and promises "another great day with clear skies and no rain." They get up every morning and squint into the marshmallow sky and hope that the weatherman will be wrong, although he seldom is. There are times when it doesn't rain more than 12 inches in a whole year, when many of the deer that run wild on the range die of hunger, when the bucks are so undernourished that they grow not horns but little spikes. Sometimes when you shoot one, the fur flies. That's when you know that your bullet barely reached the deer before starvation.

Even when the average rainfall of twenty-five inches is equaled

---

Jack Dunn, who can tell you what cowboys were really like.

in a year, there is no guarantee that times will be average. That's because it's been known to rain twenty inches in one day, as it did in 1967 when Hurricane Beulah swept up from Mexico and devastated Corpus Christi. That doesn't leave much rain for the rest of the year, and this is when the pastures burn brown in ninety-five-degree heat, when one cow on 220 acres can't find enough grass to sustain life.

In the grip of drought some ranchers go to church and pray for rain. Others go to the bank and ask to be refinanced. Some end up owing the bank more than their herd is worth, and they surrender their land and go to work for somebody else. Others hang on and survive with a tenacious optimism that they describe as "hoping for something that seldom comes."

It's 6:30 in the morning when I leave my motor inn outside Corpus Christi, on the Gulf of Mexico, and drive one hour west toward Alice, which is 120 miles north of the Rio Grande, the border between the United States and Mexico. The darkness begins to melt after thirty minutes, revealing land so flat that I can see from horizon to horizon. It's as if somebody has taken the lid off the top of the world and made the sky twice its normal size.

Faint white clouds, streaked with the pinkish-orange glow of a new day, offer no hint of rain or relief from heat that is as intense as a sauna bath. At ten o'clock last night, it was ninety-two degrees. This morning Alice radio station KBIC, boasting "the best in radio entertainment in south Texas," already reports eighty degrees.

Off to my right a farmer plows, headlights blazing on his tractor, a solitary figure in endless acres of brown dirt that looks powdery enough to fly away with the slightest wind. On up ahead a lighted signboard, in brilliant blue and white, urges customers to "lose wait" by getting in line at the Bank of South Texas. I pass through Robstown, a town that looks like all others, except that the municipal water tank is painted red and white and bears the name of the high school's athletic teams: "Robstown Cotton Pickers."

And then I'm in Alice, population 20,121, the home of Jack Dunn. Alice was born not quite 100 years ago when the Southern Pacific Railroad was routed through the area. Originally, the story goes, they were going to call the town Kleberg, the name of a famous rancher of the day. But there already was a Kleberg,

Texas, they discovered, so they named the town Alice, after one of rancher Kleberg's daughters.

As a railroad town to which ranchers drove their cattle for shipment to market, Alice prospered. When oil was discovered, Alice boomed. But then the oil played out, and attempts to revive the wells were not successful. Today, they say, Alice is only a shadow of what it was in the boom times, but the Chamber of Commerce slogan remains. Alice is "the hub of south Texas."

In the long-ago days, the railroad divided the town and the Mexican minority lived on the south side of the tracks, the "Anglos" on the north side. Even the four Catholic churches abided by this unwritten rule. The churches to the south were for Mexicans; the church to the north was for whites. Now the Mexican minority has become the Mexican majority, and the railroad tracks are no longer a dividing line. The whites haven't turned cartwheels of joy because of this, but they also haven't made an issue of it. They live in surface peace, a resident told me, "sort of like between blacks and whites up north."

I drive almost through town before I see a pay telephone. It's in front of Canale's Cafe, a white, one-story concrete-block building with a sign that says: "Congratulations to our working people. Open 4 A.M. to 3 P.M." I feed a dime into the telephone and dial Jack Dunn to tell him that I've arrived.

"That's mighty fine," he says in a mellow voice.

"How do I get to your place?"

"Tell me where you are, and I'll come get you."

I tell him that I'm at Canale's Cafe and his answer is: "Mighty fine. Be there in a minute."

Jack Dunn is somebody I'm eager to meet. We've talked half a dozen times by telephone, and he has been reserved but polite. I'm told that Dunn is every bit as tough as the brush country, that he is curt and abrupt and difficult to get to know. But I'm also told that once Dunn likes you, he treats you as kin and can tie you in knots for hours with his tales of how it was in the old days, during the Great Depression, when cowboys lived on the range, spent nights on the ground and days on horseback, and worked just as hard as they played.

Inside Canale's Cafe everybody looks Mexican. Most of the customers are men in work clothes, and they are seated, in groups of four, around square tables. Mostly they seem to be speaking Spanish. There is one empty stool at the counter, and I slide onto it, looking up at the two menus that are posted on the wall above the cash register. One menu is in English, the other in Spanish. The menus list eggs, chicken, tacos, tamales, hamburgers, pralines and Carta Blanca beer for sixty-five cents a bottle. An olive-skinned waitress in a white uniform approaches me, smiles and, by waggling her pencil, asks for my order. I tell her I want only coffee and she responds in flawless English: "Will that be to drink here or to take with you?"

For forty cents I get super-dark coffee in a plastic cup to take with me. The sun is bright now and, to kill a few minutes, I walk next door to Tavo Salinas's Exxon station, where five attendants who speak a curious mixture of Spanish and English already have stained their uniform shirts dark with sweat. A steady line of cars inches past the gasoline pumps. Mostly they are dirty cars, four to ten years old, driven by Mexicans who appear dressed for factory work. The drivers exchange greetings with the attendants, often on a first-name basis. Everybody seems happy and although the attendants are rushed, they remain pleasant, not only filling gasoline tanks but also washing windshields, offering to look under hoods and even to check tire pressure.

I return to my car, beside the pay telephone, and wait for Jack Dunn to appear. In two minutes a dusty green Chevrolet pickup stops alongside my car, and a tanned, lined face peers out from under a straw hat. It is Jack Dunn, Texas rancher.

His handshake is dry and firm, and he invites me into the cab of his truck, which is as dusty as the outside. The truck is a 1979 model with only 11,205 miles on it, but they have been rugged miles, through the cactus-infested rangeland and also on the open road, pulling cattle-filled trailers. A bag of matches hangs by a leather thong from the radio knob, and the glove compartment door is open, bulging with tools, rags and pain relievers for Dunn's arthritis. He needs everything at hand because he spends so much of his time not on a horse but in this truck.

But what freezes my eyes is a leather-sheathed rifle on the seat between us. Dunn carries it "mostly from habit—certainly it's not for protection." It is a .243 caliber rifle, which Dunn describes as smaller than a .30-30, "but a lot hotter. I use it to kill deer and stray dogs, hawks, coyotes. I don't believe it's big enough to kill an elephant, but it's a mighty fine weapon. Mighty fine."

Dunn is lean and he looks in good shape, certainly not like a man of sixty-four. He wears a blue and white checked shirt and khaki-colored trousers that are stuffed into $250 leather boots that Dunn has handmade in San Antonio—not because he's a boot snob but because of a half-size difference in his feet. If he bought ready-made boots, he'd have to buy two pairs to get one pair that fit. Boots, like everything else, have climbed the inflation scale. The first handmade pair he ever bought, when he was eighteen, cost $22.50. But he considers his boots, even at $250, a good investment because "you can wear them for years—these are five or six years old—and they never wear out. I don't wear shoes anymore. The last shoes I bought were the ones I got married in. You get comfortable in boots and shoes seem uncomfortable."

There's a practical reason beyond comfort, however. "When you're ridin' or walkin' through the brush, you got to have protection for your ankles. If you didn't, you'd get so scratched up you'd think you'd been in a fight." And then there are the rattlesnakes, which sometimes get up to six feet long and four-to-six-inches in diameter. Dunn looks at the sandals I am wearing, laughs and says, "Son, you are going to have fun."

We head out for the ranch where Dunn was born, eight miles from Alice. He was one of five children—four boys and a girl—and "we went horseback to school, a 7½-mile ride. But little sister couldn't take it, and so Daddy bought a place in town." Dunn also has a place in town, which he bought in 1958 shortly after he was married. The mortgage is just about paid off now, and the house, on a tree-lined street not ten blocks from Canale's Cafe, is where Dunn and his wife, Dorothy, raised their two children, Peggy Ann, a senior at Trinity University, and John, a junior at Texas A & M.

Dunn's sister was killed in an airplane crash in 1948. The three brothers still live in the area but none is a rancher. Jack Dunn took over the ranch when his father died about thirty years ago. How big is the ranch? How many cattle does he own? Dunn grins and tells me it's none of my business. "That's like asking how much money I got in the bank, and around here that's something nobody asks." But as we get to the ranch, fenced land that seems to go to infinity, it is obvious that Dunn has both considerable acreage and lots of cattle, although he describes himself as a small rancher. "Around here 10,000 acres is a big ranch. Other places 500 acres might be big. In west Texas 40,000 would be big, maybe even 100,000."

Dunn is up every morning at dawn and he puts in his entire day at the ranch, a one-man operation except during branding, vaccinating and weaning times, when he hires outside help. What he does depends on what needs to be done, cleaning out a water line, mending fences, fixing a broken windmill that pumps water from a 330-foot-deep well into a concrete tank from which the cattle drink. "You have to be a mechanic. You have to learn how to do everything—all by yourself. It's hard, being nailed down to a job like this. When you get sick, it's a helluva note. There was a boy here I hired the last time I was sick. But I don't get sick often. I like what I do. I can't feature myself at anything else. But I wouldn't advise anybody else to start. It seems like the cards are stacked against you. You can't get good help when you need it, there's no available land to run the cattle. If you had an oil well, maybe you'd have enough money so you could hire people to do the work. Maybe if you married a rich woman, it would be OK. But, aw, shoot, I sound like I don't like it. I do, and I wouldn't be happy in nothin' else."

The cattle that Dunn breeds and raises are Beefmaster, recognized by the United States Department of Agriculture as an American breed. They are a fraction less than half Brahma and about one-quarter Shorthorn and one-quarter Hereford. They are mostly brown or tan with white trim, and they are built low to the ground, like a good football running back. A Beefmaster bull can reach 2,000 pounds or more; a cow, 1,300 or 1,400 pounds. Most of the bulls and cows are sold for reproduction and only what Dunn calls "the low end" goes to market—the cattle that, for whatever reasons, are considered undesirable breeding stock.

A good bull, Dunn says, is almost worth its weight in rain water. Dunn has paid as much as $18,000 for a bull, but that is chicken feed compared to the prices commanded by bulls with established siring records. "I have heard of somebody paying $150,000 for a bull," Dunn says, wincing. "I once sold a young bull for $1,250 to a Florida man. A few years later he had a sale and sold three-fourths interest in that same bull for $66,000. That's the difference between a two-year-old bull and a bull that's a proven herd sire."

As we bounce along rutted trails, some of the cattle seem almost to recognize Dunn. They walk near the truck and when he gets out to open a gate, they seem unconcerned. "Cows are smart. They recognize you if you're familiar. If they don't know you, they run away. They have personalities, just like people. Some are shy, some are aggressive."

Some of the cattle have horns, others don't have horns. Why is that? Dunn doesn't know why. "Some guy asked me about that the other day. He wanted to know how some could be born with horns. I told him they weren't born with horns; they grow horns after they're born. I dehorn some of them. But I think it's a mistake to dehorn bulls. That's because some bulls spend so much time fighting. If they have horns, they get skinned up, but pretty soon one is the boss. If they don't have horns, they fight for hours, and they're not in much shape to breed."

What is a desirable ratio between bulls and cows? "That depends. If they're in the brush, maybe twenty cows to one bull. If they're on improved land, maybe forty cows to one bull. I had forty-one cows in an area with one bull and I got thirty calves. This year I had thirty-four with one bull and I got thirty-two calves. Years ago Daddy told me he had forty-three cows with one bull and got forty-one calves."

If a cow is regular, she comes into heat every eighteen to twenty-one days, but, Dunn says, "you can't always be sure when. With some the only way you can swear they're in heat is when the bull follows them. The cow's gestation period is 287 days. But there's no set rule. I've seen two cows take a bull the same day and there was a week to ten days between births."

The calves are weaned at about eight months and their mothers are given a rest period of two or three months before they are bred again. Calves that are not to be bred are sold right after weaning.

I tell Dunn that I can't understand how he decides which calves will be bred and which won't be bred. Dunn laughs. "You learn to tell by looking if a calf's good for breeding." He stammers and continues. "I don't know exactly how to tell you this in a polite way. But it's like going to a dance and seeing a girl who appeals to you. It's that way with cows. Do you understand?"

When I tell him I don't understand, he tells me just exactly what he looks for, and he's right: There is no socially acceptable way to explain it.

How do bulls feel about this whole business? Do they grow fat and happy? "Well," says Dunn, "if you keep one bull with a lot of cows, he sort of gets tired of it. He starts not to pay attention to the cows. He's just like some men I've known. He gets to where he hates to see the sun go down." But a good bull, if he's taken care of, can stay productive for ten or twelve years—before he wears out and is trucked to a slaughterhouse.

Dunn's brand is a dot inside a circle and his cattle are called "Circle Dot Beefmaster." But even a brand is no absolute protection against cattle theft. Yes, that's right, even in this day and age there are cattle rustlers, some big-time operators who drive cattle into a truck and haul them to market, others who cut a single cow from a herd and butcher her right on the spot for meat to put in the freezer.

"Sometimes you never know what happened. You know a cow has a calf and then the next time you see the cow, there is no calf. Did the coyotes get it? Did it just die? Or was it stolen? A lot of times you never find out—unless you see buzzards circling. I had a $1,500 calf that was contracted to go to Florida and it just disappeared out of pasture. I know somebody stole two calves from me. I found their guts. They had been butchered, and the guts were all that was left."

Dunn's ranch has no name—he jokingly calls it "Poverty Flats"—and it definitely does not have the glamour of ranches as depicted in novels and cowboy movies. The ground is flat, and much of it is brown—except for about 400 acres of pasture that has been improved by clearing brush and planting perennial grass. This pasture is fairly green, the result of what Dunn calls a summer that "hasn't been particularly dry. It's drier than I'd like, but I'm not complaining—not after some of the years we've had."

Cattle that are to be fattened rapidly are turned into this improved pasture. But the rest are left to roam the dusty soil, nibbling Johnson grass, leaves from mesquite trees that grow in abundance, and yes, even cactus leaves.

Cactuses seem everywhere. Big cactuses, little cactuses, middle-size cactuses. But all have thorns as sharp as knives. I try to touch a cactus leaf, and it's like sticking my hand into a pincushion after somebody has played a dirty trick and reversed the pins. A cactus, Dunn says, will grow anywhere. "You could break off a leaf, put it on a fence post and it would grow." Cattle eat it because it has high moisture content, but they pay a heavy price since the thorns lodge in their mouths and often cause infection and swelling. So it's only when the cattle are driven nearly mad by heat, humidity, hunger and thirst that they attack a cactus, unless the thorns have been burned off. Sometimes when it's very dry, Dunn will singe off the thorns with a butane torch and the cattle, familiar with the sound of the torch and what it is doing, will follow Dunn around the range and eat behind him.

Singeing the thorns is called "burning pear," because a cactus, in this part of the country, is referred to as "prickly pear." Back in the old days, when a rancher could hire a hand for forty cents a day, the burning was done by vast numbers of people who cut pear and held it on a stick over a wood fire and then threw it to the cattle. Later kerosene-fired blowers were used, until they gave way to the butane torches. Now it's possible for Dunn to burn as much pear in a day as dozens of men could have burned fifty years ago.

Dunn has six wells on the property, all pumped by windmills that need winds of about ten miles an hour to sustain them. When windmills break or when the winds falter, the cattle are in danger of water shortage. Three or four times in his life Dunn has bought water and trucked it to his ranch; but he's been lucky, he says, because breakdowns have been seldom and the wind manages to keep the windmills turning.

There are no living quarters on the ranch now. The house where he was born has tumbled down with age. A few storage buildings remain and in one of them there is a dusty, spiderweb-filled cot on which Dunn has slept, when his presence on the ranch was needed around the clock. But this doesn't happen much anymore.

It used to be that hired hands slept on the range, going to their homes and their wives and children only on weekends. But today hired hands, most of them anyway, commute from their homes in town to the ranch and retreat at night back to their television sets and six-packs of beer. Nobody wants to rough it anymore, Dunn says, and there is an unmistakable trace of sadness in his voice. "But times have changed. I'd rather go home, too, and get a hot meal and sleep in a clean bed."

There was a time, many years ago, when the oil companies swept across the rangeland in search of oil, drilling as deep as 7,200 feet for the black gold that overnight could make a rancher rich. Twice they drilled on Dunn's land and both times they came up empty. "It could have meant a lot of money. They pay maybe $1.5 million for a twenty-year lease. I'd have been a fat cat with a new house. Naturally, I was disappointed when they didn't find oil. I didn't cry, but I was let down."

Some of his friends and neighbors were more fortunate. Their land yielded oil, and some of them became wealthy. "It's kind of funny to see what happens to somebody like that. A lot of them got constipated, all puffed up. One day they were on their tail, without a pot, and the next day they had all kinds of money. I knew this one guy who for years had only one pair of brogan shoes to his name. Then they found oil on his place and when I saw him a few years later he was wearing handmade boots. He said that everybody should have two pairs of boots—in case one pair got wet. I said, 'You son of a gun, you used to have just one pair of shoes.' I don't think he understood what I meant.''

Today Jack Dunn trucks his cattle to market or to the buyer, but in the old days he and the hired hands drove the cattle to the railroad stations, to Alfred, twenty miles away; to San Diego (Texas), eight miles away, or to Alice. "The longest drive was about twenty miles. We did that once in October when it was cool. I'd be dead if I tried to do that now, but then I wasn't so tired.''

The horses, as well as the men, were tougher back in the old days. The horses seemed able to go all day. "Now you can't ride a horse twenty miles on a hot day. He lopes five miles and he's tired. I've seen a man cut 100 fence posts in a day. I mean to tell you that he slept well at night after he cut 100, but today you'd be lucky to find a man who'd cut 40 or 50. Everything is different now.''

We bounce along the trail that has been rutted through the sagebrush, grass and cactus, and, off to the left, there is a jackrabbit, gray, sleek-looking, about the size of a small dog, ears laid halfway back along his body. Then there is another jackrabbit, and another and still another. Before long we're following half a dozen jackrabbits as they flit through the brush, seeming to enjoy playing hide-and-seek with the truck. "There's a lot of them around here," Dunn says. "You ever eat one? The meat is black, but it's good.''

We've just shaken loose from the jackrabbit patrol when something happens so rapidly that I can't be sure what I've seen. There is a blur across the road, in front of us, something that looks like a chicken—or maybe a pheasant. But it's moving much too fast. What was it? Dunn laughs and asks if I've never seen a roadrunner.

A roadrunner. Can you believe that? I thought a roadrunner was a bird that somebody invented for cartoons, a bird that forever seems to be chased by a coyote that always is outwitted. By golly, there's another one. Dunn points it out, up ahead, off to the right, and it is a chicken-like bird that runs at blinding speed, kicking up dust. I expect to hear it go "beep, beep" and roar away with the coyote in hot pursuit. But there is no "beep" and no coyote. At least that much was created for film.

Say, Jack, how fast can a roadrunner run? "Pretty fast. I've been in a truck going thirty-five miles an hour, and they kept up with me."

I ask Dunn if he ever plans to retire, and he says, no, he doesn't have the money to retire. "Besides, if I retired, there'd be nothin' left to do but die." He hopes his son will find something else to do for a living. "It's a good life, but it's hard, too. I enjoy it, but then I never did nothin' else. I grew up in the depression; I got out of high school in '32 and I know what it is to have a menial job. I don't mind menial jobs a bit. I guess that's why I can be happy on the ranch, fixing windmills and repairing water pipes. But kids today don't like to do menial things. They don't know what it is to have to work at a job like that . . ." Dunn's voice trails off and his eyes turn away. Then he finishes: "And I hope they never do."

Dunn and a hired hand or two give the cattle all their shots except the brucellosis injection. At the mention of brucellosis, Dunn bristles and his words are venom-coated as he spits them out:

"The government says we must have a veterinarian give the brucellosis shots. I call it the 'vet relief bill.' The shots aren't worth a damn. Sometimes they cause a reaction and then the government thinks your cow has got brucellosis. They say if a cow once shows brucellosis, it never clears, but some of mine have."

It's all crazy, Dunn says, and the way he explains it, I have to agree: It does seem crazy. Brucellosis is a fancy name for undulant fever, which can be transmitted to humans only through drinking the milk of infected cows—not through eating the meat of infected cows. "I can see a problem if you've got a dairy herd and some cows are infected, but not in beef cattle. They're condemned and killed and then they hang the meat right next to other cows that weren't infected. I wish the government knew enough to stay out of our business."

Dunn turns the truck toward a fenced area where he keeps one of his six horses. "You know, it's crazy. I got more horses than people to ride them. For eleven months they're a dead loss. For two weeks when we're branding and weaning we ride the horses, but the rest of the time, they're in the way."

On the open range Dunn can round up his cattle with his truck or with a Jeep. But when he has to go through thick underbrush, he mounts a horse, just as he has for more than fifty years.

Horses are very much like people, Dunn says. "Some you can fuss at and they'll try harder. Others fuss right back at you. You don't give in to them but you don't handle them the same way. I never get on a horse without wearing spurs, but it depends on the horse if I use the spurs—or how I use them. Some people use spurs to punish and they can cut hell out of a horse. Some horses are docile and respond to spurring. Others buck and go crazy. You got to know your horse.''

Dunn parks beside the fence and we go through a gate, beneath a mesquite tree that Dunn says is "the worst shade tree in the world because it has little leaves and lots of space between leaves." Right in front of us is an oil tank, thirty feet in diameter, that Dunn trucked to the ranch. Only this tank has no oil in it. Dunn bought it years ago and now he uses it as a storage building. He has painted it silver, cut a door in it and even run electricity into it. We walk inside and there is a sight to behold—old saddles, saddle blankets, ponchos, ropes, hats, chaps, jackets. What I'm looking at is three-quarters of a century of history, Dunn family history. There is his first saddle, his father's poncho, a rope that Jack Dunn used when he was a kid, a saddle blanket trimmed with leather to keep the rider's legs from wearing out the wool.

I ask if I can try on a pair of leather chaps, because they look just like the ones worn by the cowboys who starred in the Saturday movies I attended as a kid. "We don't call them chaps," Dunn tells me seriously. "They're leggins. They only call them chaps in western stores. But they're important on the range. You can't ride through brush without them. If you did, you'd cut your legs to shreds." He hands me a pair of leggins worn by his father in the early 1920s and, all of a sudden, I don't want to put them on. There are some things you don't disturb. It would be like taking the bat with which Babe Ruth hit his sixtieth home run and using it to drive nails.

The saddle that catches my eye is dark brown and surprisingly heavy, about seventy pounds. The leather is tooled and, although worn, it still is elegant. Dunn paid $180 for the saddle in 1951. If you could buy one like it today, you would pay about $900.

Jack, did you ever rope a cow?

Yes, he did, but not very often. "You rope a calf only as a last resort because you might hurt or cripple it. You rope a cow once and you always have to rope that same cow—because it never forgets. You look at the rodeo cowboys today, and they're the best in the world at what they do. But the problem is that what they do never would be done on a ranch. These guys really are drugstore cowboys. You put them on a ranch and they wouldn't know what to do.''

The reason, says Dunn, is that rodeo cowboys get their kicks—and their paychecks—from manhandling cattle. "A real cowboy wouldn't rope and drag down a cow. He'd spend an hour or two trying to get it into a pen without using a rope. You handle a cow like you handle produce—very gently. If you establish a reputation for being rough with cattle, you can't ever get away from it. And nobody will want to buy them.''

We've left the oil tank and Dunn is carrying one iron chair and motioning for me to pull down another chair that is wedged, for storage, into the mesquite tree. He invites me to sit down, and I do. For a while he says nothing. Not a word. Miles in the sky, a silver jet leaves a white vapor trail, a reminder that we're still in the here and now, not the there and then. Slowly, Dunn begins to talk about the old days and how nobody seems to remember them the way they really were.

"In one of the movies, a cowboy rode his horse from Dallas to Ft. Worth in a dead run and the horse didn't even sweat. I think that was Gary Cooper. John Wayne rode to Arizona and never changed horses. If you ride a horse hard, he's through for a day or two—just like a man. If you ride a horse hard through brush, you'll kill him in a mile or two. Or even if he lives, he won't be worth a damn after that. He'll be wind-broken. He won't ever have any strength.

"About 300 yards is all you can get out of a horse at top speed. After that, he's tired. You look at racehorses and they can run only a mile and a quarter. or so—and they're in shape and bred for it. On a cattle drive, you walked the horses and you walked the cattle. You didn't trot them—like in the movies.

"The chuck wagon, well, there really was a chuck wagon. That's where the cook worked and made up his beans, potatoes, rice and meat. There never were any eggs. I never had any eggs. For breakfast you had whatever was left over from the night before, maybe fried potatoes and beans. The coffee was boiled, and I thought it was good. You'd get a fifty-pound bag and grind it yourself. Then you'd take a handful and throw it in a pot of boiling water. After the grounds settled, you had yourself some really good coffee.

"A good cook was harder to get than a good cowboy. You had

to have a good cook. If you didn't, then everybody would gripe and nobody would work for you. A good cook got paid more than the cowboys, too. I guess that was because he had to get up earlier. The going rate then was from seventy-five cents to a dollar a day for cowboys. Now hired hands want from $17 to $25 a day. Some want $25 a day and board. It's not like it was.''

OK, Jack, what about the campfire scenes in the movies, where the cowboys sat around and sang?

"I never saw a campfire unless it was cold as hell. Nobody wanted to sit up anyway. You were tired and you wanted to go to sleep. Usually you slept on the ground, sometimes on a cot, if you were lucky enough to have a cot. I'd say cowboys were happy, but I never heard anybody sing.''

You mean there were no singing cowboys?

Only in the movies, Dunn says. Cowboys didn't drink much when they were working, mostly because they didn't have the money to bring liquor from town. But weekends were another story. By the time they got back to town after a week on the range, they were thirsty. The drinking might last for the weekend, but when Monday morning came, they'd all be ready to work, red eyes notwithstanding.

Dunn is leaning back in his chair and searching the corners of his mind. "In the movies you see a man break a horse, and in twenty minutes he's got the horse eating out of his hand. It's possible to 'green break' a horse in a few days—so one man can ride him. But not just anybody can ride him. It takes a year to get a horse in the riding shape they show in the movies after twenty minutes.''

The motion picture kind of romance never existed on the range, Dunn says. Much of a cowboy's time at night was devoted not to making love to the queen of the roundup but to swatting mosquitoes. When the mosquitoes were really bad, as they often were, cowboys would huddle around a smoking fire "so close that you'd almost choke. But at least there were no mosquitoes.''

One night, Dunn remembers, a skunk slipped up and walked right over him and the cowboy sleeping next to him. "We were scared to move, even though we both woke up. We were lucky. The skunk just kept right on walking.''

While he saw plenty of snakes on the range, he never had any encounters with them during sleep time. "I always heard that if you laid a horsehair rope around where you were sleeping, a snake wouldn't cross it. I don't know if that's true or not, but a lot of cowboys believed it.''

He ridicules the lack of realism in cowboy movies, but Dunn does watch some of them, mostly on television. Which of the movie cowboys is the best horseman? Dunn hesitates not an instant before he answers: "Ben Johnson is the best. You can tell that he knows how to ride. He just knows how, and nobody taught him so he would ride in a movie. Audie Murphy was good, too. John Wayne knew how to ride a horse, but he wasn't a real horseman like I was used to seeing on the range.

"Gary Cooper was OK. I always liked Gary Cooper. He knew how to ride, but he held one of his legs up in the air, and he always looked kind of funny to me.''

All of the movie cowboys, Dunn says, managed to get twenty-four shots out of a six-shooter without reloading, and they rode on 1970 saddles in movies that were supposed to take place in 1870. "They weren't very realistic, the movies, but they were fun to watch and they didn't hurt anybody.

"I guess that's why I've always liked John Wayne so much. I mean when he died, it was almost like a death in the family. He spanned the generations, just like Spencer Tracy. He was a very special guy, John Wayne. He never used profanity to get a point across. There never was any nudity in his films. You could take your children to see them and know that they weren't going to see anything they shouldn't see. It's not like that anymore. And there aren't many like John Wayne anymore.''

I ask Dunn what it was like, as a boy, working on the ranch with his father.

"Sometimes he raised hell with me, but the only time I talked back was after he'd gone, so he couldn't hear me. One thing you never wanted to do was lie to him. He was very strict. I'm not that strict with my children. Nobody's that strict anymore.''

His father taught him the rules of life, Dunn says, and he did it in ways that Dunn never forgot.

"There was a time when I was not yet twenty. I got Daddy's car to go to Corpus Christi to see a football game. I didn't get back until 4:30 or 5:00 the next morning. Daddy didn't say much. He woke me up and told me: 'Let's go to the ranch, Son. We're going to rebuild this piece of fence today.' And we dug post holes all day. He never said anything else, but I knew what he meant. I knew I was being punished, and he knew that I knew. It was one of the best lessons I ever learned. After that I always got in at a decent hour.''

While we have talked, the time has flown. Dunn looks at his watch and is surprised that it is midafternoon. "No wonder I'm hungry. It's past time to eat. Let's go home. I told Dorothy I'd be bringing you for dinner."

We climb back into the truck and we're off again, bouncing, bumping, the sheathed rifle rattling around on the seat. Dunn strokes the rifle and begins to talk about coyotes:

"I've never seen coyotes run in a pack. I've seen one run a calf or a fawn. I've heard old-timers talk about watching coyotes separate a cow from her calf and then getting the calf, but I've never seen that happen. Coyotes are afraid of people. I've never heard of them biting, but there are stories that people have been bitten and then get rabies.

"I shoot maybe six to ten in a year. Once a cow died near where I had parked the truck while I'd been deer hunting. I came back and there were twelve to fifteen of them, coyotes, eating on the dead cow. I shot them all. Then I burned them on top of the dead cow."

There are some people who want to glamorize the coyote, Dunn says, but really it is a skinny animal that is full of fleas, lice and ticks. "They are mangy. I've killed some that had almost no hair. I used to set traps for them, but they are very cunning. If they get away from a trap once, they never come back again."

The eight miles slide by quickly and now we're back in Alice, past St. Elizabeth Catholic Church, where Jack and Dorothy worship, and then three blocks later we're home.

Dorothy Dunn was born in San Antonio, 125 miles to the north, but moved to Alice with her parents when she was four. She has known Jack "since I was a little girl" and her mother and Jack's mother were close friends.

It is obvious very quickly that she enjoys sticking the needle into her husband. "Jack's the only man I know who puts on his hat to go out the front door to get the paper. He says he doesn't feel dressed without it. You remember that movie, *Giant?* There was a scene when the man argued with his wife and put on his hat and boots and left. I thought I'd laugh until I died over that, because it hit so close to home. That guy was just like Jack—hat and boots all the time."

The house where the Dunns live is sided with green asbestos shingles and is as modest as any on the street. Dorothy Dunn doesn't help Jack on the ranch—she calls herself a housewife—but she understands a rancher's problems. "It used to not matter to me if it rained or not. But now I watch the clouds just like Jack does."

They've taken just one vacation in twelve years—that was to West Texas—but Dorothy says she knows that Jack is happiest when he's working at the ranch. She goes with him several times a year when he travels to cattle sales, and she has been hostess at his cattle sales, supervising the feeding of 200 or 300 people on a menu that invariably features beans and homemade tamales that are filled with beef, pork or venison and then wrapped in corn shucks and cooked. "You skin them and eat them like bananas."

For our meal Dorothy serves beef roast, venison, green beans, macaroni, tomatoes and homemade biscuits. Jack leans back in his chair and says that when people talk to him about the high cost of beef, he tells them that his fondest hope is to get his bank note paid off. It's his way of saying that he isn't making the big money that you might think when you pay $5 for a pound of steak.

He is paid, he says, about forty-five cents a pound on the hoof for cattle that are shipped to the slaughterhouse, and the difference between that and the market price means that "several guys are making a living off me before the meat gets to the supermarket. They kill it, process it, freeze it, haul it. And the consumer pays for all of that. It's a funny economy. Lettuce pickers in California are getting $5 an hour. I've got half a million dollars worth of property and I'm not making any money.

"A farmer may have a bad half year. Maybe he'll have a good spring but not a good fall. If that happens, he can park his tractor. But a cow has got to eat. A rancher's expenses go on, regardless of the weather. So you start to buy supplemental feed, and that's expensive. A lot of so-called ranchers sell out in tough times. This floods the market and prices go down. Then we have two or three good rains and they want to get back in. Doctors buy ranches so they'll have a place to hunt birds and deer. They don't care how much they pay. And this drives prices up." There is no relationship, Dunn says, between the price of the land and the profit that can be made from the land through the cattle that graze on it.

Dark clouds are starting to form now, and Dunn says with conviction: "Rain is on the way."

Does he really expect rain? "Well, it can be pretty spotty around here. Last night we had a big rain in town, but hardly enough to settle the dust down the road."

How does Jack Dunn find buyers for his cattle? While he runs some advertising in the *Beefmaster Cowman,* the publication of Beefmasters Breeders Universal in San Antonio, most of his business comes through recommendations of satisfied buyers. One of his recent buyers was Lee Roy Jordan, the former all-pro line-backer of the Dallas Cowboys. Jordan, now retired, owns a ranch not far from Dallas, and both Jack and Dorothy Dunn beam when they tell about the time that Jordan came to their house and "sat and talked with us just like an ordinary person." They shook hands and Jordan bought twenty-three head of cattle before he left that day.

Speaking of leaving, it's time for me to leave now. It's getting on toward sunset, and we walk outdoors to find that the dark clouds that promised rain have disappeared. Only a few drops of rain are in evidence from the spatters in the dust on Dunn's truck. "Oh, well, maybe we got some out at the ranch."

Dunn takes me to my car, and then I'm off, back east toward Corpus Christi on State Highway 44. The sun is behind me, and the glare is so bright that I turn the rearview mirror away from me. As I get near Robstown, home of the Cotton Pickers, I notice that traffic is heavy and moving very slowly. At an intersection I find out why. The intersection is flooded, almost impassable. Within the hour, somebody tells me, a rainstorm has deluged Robstown, a rainstorm like you wouldn't believe. Now I know where Jack Dunn's rain went, why he didn't get any. Robstown got it all.

I'm back in Corpus Christi, a sleepy-looking town of about 200,000 that still bears the scars from Hurricane Beulah in 1967 and Hurricane Celia in 1970. They've never rebuilt some of the business district, and a few stores still are boarded up, vacant, silent, just as they were in the days immediately after those two storms, which, together, killed eighty-five people as they ravished Cuba, Florida, Mexico and Texas.

I drive down to Corpus Christi Bay, along Shoreline Boulevard, a beautiful street that parallels the water, like something you'd see in Miami. I cross the ship channel and park near the bathing beach—not because I want to bathe but because I want to walk in the sand. But I do stick my toes in the water, and it's like dipping into a heated swimming pool. The water is eighty-seven degrees, just about the temperature of our pool in the condominium back in Philadelphia.

I'm at my motel in ten minutes and then I'm showered, shaved and out for the best Texas gulf shrimp dinner of my life. There are only four shrimp on the plate, but they are so big that I can't eat more than four. I also have a salad and a baked potato and wash it all down with a full carafe of rosé wine. The bill is less than $15.

I take another drive, in the damp evening air, and then I'm in bed, early. I have to be up at 5:00 in the morning because the jetliner out of Corpus Christi leaves at 6:15. I wake up in a rain-storm, an honest-to-goodness rainstorm. We take off on schedule and as we climb into the dark sky, the pilot announces that the rain is localized and we should be out of it in a few minutes.

Through my rain-streaked window I look beyond the lightning, off to the west, and hope that Jack Dunn is getting his share.

Epilogue

At the end of my travels, I was both tired and satisfied. I was tired of packing my suitcase, leaving my wife, eating my dinner on airplanes. I was satisfied because I felt that I had done what I set out to do—scratch through the surface of rural America and gain some insight into those of you who live there and why. I also was sad—because of the death, two months after my visit, of Mrs. Viola Retzlaff, mother of Cedarburg, Wisconsin, dairy farmer Henry Retzlaff Jr.

What impressed me deeply about many of you was the rich sense of satisfaction and fulfillment in your lives, a glow that, like an eternal flame, remains fixed, neither fanned by good times nor snuffed out by hard times. Out in the country, self-measurement seems involved less with what a person does and how well he does it than with the kind of person he is and the extent to which he shares himself with his family and friends, even with strangers. This is what makes rural America what it is, not the crops, which are beautiful, but the people, who are more beautiful.

There are families that seem bound together not by necessity but by love and common goals, families whose young members work and sweat and then instead of asking if they can quit now, ask if anything else needs to be done.

There is hard work on the farm but almost no profanity. There is absorption of religion into daily living and a shortage of the games that people play. Few of you seem to worry about keeping up with the neighbors. Many of you seem to focus your energies on doing your best. If that is not good enough, you see it as a momentary setback, not as a crushing defeat. Tomorrow will be better. Hope is contagious.

On the farm, wives seem to have full-fledged partnerships not because the times demand it but because husbands and wives need it. My guess is that women's liberation, by whatever name, had slipped quietly into rural America long before it crashed into the cities.

There are problems on the farm: Prices are down; costs are up; young adults who want to stay on their family's land can't because the land is unable to support their parents and them, too.

There are changes on the farm: Little farmers are being squeezed out by rocketing land costs that make it impossible for them to add acreage and survive; big farmers are wondering if they can continue to compete successfully with the growing numbers of corporations that are branching into farming.

There are some who say that the quality of life on the farm has diminished. I didn't see evidence that it had diminished very much. What I did see was a rural America that, despite its problems and changes, still offers what many of us hunger for, a chance to see with our own eyes the clear-cut results of what we do with our own hands and minds.

That kind of basic simplicity is what made this country great. It is, I believe, our guarantee that rural America, as we know it, always will be with us.